MY DANCING DAYS

MY UNCLE SAM

MY DANCING DAYS

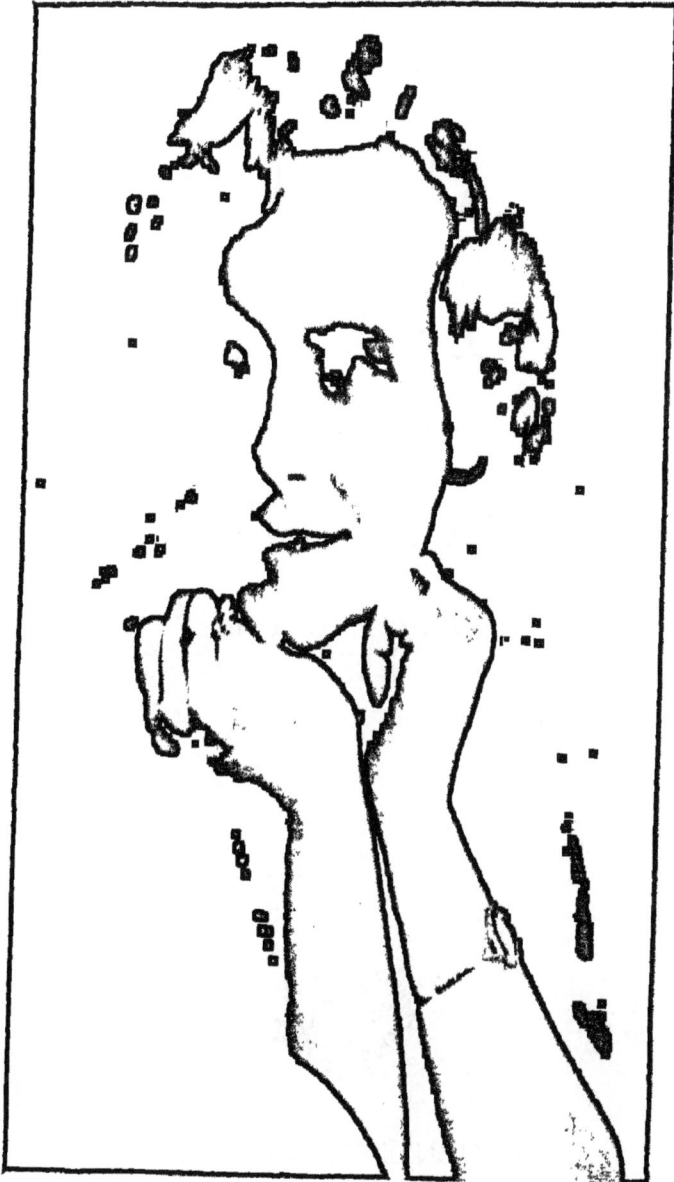

Gordon Anthony

MY
DANCING
DAYS

Phyllis Bedells

WITH 63 PHOTOGRAPHS

PHOENIX HOUSE LTD
LONDON

Dedicated with deep affection to two great artists,
DAME ADELINE GENÉE, D.B.E., D.Mus., M.I. et A., B.M.,
who was my inspiration, and
MISS MARGOT FONTEYN, C.B.E.,
who has realized my ambition and become England's
PRIMA BALLERINA ASSOLUTA.

Printed in Great Britain by
The Aldine Press at Letchworth for
Phoenix House Ltd, 38 William IV Street,
Charing Cross, W.C.2
First Published 1954

Illustrations

I

MY PARENTS never had too much money. But my grandfather was a fairly well-to-do Nottingham merchant. Each of his nine children played some kind of musical instrument and the little family orchestra they made up between themselves was at one time a feature of Nottingham's social life.

A liking for music, which they shared, first drew my parents together. My father used to meet my mother at musical functions. He was eleven years her senior and when they became engaged it was understood they must wait for five years before marrying as she was considered to be too young.

Father had obtained the post of organist at Emmanuel Church in Nottingham. When his parents died the family fortune was split up and divided between the children. With his share of the legacy my father was unfortunate: he was persuaded to invest it all in a business in the North of England. The day he married he was also made bankrupt. That clouded the happiness of the honeymoon and married life was begun in what must have been very difficult circumstances.

My father took a position as junior clerk with the Bristol Gas Company. He had decided to play for safety and he and my mother lived in furnished rooms until they could afford to have their own home. But it was not long before they moved into a tiny cottage near the church at Barrow Gurney, near Bristol, and Father—as he loved to do—was playing the organ again. Mother could be very amusing about those early days which, in spite of all the difficulties, she seemed to have thoroughly enjoyed. We would often laugh when she described how she made furniture out of sugar-boxes and cretonne, and did most of her housework with a crumb brush and tray.

My brother was born first; and nearly four years afterwards on 9 August 1893, I made my first appearance. By then my parents had moved again, to a charming cottage on the outskirts of Knowle, then a new suburb of Bristol and still very rural.

It was the year before I was born that my father founded the Bristol Amateur Operatic Society, of which he remained musical director and producer for thirty-one years. At first Mother used to play principal parts in their annual productions of the Gilbert and Sullivan operas and other light works. All my early years were spent among people who liked music and it was natural, therefore, that as soon as I showed a talent for dancing I was encouraged as few children were fortunate enough to be in those days.

Rose Mount, as our cottage was called, has long since disappeared in the rebuilding of Knowle and I do not remember much about it. There was a pleasant garden which my mother looked after. When I was about four years old we moved to another house in Knowle, next door to some great friends of ours called Valentine; but we were there only a short time before moving into a larger but very old house with a heavenly garden and a terrifying basement. My earliest memories are of climbing the fruit trees in the garden and eating the delicious Victoria plums I can also distinctly remember the year we had most magnificent sunsets, which I was told were caused by Vesuvius being in violent eruption.

Summer holidays were always wonderful times when I was small. We went with several of my parents' friends, most of them members of the Amateur Operatic Society, to Crantock, a village near Newquay in Cornwall, where there were only some ten cottages, a farm, and a lovely.old church. Usually there were about fifteen or twenty in our party. Year after year we occupied every available room. We used to devour splits and strawberry jam and Cornish cream. In the evenings, as I lay in bed, I could listen to the grown-ups singing the lovely old songs and hymns in harmony.

When I was about five years old we went for a long day out to picnic and explore some caves. We forgot the high tides and were cut off. Everyone had to wade, waist deep—I was carried on my father's shoulders. Suddenly he uttered a sharp cry and almost fell with me. He had stepped on a broken bottle and his foot was badly cut. I had to be carried by another man while my poor father was got to safety. We all got back to Crantock feeling very miserable. That ended our holiday, as we had to return to Bristol with my temporarily crippled father. For a small child it was a dreadful experience.

Another childhood memory was of sitting astride my father's shoulders among the crowds celebrating the relief of Ladysmith. I was rather frightened. Everyone seemed to have gone mad. All the cheering and flag waving amazed me. I didn't understand what was happening.

8

I specially liked to be in Nottingham with my mother's relations for the Goose Fair at the beginning of October. It remains vividly in my memory. Brandy-snaps and Grantham gingerbread were sold. Naphtha flares lit the stalls and sideshows and there was the glorious noise of roundabout organs and the men shouting outside the booths. . . .

My mother, who had a lovely voice, and was really a most beautiful woman, decided to go on the stage to help my father with the cost of educating my brother and myself. So a housekeeper and her husband looked after us: both I remember disliking intensely. They had a little girl of about my age; and my parents did not know until much later how unkind these people were to me and how spoilt their own child was. I had always hated slugs and snails and they used to send me out into the garden at dusk with my little seaside bucket to gather as many as could be found. I always believed the housekeeper cooked them for her husband's supper! I was also made to fetch and carry for them as if I were their servant. The basement passages seemed to me filled with unimaginable horrors. In spite of its garden I was glad when we left that house and moved yet again to a smaller and more modern house in Knowle and the married couple were dismissed.

My mother's stage name was Phyllis Stuart—a combination of my own name and my brother's. She frequently toured with George Edwardes's number one companies in such musical comedies as *San Toy* and *The Country Girl*. At Christmas she played in pantomime. Between engagements she came home to spend as much time with us as possible. I never tired of listening to her tell of her experiences.

As children both my brother and I were very theatre minded: our favourite game was to make a stage under the dining-room table, using my mother's potted ferns for trees and the tiny dolls from my dolls' house as actors. The big chenille tablecloth with its bob fringe was our drop-curtain. Sometimes we wrote the plays ourselves. Our chief delight, however, was to arrange the *décor*. We were for ever inventing new ways of setting and lighting our stage. It is remarkable we did not set the house on fire with lighted candles.

We charged our parents and their friends a halfpenny each for admission. I fear we were mercenary young monkeys!

9

⋯⋯⋯⋯⋯⋯⋯⋯⋯⋯⋯⋯⋯⋯⋯⋯⋯⋯⋯⋯⋯⋯⋯⋯⋯⋯⋯

2

I FIRST went to school at the Convent of St Agnes at Knowle, as a day girl, and the needlework I learned there stood me in good stead in later years. We were taught to make an exact replica in miniature of a cooking apron and we had pieces of white stockinet with holes cut in, which we had to darn, and catch up every single thread. Only when we had mastered such plain sewing were we allowed to do fancy needlework.

While I was still at the convent it was decided I should be taught dancing and I was taken once a week to Clifton, which seemed a long way off in those days. My first dancing mistress was one of the most beautiful women I ever saw: Miss Edna Stacey (in private life Mrs Richard Tuckett). She had a large connection, and I went to the 'fancy' dancing class, and lived for just that one hour every week. I learned much at those delightful lessons that I have never forgotten. I can remember, step for step, some of the solo dances; and I now know that these were very well arranged and suited to our age and slight technique. We were never forced, always encouraged, and I adored Mrs Tuckett. We were also taught deportment—a subject that is much neglected nowadays. We had to walk across the huge room and greet our hostess, sometimes with a curtsy and sometimes by shaking hands. Classes ended with a slow waltz round the room with us holding out our very full skirts; then we walked slowly and gracefully the full length of the room again to say good-bye to our teacher. No dashing about or chatting in class was permitted.

While still at St Agnes I had an accident which was to have far-reaching consequences. In our playground there was a swing, a giant stride, and a seesaw. It was a strict rule with the nuns that the moment the handbell was rung we must stop playing and stand to attention. I jumped from the giant stride one day on hearing the bell; but the others were not so prompt. One of the girls came swinging round and knocked me face downwards on to the asphalt. When I was picked up not only was my lip cut but one of my teeth was broken. For many years, until I had it crowned, I was very conscious of it.

When I was eight I made my first appearance on the stage, at Lowestoft, with Paul Mill's concert party which performed in the

Olympian Gardens and at 'Sparrow's Nest', the open-air theatre. I used to go with my mother, who was their mezzo-soprano for the summer holidays. I would sit on the stage at her feet, wearing a pierrot hat; and I 'appeared' as a very cramped baby in a cradle in one of the Paul Mill numbers called 'Baby Bill'. Only my hand was visible, but it added a touch of realism to the song.

I was nine when we next went to Lowestoft by way of London. As I had never been to London before, Mother decided to show me some of the sights. I recall feeling very proud of myself in a navy-blue kilt, a fisherman's jersey, and a little sailor hat turned up all round. It was Sunday, and we watched the church parade in Hyde Park—and the parade of fashion in those days was something worth watching. Scarcely a motor-car was to be seen, but there were many carriages and hansom cabs going past us under the trees. We went from the park on the top of a horse-bus all the way to Petticoat Lane where I was amazed and a little shocked to see all the shops and stalls open for business.

That summer Paul Mill suggested I dance for him occasionally at matinée performances, and promised to pay me pocket money. Mother agreed and I had a very thrilling time. The patrons made a great fuss of me because I was so tiny and ridiculously inexperienced. I was also prompter to the company, which made me more self-important than ever. But one day, when my mother was reciting *The Matinée Hat*, someone called me away and, as luck would have it, Mother turned her head and saw I was not there. She immediately dried up and had to walk off after apologizing to the audience. I was very ashamed of having failed her. It was a long time before I got over it.

Mr Airlie Dix, the composer of the famous song *The Trumpeter*, spent one summer with us. His wife was the concert party's accompanist. It was he who first gave Mother the idea that I might become a successful professional dancer. While I waited for her to dress after the show he and I used to go on to the stage and he would play the piano while I danced. We became the greatest of friends, and he wrote a charming mazurka for me which I have kept to this day.

When the Lowestoft season finished the company went to Torquay and Plymouth, and I remember climbing the cliffs at Babbacombe with Jimmy Taylor, our comedian, and his small son—a feat which nothing on earth would have induced me to perform in later years. But I was quite fearless then.

While I was at Plymouth I received my first proposal of marriage. It was one of the most beautiful and romantic moments of my life. We sat together on a free bench on Plymouth Hoe. I felt, however, that he was a little too young for me—I was nine then and Jimmy Taylor's son only seven!

Back in Bristol my parents took me to the Prince's Theatre whenever there was a suitable play. I saw *The Tempest* with Sir Herbert (then Mr) Beerbohm Tree as Caliban. I remember I was greatly impressed by his horridly long finger-nails. One night my belief in fairies was rudely shattered. Iris Hoey, then a young girl, was playing Ariel, and stumbled over a tree trunk. She fell so heavily and made so much noise that all the illusions I had been entertaining vanished.

I appeared in one of my father's productions as the second royal page in *Merrie England*. My mother played Jill-all-alone and my brother was the Queen's Fool—it was quite a family affair. I shall never forget how people laughed when I first appeared in my doublet and hose. I had very thin legs and knobby knees and was very small. The firm from whom the costumes had been hired had sent me a full woman's size in cotton tights which fitted like concertinas. But the thrill of being on the stage was compensation for the audience's laughter. I had a speaking part and thoroughly enjoyed denouncing Jill, my mother, as a traitor.

In 1905 we were living on Durdham Downs and I went to a small private school where I made good progress with my general education. The Principal was a charming woman and also interested in the theatre. She and I often discussed the plays we had seen at the Prince's Theatre and from her I learned to be discriminating.

Next summer I went to Lowestoft again with my mother, and danced regularly for Mr Mill which brought me a salary of ten shillings a week. I appeared as a pierrot, and a coon, danced an Irish jig, and was in a pseudo-Eastern number.

I was eleven years old. When we came back to Bristol, Seymour Hicks and Ellaline Terriss were at the Prince's Theatre in *The Catch of the Season*. Edna Stacey said it might be a good plan to ask Seymour Hicks to see me dance and give a candid opinion on my possibilities. That was the real turning point in my life. An appointment was made for him to see me after his matinée. When we arrived on the stage he had not had time to change his clothes and sent his musical director to find out whether I could sing. It was an awful moment. I had no music with me; but, unaccompanied, I sang *A Little Bit of String* in at least six keys. When I finished the musical director looked very glum and said, 'Well, perhaps you can dance.'

At that moment Seymour Hicks came hopping out of his dressing-room and I began to dance. He was very charming afterwards and told Mother he would like his stage director, Edward Royce, to see me dance on the following day. Once again I had the thrill of an audition. My mother was advised to have me trained seriously for the profession. Mr Royce told her that I ought to go to London and be given daily lessons under a first-class teacher. That was depressing because we had no money to spare: however, my grandmother, hearing of our difficulties, wrote to say there was a very good school in Nottingham with Theodore Gilmer as Principal, and offered to pay for my training.

3

❖❖

I WAS the youngest student at the Gilmer school. Most of the girls were over sixteen and studying to become teachers. Our work was very strenuous but I loved every moment of it. After one term as a day girl my grandmother decided it would be better if I became a resident student to save my making the early morning journey and coming home in the dark.

At Gilmer's we were called at seven-thirty and had breakfast at eight o'clock, after which we had to tidy our rooms and make our beds and be in the studio by nine o'clock. We worked for two hours under assistant teachers on classical ballet technique; then there was a general class for outside pupils, and we were expected to help with the instruction. Almost every afternoon there was a big fancy dancing class for which the richer children used to arrive in the expensive motor-cars which were just becoming fashionable. Among them were the children of Mrs Charles Birkin, one of whom afterwards became the beautiful Mrs Dudley Ward. I remember I felt very envious of the party frocks. While I had to make do with one frock they never seemed to come twice in the same.

Mr Gilmer was extremely kind to me and frequently gave me

13

extra private lessons in the evening. He gave all his lessons, other than ball-room dancing, to his own accompaniment on the violin in the good old way, rather like the Dancing Master in *The Rake's Progress.* His father had studied at the Paris Opéra; his brother managed the famous old Oxford Music Hall.

I enjoyed going to the gym class, although attendance was not compulsory for us. Once a week a Cinderella ball was held and we were allowed to sit up until midnight.

In order to go to Gilmer's I had to give up school, of course;

Dancing

Dancing is by no means an easy task To make a perfect dancer it is necessary to practice for hours a day. In fact no dancer has ever finished her training as there is always something to learn When

Part of an essay written by the author at the age of eight

but I worked at my general education in my spare time, read a good deal, and practised the piano whenever I could manage it. My parents had made me realize how important it was not to neglect my studies at such an early age.

Saturday at Gilmer's was a fairly slack day, so I used to beg Mrs Gilmer to allow me to do some of her household shopping. There was a fascinating market in the centre of Nottingham which has since disappeared to make way for the War Memorial gardens. On these shopping expeditions I used to wear the snug Little Red Riding-Hood cape my grandmother had made for me and carried a basket on my arm. To the stall-keepers I was soon a well-known figure. In later years Mrs Gilmer told me that the market people were so much amused to see a youngster like myself taking the business of shopping so seriously that they used to give me particularly good value for what money I spent. Certainly I did feel very proud of myself, and I think that doing the marketing taught me the value of money. But there were times, too, when I would sit in a café and eat cream buns and drink hot milk.

In the summer of 1906 I paid my last visit to Lowestoft and this time, on our way there through London, I went to see my first ballet. I had never been inside a music-hall. We went to the Empire in Leicester Square to see Adeline Genée in *Coppélia*. We sat up in the gallery. My joy was unbounded; and, from then onwards, my one dream was to be anywhere on that stage, even in the back row, if only I could be near so divine a dancer.

Fred Farren's performance as the old doll-maker also impressed me deeply. He was a magnificent character actor and made more of the part than anyone has done in recent productions I have seen. He made me cry then. For a long time I dreamt of how the poor old man was ill-treated by the villagers and of Swanilda's and Franz's heartless behaviour to him.

How I wish that critics and balletomanes of to-day could have seen that production of *Coppélia* at the old Empire. They would know then that ballet in England was flourishing long before Diaghilev was heard of here. Much as the art in this country owes to the Russian Ballet—as I would be the first to admit—I feel we owe still more to the influence of Adeline Genée.

I was back at Gilmer's and studying hard when, in December 1906, Mother arrived unexpectedly just before term ended. She showed us a telegram she had received early that morning. BRING PHYLLIS TO LONDON   AUDITION PRINCE OF WALES THEATRE TOMORROW AFTERNOON   SEYMOUR HICKS.

Excitement was immense. Needless to say I was whisked off to London next day. We went straight from the station to the Prince of Wales to find everyone in the midst of rehearsals for *Alice in Wonderland*. We waited in the wings for a while and then everyone was told to clear the stage and I was given my audition. I was engaged on the spot to appear in 'Alice' within a fortnight at a salary of four pounds a week. I had two solo dances which were arranged by Edward Royce, although the other dances in the show were produced by Will Bishop. We opened on 20 December and did five matinées a week. *The Vicar of Wakefield* with Isabel Jay and Walter Hyde filled the evening bill and the Saturday matinée.

15

There was a wonderful cast for 'Alice'. Stanley Brett, Seymour Hicks's brother, played the Mad Hatter; Tom Graves, brother of George Graves, played the Mock Turtle and Tweedledum; Will Bishop, himself, was the First Lobster and the Golliwog; and Alice was played by the beautiful Marie Studholme. The rest of the cast were: J. C. Buckstone as the Gryphon and Tweedledee; Florrie Arnold as the March Hare; Rita Leggerio as the White Rabbit; Harry Ulph as the Caterpillar and the Red King; Alice Barth as the Duchess and the Red Queen; Euphan Maclaren as the Cook; Marjorie West as the Cheshire Cat; Ivy Sawyer as the Dormouse; Margaret Fraser as the Second Lobster; Alice Dubarri as the First Fairy and the Rose; Julian Cross as the King of Hearts and the Walrus; Florence Lloyd as the Queen of Hearts and the White Queen; Harold Borrett as the Knave of Hearts and the White King. H. H. Cameron took the parts of the Executioner, the Carpenter, and Humpty Dumpty; Carmen Sylva, the Lily; Dorrit MacLaren, the Red Knight; Leslie Bilbe, the Lion; John Hobbs, the Unicorn; Tom Jones, the Leg of Mutton; Ethel Evans, the Plum Pudding.

In Act I, I emerged from a large oyster shell, dressed as a little sailor boy, and danced a hornpipe. This seemed to me slightly incongruous, as I was supposed to be the First Oyster; but nobody minded Act II was Through the Looking Glass, and Carmen Sylva, a child with a heavenly voice, appeared as the Lily. She changed her name later to Sylva Van Dyck and had a great success as a singer. To-day she is well known in the theatrical and social world and is married to Stuart Watson, General Manager of the Haymarket Theatre. I was the Cornflower in the garden scene. I realize now what a ghastly dress I wore: instead of the usual tarlatan or ballet net the skirts were made of yards and yards of accordion-pleated blue chiffon with ruching on the edges. It was doubtless expensive; but it was most unsuitable.

At our dress rehearsal Seymour Hicks made me run on to take curtain calls in the empty theatre and insisted that as I curtsied I say 'Thank you'. This was one of the many valuable lessons I learned from him and since then, whenever acknowledging applause, I have always said 'Thank you' under my breath. It is surprising how much difference such a simple thing makes to the sincerity of the curtsy.

Mother took a furnished bed-sitting-room, an attic in Maryle-bone Road; and I remember so well the meals we cooked on a

16

gas ring when my father and my brother, who was on leave from the navy, came to visit us at Christmas. The sloping ceiling was a trial to my father, who was constantly bumping his head against it.

For two of us to live on my salary we had to be very careful; however, as we were free in the evenings, we went to theatres, in the galleries. We used to queue or, if we were lucky, arrive early enough to spread newspapers on the steps leading up to the pay box and sit down for the long wait. Hired stools were unheard of in those days. One of the plays I saw that remains in my mind was *Truth* with Marie Tempest and Dion Boucicault. It was, of course, the first time I had seen these two great artists, and after that I felt I wanted to see whatever Marie Tempest did. I went with Mother to see Genée in *The Débutante*, a most finished production and one which had to be revived many times. I had begun to idolize Genée to such an extent that finally Mother wrote to her about me, and the great lady invited me to go and see her in her dressing-room.

Details of my first meeting with her will, I suppose, stay in my memory as long as I live. I felt very nervous as I passed through the stage door and, with my mother, went stumbling down a dark and narrow staircase. Number 1, Genée's dressing-room, was at the end of a corridor from which swing doors, used only by the star, led directly on to the stage.

And it was such an ordinary and even shabby little room, with a coal fire burning in the grate, in front of which was a nursery fireguard. Daylight filtered in through a grating up near the ceiling. I could hear the footsteps of the people passing overhead along Lisle Street. I stood there, tongue-tied with excitement, staring at all the ballet skirts hung on pegs and at the ballet shoes ranged on either side of her dressing-table. My impression was that there were shoes everywhere.

She received me most kindly and, when I left, gave me a signed photograph of herself as Swanilda.

This, together with the doll Marie Studholme gave me at the end of the run of 'Alice', made me the envy of all the other students when I returned to Gilmer's. It was a lovely doll; and Miss Studholme had made the clothes for it herself, even its white satin corsets, which laced up the back and were properly boned.

4

AFTER my London début I appeared in several charity shows directed by Mr Gilmer. At the first of these, in Nottingham in the early spring of 1907, I danced an arrangement of the Doll Dance from the second act of *Coppélia*. The Duchess of Portland, who was present, sent for me afterwards and was very encouraging. I next met the duchess in 1920 at a Norfolk house party, where I was giving a recital with Prince George Chavchavadze and we recalled our earlier meeting. I was able to tell her how grateful I had been for what she had said.

I went to London for another of these charity performances, which was given at the Royal Albert Hall Theatre by Mr Gilmer for his London pupils. My mother had had leaflets printed with a photograph of me *sur les pointes* and excerpts from my 'Alice' press notices. She sent one to Alfred Butt at the Palace and one to Walter Dickson at the Empire and asked for an appointment while I was in London in Mr Gilmer's show. Both replied, making appointments on two successive days. After I had danced for Alfred Butt he suggested to Mother that we prepare an act lasting from fifteen to twenty minutes with our own scenery and costumes which he would be willing to put into the programme at the Palace. We came away from the interview very crestfallen. We could not possibly afford to do it.

However, the following day I had my audition at the Empire. About ten or twelve men sat in the stalls. I had the whole of the huge stage to myself and the services of Harvey Pinches, the Empire's official accompanist. When my first dance ended I ran to the footlights and called out, 'Would you like to see another?' And I went on in that way to dance no less than eight solos. I did not know that as a rule the management rarely sees more than a few bars of a dance before the performer is stopped and told that she will be written to. Apparently I amused my small audience so much that they wanted to see how long it would be before I tired. The entire board of directors were there, I heard afterwards. They had come from a board meeting and eating a good lunch, and must have been particularly well disposed. Mr Dickson, the Managing Director, came on to the stage when I eventually exhausted my repertoire and immediately offered me a ten weeks' contract.

I was to start work in three weeks, on 27 May, in a revival of the first act of *The Débutante*. He asked my mother what salary I wanted. We were both so dumbfounded by my success that we scarcely knew what to say. Mother told Walter Dickson that I had been receiving four pounds a week in *Alice in Wonderland* and he said, 'Will that suit you?' We agreed, and the contract was signed before we left the theatre.

I have no doubt that Marie Studholme's kindness was instrumental in my being given the audition. She was a friend of Walter Dickson and had already spoken to him about me.

There was more excitement for me that night. It was the opening performance of a new ballet, *Sir Roger de Coverley*. We had booked seats in the front row of the circle. It was my first experience of a West End *première* with its noisy enthusiasm and crowds of well-dressed people.

At the end the ballet mistress, Katti Lanner, took many curtain calls. With this dear old lady was my adored Genée. The contrast between the two was very amusing. They did not come on together; but Genée, with her merry little face, flitted across to the footlights, and Katti Lanner followed her, stumping along with a not very straight back, swinging her bouquet upside down like a market-bag.

The ballet at the Empire in those days and for a good many years afterwards was hampered by there being no classical male dancers in England. Several men appeared in character parts: Tom Walls was generally a villain or an old *roué*; and his acting, needless to say, was of a very high order. The main male character was usually played by Fred Farren, who was an extremely nimble dancer in *demi-caractère*. There were a few other men in the company; but as a rule younger male parts were played by a tall, handsome woman who was known as a *travestie artiste*. Among the women who took these parts I remember Dorothy Craske, Flo Martell, and Hilda Edwardes who married Tom Walls. The *grande dame* was magnificently played by Madame Zanfretta whose miming will be remembered by all who saw her as the most finished work of its kind. No Empire ballet at the time would have been complete without her. Incidentally, it was with Madame Zanfretta that Ursula Moreton studied mime; and Miss Moreton, after a very successful career as a mime, is now the chief teacher of the subject at the Sadler's Wells School.

5

WE STARTED rehearsals for *The Débutante* at once. Although the production was originally Katti Lanner's my two solos were arranged, or rather adapted, by Fred Farren from two that I had danced at my audition. Madame Lanner was none too pleased at my being engaged, as she had quite a number of her own pupils whom she naturally thought ought to have been given the opportunity. She was not particularly nice to me; but I am very glad I came into contact with her. There is no doubt that she was a great influence on the ballet of the day. I can see her now, sitting in the prompt corner, yelling at the *corps de ballet* if she saw the slightest defect in their work or if they were out of line, not realizing that she could be heard by the audience out in front.

My path was made smooth by the kindness and help of Fred Farren who taught me little tricks of the trade and showed me how to make the most of my opportunities. He was greatly loved by the public and by everybody on the other side of the curtain as well. Many were the talks we had together and much of my success in later years I owe to his advice.

Genée's part in *The Débutante* was taken in the revival by Elise Clerc. Fred Farren played his own role of the Dancing Master and I was the Naughty Pupil. This work formed the first part of the programme and began soon after eight o'clock. Three or four first-class variety acts followed; then came the final item of the evening, *Sir Roger de Coverley* with Genée dancing. This started about ten o'clock.

There was a really first-rate orchestra of forty-five instrumentalists under the baton of Cuthbert Clarke, who composed the music for many of the ballets.

Four weeks before my contract expired Mother was sent for by the directors and given a further three years' contract for me at the same salary, plus ten shillings a week which they insisted I should keep as pocket money. We were able to say good-bye to the boarding-house in Woburn Place where we had been living, and take a three-roomed flat over a shop in Haverstock Hill (opposite The Load of Hay), which we furnished on the hire-purchase system. By the time I was fourteen I had a home of my own. Out of my salary we managed to save a little for a rainy day as well as pay for my dancing classes, and instalments on the furniture.

For my father these were years of self-sacrifice: his work kept him in Bristol and he was only able to come to us occasionally at week-ends. Even though he was kept busy with his Amateur Operatic Society he must have had many lonely evenings.

Adeline Genée recommended my mother to put me to study under Madame Cavallazzi. At our first interview Madame, in broken English, asked me: 'What ees your name, darleen?'

I answered: 'Phyllis, Madame.'

'Ah, Joseph!' she said.

'No,' I said. 'Phyllis.'

'Joseph.' She seemed to reflect. 'Joseph will do,' she said.

And from then on that was the name she called me.

I enjoyed my classes, which were for two hours three times a week. We worked hard—very hard—on the technique of the Italian school. Cavallazzi, in her early years, had been a very great dancer and was later a famous mime; but when I was studying with her she had grown elderly and had rheumatism. She rarely moved out of her chair. She taught us by cleverly using her hands. We had to be very quick if we were to understand what *enchaînements* she was setting for us. It became a private game with me to see if I could be first; and soon she began to rely upon me to lead the rest in spite of my being almost the youngest. The youngest was a tiny girl called Olive Walter who wore little white woollen combinations at class and nothing else. she made a name for herself later as Tyltyl in the Haymarket production of Maeterlinck's *Bluebird*. Nearly all the other girls were in the ballet at Covent Garden.

We seldom had any music. In a very cracked voice Cavallazzi used to hum for us and beat time with her feet. 'Ra da da; ra da da.' It might be thought this was uninspiring; but, believe me, Cavallazzi could have inspired a log of wood! And she had a frightening temper: if her pupils displeased her she frequently picked up a chair and threw it against the wall. I have known her lay hands on two girls and knock their heads together. After these bouts of fury she invariably flung out of the room and we heard her swearing in Italian. Her anger spent, she would return and, with tears in her eyes, speak falteringly and quietly to us all: 'Darleens, darleens; what for you do thees to me?'

The classes were held in a basement in Henrietta Street,

21

Covent Garden. Two pillars supported the ceiling, and we became adept at avoiding them. The dressing-room accommodation was extremely cramped and we worked all the time in the smell of apples from a warehouse next door.

Cavallazzi had complained to my mother that my legs were too thin and advised her to order some pads for me to wear under my tights. Burnets, who made all the tights, were given the order, and eventually the pads arrived. I cannot describe how I looked. My very skinny arms and thin body, I suppose I had learned to accept; but, when I looked down, the bulging legs I saw did not seem to belong to me at all. I wore the pads once—and only once. They completely altered my appearance, and not for the better.

There were six evening performances weekly at the Empire, and no matinées. I spent much of my time in the theatre. I used to wander into the property room, which was full of fascinating junk, and go up to talk to the electricians, who were very proud of the theatre's lighting equipment which, I believe, was a long way in advance of that in other theatres. With the stage hands I always got on very well, and made many good friends among them. And they helped to make my life as happy as it was at that time.

I used to practise for about three-quarters of an hour on the stage each evening before the audience was admitted. It was very thrilling, and an eerie experience, to be on that vast stage with just a pilot light burning in the flies. The great safety-curtain was down and swayed heavily, sometimes sufficiently to disturb my balance as I danced. It was a greyish, dirty white.

Sometimes I had the company of Theresa Heyman, another ambitious *coryphée*. She was a very serious worker; we did not chat to each other, but kept to our own portion of the stage.

Whenever ballet skirts were worn, the principals—myself included—had new ones every week, while the *corps de ballet* never wore theirs for more than three weeks before having them renewed. All our costumes were made of expensive materials. Satin shoes and silk tights were provided. The theatre staff, too, like the majority of the company, were permanently employed, and were so well looked after by the management that there was a perfectly genuine feeling that we were all part of a big, contented family.

Most of the *corps de ballet* were girls and women who had grown

22

up in the theatre, and they lived a very strict and steady life. Whatever was true of the front of the theatre, on our side of the curtain we had reached an extreme of rigid respectability. I can remember an occasion when the *corps de ballet* were so shocked at being given dresses to wear without sleeves that they threatened to go on strike. If bare midriffs or bare arms were to be shown the girls were given flesh-coloured stockinet leotards to wear.

There were most extensive wardrobe and dressmaking departments on the premises. Above the front of the theatre were three very large rooms: one occupied by a dozen sewing women, another used by the three assistant wardrobe mistresses who did most of the fittings, and a third, very comfortable room, the sanctum of Miss Hastings, the chief wardrobe mistress, a remarkable character who ruled her domain regally. She used to wear a black taffeta dress and a boned bodice with a high boned collar which always reminded me of Queen Victoria. I never lost my awe of her.

There were also two enormous rooms at the back of the theatre used during the performances by an evening sewing staff. One of the rooms contained dozens of stands with pegs on either side where dresses were hung after each performance for overhauling and renovation. Everything we wore was kept spotless: our tights and any muslin or silk cravats were washed before every show. This had the effect of making us all take a special pride in our appearance; and, I am sure, it added something to the quality of the performances we gave.

It was in this big room with the rows of stands that I first dressed with the two youngest members of the *corps de ballet* because we were considered too young to be in the grown-ups' dressing-rooms. Not that we cared. It was far more exciting for us to be where we were and especially so for me. I was near the stand where Genée's dresses were hung. I used secretly to finger them lovingly and dream of the day when I, too, might reach the heights.

23

6

THEN I received my first present of jewellery from an unknown admirer: it was a beautiful necklace of nine heart-shaped amethysts strung on a gold chain. My mother, even so early in my career, had insisted I should not accept presents from men. As I held the necklace in my hand and watched the light winking in the stones I felt excited and a little sad. I might be allowed to accept flowers, Mother had told me, but nothing else. We made some inquiries at the stage door and were told that the box containing the necklace had been delivered by the driver of a hansom but that there had been no passenger in the cab. There was a charming little note, but we did not recognize the handwriting and there was no name and address. So the necklace could not be returned and I have always kept it.

We in the ballet were always extremely well treated by the management during the last week of rehearsals for a new production when we had to be in the theatre for long stretches at a time. Food was provided in the foyer at the back of the circle for the *corps de ballet* and the stage staff. Principals were given excellent meals at the Queen's Hotel, next door, where a large table was kept laid and ready for any of us who were able to slip out of the theatre for half an hour or so. This arrangement continued until the end of Walter Dickson's management.

I had my fourteenth birthday while we were rehearsing for the new production, and was allowed to join the ladies. I moved into a principal's dressing-room on the ground floor, which I shared with Elise Clerc and a girl from one of the star variety acts. In those days there was no central heating, but in No. 6 we always had a big coal fire in the winter time, which made the place very cosy. An enormous kettle was on the hob boiling water for washing.

Mother used to come with me to the theatre and take me home. She looked like a frightened mouse as she sat in the dressing-room, for she was desperately anxious not to become the typical 'theatre mother'. But she was different from the majority of the dancers' mothers. She never told me when she was going in front to see a performance in case it worried me, and never praised me unless she thought I had done particularly well, whatever

24

flattery I might be receiving from the press and well-meaning friends.

Our new production, *The Belle of the Ball*, was presented on 30 September 1907. It had been written by C. Wilhelm, designer of scenery and costumes. The music was arranged and composed, as it so often was, by Cuthbert Clarke. Fred Farren, who played one of the leading parts, arranged the dances. It was the last ballet in which Genée starred before leaving London on her first visit to America. She played the title role.

The scene was set in Covent Garden market, outside the Opera House, which afforded opportunities for dancing by costers and flower girls, and for excerpts from various light operas performed by people coming away from a fancy dress ball. Madame Zanfretta appeared in *La Fille de Madame Angot* and *La Grande Duchesse*. An arrangement of *Rip Van Winkle* gave a wonderful chance to Genée as the Spirit of Wine. Young Rip was played by Flo Martell and Old Rip by Tom Walls. I played the Demon Dwarf in this scene with a humped back, false nose, and a long grey beard and wig. My shoes and stockings were padded out to make me look old, and I carried a barrel of wine on my shoulder for Genée to use when she tempted Young Rip. I revelled in the part. Sickly green light from one of the spots followed me as I moved round the stage. Later in the ballet I was a cheeky little coster girl, dancing to a popular tune of the period, 'Poppies', played on a hurdy-gurdy. A hefty policeman ordered me off and I slipped away, making a long nose at him and hearing the audience laughing out in the theatre. Genée was also a delicious Veronique. She made her entrance seated on a dear little live donkey led by Hilda Edwardes, who was playing Florestan.

Genée was a tremendously hard worker. For two hours each day the stage was left for her use. She studied generally under her uncle, but alone if he were not there. It was a rule, strictly observed, that nobody disturb her during that time. I had a great friend, one of the stage hands up in the flies, and used to climb the iron steps and creep along the bridge among the hanging backcloths and sky-borders to watch my idol. I was terrified lest she should discover that I was playing Paul Pry; but she never did. I learned much from watching her. During performances, too, I would stand in the wings whenever she was on and I was not actually dancing myself or changing.

I wish that the great ballet public of to-day could see her as she

25

A NEW AND ORIGINAL DIVERTISSEMENT.

7 "THE BELLE OF THE BALL."

AN EPISODE OF COVENT GARDEN.

By C. WILHELM.

A Terpsichorean Pot-pourri of Popular Melodies, past and present.

Produced by C. WILHELM and FRED FARREN.
The Music Composed and Selected by CUTHBERT CLARKE.
The Dances and the Action arranged by FRED FARREN.
Scenery by JOSEPH HARKER.

The Costumes (from Mr. WILHELM'S designs) by Miss HASTINGS and MORRIS ANGEL & SONS. Machinist, W. SHELDON   Properties by P. GRIEVESON.   Electrician, C WINTER. Wigs by CLARKSON   Floral Accessories by GATTI & CO

Period—TO-DAY   Scene—COVENT GARDEN MARKET   Time—DAYBREAK

CHARACTERS.

NAT NIMBLE (a Cos'er Lad)............	Mr. FRED FARREN
ARAMINTA (his "Donah")......	............Miss ELISE CLERC
Captain JACK JERMYN (a Man about Town).................	Mr. TOM WALLS
MONTY GRAFTON .... }"his "Pals")	{.. Miss F. MARTELL
PERCY MADDOX ..... }	{ Miss B. TREVESICK
Col. BURLINGTON..... }	{ .... Mr. JAMESON
JUDITH LEBRUN (A Parisian Artiste)................	Mlle. F. ZANFRETTA
GERTIE GAYSPARKLE } (Popular Actresses)......	{..... Miss M. PASTON
ALMA EGERTON ...... }	{ Miss EVA McFARLANE
BIRDIE BELLAIR ....}	{.. Miss ELSIE COLLIER
MAX RITZHOPPER (of the Moravian Embassy)...	Mr. PAUL BUNDBERG
BLACK BEN (a Loafer)	Mr. H. FORD
NANCE (his Wife, a Flower-Seller)	.................Miss B. HILL
TINY TRIPPIT (a Child Dancer)	Miss PHYLLIS BEDELLS
ALGY ALBEMARLE .... Mr. A. YOUNG BOBBY BUNTING . . .. Mr. HILTON	
AUCTIONEER.............Mr. LEWINGTON POLICEMAN. ....Mr. RODFORD	

AND

STELLA DARE (Queen of the Dance)....... ..Mlle. ADELINE GENÉE

Mlle. Genée's Dances and Action arranged by Mons. A. Genée.

DANDIES................. ..{ Misses COURTLAND, KAYGILL, H. EDWARDS, ROULLRIGHT, DAWSON, RUBY, WILLEY, and REEVES.

PARASOL LADIES..... ....{ Misses MANSELL, G. TREE, G THOMAS, BANKS, B. HILL, DENTON, BANBURY, and BEACON.

MARKET ORDERLIES......{ Misses OSMOND, B. COLLIER, PAYNE, FARRANT, RUSHTON, BOSETTI, ARIGONI, and CUNNINGHAME.

COSTER BOYS AND GIRLS, MARKET PORTERS, DANCERS, FOOTMEN, HOSPITAL NURSES, &c., &c., by Misses LYONS, DESMOND, CARTHEW, JONES, WADE, HEWITT, and SHEPHERD, Messrs. WHITE, FREWIN, ORAM, G. T. VINCENT, L. GREVILLE, and the Ladies, Gentlemen, and Children of the Corps de Ballet.

The Motor Car kindly lent by THE GERMAIN MOTOR CO. (with Ducellier Lamps).

The Music by kind permission of SIDNEY JONES, Esq , LESLIE STUART, Esq., Messrs BOOSEY & CO., Messrs. ASCHENBERG & CO', and the respective Composers and Publishers.

was then. For ten years she had reigned supreme at the Empire and was advertised all over the town—I believe, with reason—as the world's greatest dancer. Her technique was so perfect that I am quite certain if a film of her dancing had been stopped in the middle of any movement she would have been found in an absolutely correct position. This cannot be said of many of the dancers of to-day, as the action photographs which are published demonstrate. And it must be remembered that Genée did not have the support of a male dancer at the Empire to enhance the beauty of her movements. She had to do without lifts and supported pirouettes and the fouettés which we see so much of to-day but her elevation was wonderful, her *batterie* brilliant, and her pirouettes simply took one's breath away. Mostly she danced in merry, mischievous parts and in these she was supreme.

She celebrated the tenth anniversary of her first Empire appearance on 22 November 1907. What a triumphant night it was! The crowds in the theatre and we on the stage cheered and cheered while she took call after call and the bouquets were handed up to her.

Another unforgettable night was when Genée's contract came to an end in December 1907. It seemed that the great audience in the theatre would never stop cheering. The huge stage was piled high with flowers from her devoted public. I cried my eyes out as I stood in the wings and realized that she was leaving us.

The Belle of the Ball was given a second edition when Genée had left, and Topsy Sinden was brought in as principal dancer. She was a quite different type of artist. She excelled in a light and easy kind of tap-dancing which has been much developed since, and in skirt dancing, which was very popular in the musical comedies of the period. How I missed Genée!

The Rip Van Winkle scene had been retained and I still played the Demon Dwarf; but that was immediately followed by a new selection from *The Geisha* in which I appeared as a midshipman and made my entrance to the tune of 'Jack's the Boy for Work', dancing a hornpipe. I had to make what was for those days a record quick change, discarding the clothes of the dwarf and dressing as a dapper young naval officer with a boy's wig, a collar, tie—every detail correct, even to white kid gloves. It took under a minute and a half—and I had to make my second entrance from the opposite side of the stage! Of course I used the quick-change room at the side; but it was really due to the calm, experienced

27

manner of Madame Willmain, my French dresser, that I was able
do it. We used the same routine each night. We never spoke
a word. All she said, on the very first occasion, was, 'Save your
breath.'

Whenever the weather allowed, mother and I got a great deal of
enjoyment from riding home all the way from Leicester Square
to The Load of Hay on the top of a horse-bus. We usually
managed to work our way to the front next to the driver's high
seat. We came to know all the drivers, and we used to give them
some of the fruit we were always buying, and talk to them as we
rode along. They had marvellous tales to tell.

It was one of the last London horse-bus services to be closed
down. We went on one of them on its final journey. It was a
sad day for us. And I shall always remember the face of our
driver when we got to the end of the journey and he began to say
good-bye to his horse. It was almost more than we could bear.
All of us were weeping. The last I saw of that dear old man he
had his arm round the horse's neck and tears were streaming down
his wrinkled face.

7

WHAT a glorious theatre the old Empire was in those days! It
could be said to reflect completely a part of the life of an era which
has vanished and may be sentimentally lamented by many.

Thick-piled carpets covered the high staircase which rose
through a mirrored hall to the circle. The interior was painted
sage green and gilded in the taste of the times. Wigged flunkeys
in their green liveries held the green curtains as they closed.
In the comfort of separate armchairs reclined its well-dressed,
moneyed clientele, among them the 'men about town', now an
almost extinct species, who in their leisurely way enjoyed an
evening at the theatre and a well-cooked supper afterwards.

But for those of meagre means who wished to taste this luxury
five-shilling rover tickets were sold, which entitled the purchaser
to roam through the theatre and eventually to seat himself, if he
wished, upon one of the fatly upholstered settees which lined the
walls.

Upstairs, behind the circle, was a large bar, and the promenade frequented by the 'ladies of the town'. No woman who considered herself to be a lady ever sat in the circle. Nor would any gentleman take her there.

The gallery had its professional *claque* then, composed of people who led the applause for certain of the artists. For this service they were paid—but never by me!

My mother decided to give up her own stage work and devote herself to me. One awful experience when she was appearing in Paul Mill's concert party finally persuaded her to do this. Someone had fallen ill, and she had been asked by Paul Mill to help him out of the difficulty by joining the show which was appearing at two music-halls a night and twice nightly at each. A real London fog came down—one of the worst I can remember. I came home on the Hampstead tube, which had been recently opened, and got out at Chalk Farm Station, which was near to our flat. I expected Mother to be home for supper by midnight; but the hours passed and still she did not come. I was alone. My imagination began to work, and I thought of all the terrible things that might have happened until, by three o'clock in the morning, I had driven myself half-crazy with anxiety. When she eventually arrived I did not believe it.

It took me some time to recover from the hysterical state into which I had got myself. Afterwards Mother would never leave me.

With Genée still away, in the spring of 1908 a revue was produced which I believe was one of the first of such shows to be seen in London. Arthur Playfair and Farren Souter were in the cast. For a time ballet was relegated to an earlier place in the Empire's programme.

That same spring I remember London being startled by a new dancer at the Palace: Maud Allan, who danced barefoot, clad in Grecian draperies, to music drawn from the classics. Her Salomé to Strauss's music caused a great sensation and many were very shocked by it. As a result of so much publicity there were crowded houses. We at the Empire were severely critical, as we felt Maud Allan's work lacked any sort of technique. We were unable to agree with her when she claimed that 'the dance is not an acquired but a spontaneous art and reveals the temperament of the dancer'.

She had wonderfully supple arms which she could set rippling from shoulder to fingertips. This she did so often, however, that jokes were made about it in the music-halls. Isadora Duncan was far less sensational; but, with her, 'natural' dancing was seen to have a technique of its own which was plainly the result of much careful study. It had a far greater appeal to artists.

As my real birthday was on 9 August and I expected to be away on holiday then, on the first anniversary of my début at the Empire I gave a party in my dressing-room and invited the company. Mother arranged with the Stage Director to see that his staff—electricians, stage hands, and everybody—drank my health. For nine successive years this was a regular occasion, and known as my Empire birthday.

Genée returned for a short season on 10 June 1908, fresh from her triumph in America. *Coppélia* was revived for her. My little gallery-girl's dream was realized: I was able to stand in the wings, less than a yard or so from that glorious artist whom I had seen as Swanilda from so far off only two years before. And what a reception she was given! The vast theatre was filled to capacity. Hundreds were turned away. Her dancing was, if that were possible, better than it had ever been. My excitement ran high. I was so thrilled that I bought a doll with my own pocket money and dressed it in an exact copy of the dress Genée wore in the ballet. It even had pink silk tights and satin ballet shoes. It was difficult to make the shoes look neat, and I had trouble in getting ribbons narrow enough for the sandalling. But I was very proud when she thanked me for it and seemed to guess how much devotion had gone into the making of it.

That year, on 17 August, Lydia Kyasht was the first of the Russian dancers to make her début in London. With her partner, Adolf Bolm, she presented a *divertissement* which was not a ballet, but a series of dances. Our dresser, Madame Willmain, was lent to her as Kyasht spoke no English. The little Russian was as pretty as a china doll; but I recall how appalled we were by the very short tutu she wore. Until her arrival everyone's ballet skirts had been made to reach to the knee and this new fashion was not easy to accept—though it was one that had come to stay.

Adolf Bolm had little to do and few opportunities to show what a fine artist he was. We were all interested to see for the first time supported *pas de deux* work. I am afraid that we were inclined to think everything was made much too easy for Kyasht, not realizing that a different and very difficult technique is involved.

30

Genée's reappearance had been so successful that the directors persuaded her to extend her engagement until she was due to return to America, and one of the most perfect little ballets was produced for her. It had a tragic quality about it, quite different from anything I had previously seen her do. It was called *The Dryad* and had music by Dora Bright. Genée was on stage from beginning to end. There were only two other characters: a shepherd, played by Gordon Cleather who was also required to sing, and a small walking-on part played by Connie Walter from the *corps de ballet*. Perhaps, in the true sense of the word, it was not a ballet at all; but it was a severe test of acting and dancing skill which few ballerinas could have met with success. At the end all of us watching in the wings were weeping.

Kyasht was given a contract to remain at the Empire as *prima ballerina*. She at once took over the role of Swanilda in *Coppélia* so that Genée could continue in *The Dryad*. I used to watch Kyasht; but my admiration for Genée at that time would never allow me to wax enthusiastic about a newcomer.

As she was unable to speak our language Kyasht must have had a very lonely time. The difficulty of her position can be imagined: she had to step into Genée's shoes in a strange country with no friends to whom she could talk. And her manner then gave us the impression that she was hard and cold. Later, when we knew her better and she had become used to us, we found that this was far from being true.

Madame Willmain had to devote all her time to Kyasht, and we were given a new dresser who had been a member of the staff since the Empire opened in 1884. She was Mrs Smith and she looked very austere. Although she had a splendid head of hair she fastened it back so tightly in a large bun and was so neat in her person that one would never have suspected she was a dresser at all. Nevertheless she had a dry kind of wit, and a fund of stories from which she kept us amused. She had definite likes and dislikes, but she and I became so attached that she stayed with me until the day I left.

A DAY IN PARIS.

A BALLET, IN FIVE SCENES, by Lt.-Col. N. NEWNHAM-DAVIS.

Music Composed and Arranged by CUTHBERT CLARKE. Produced by FRED FARREN.

The entire Production designed and supervised by C. WILHELM.

Dresses by Miss HASTINGS and MORRIS ANGEL & Co.

Electrician, C. WINTER. Machinist, W. SHELDON. Properties by P. GRIEVESON.

Wigs by CLARKSON.

SCENE 1.—The Place de l'Opéra	...	F. Harker.
SCENE 2.—On the Quays	...	R. McCleery.
SCENE 3.—In the Champs Elysées	...	R. McCleery.
SCENE 4.—Outside the Moulin Rouge	...	A. Terraine.
SCENE 5.—The Artists' Ball	...	A. Terraine (designed by C. Wilhelm).

CHARACTERS.

JACQUES BONFAIR (a student of Montmartre)... Mr. FRED FARREN
GEORGES LEGAY } (his Friends) ...... { Mr. FRANK BENTON
PAUL SOREL   { Miss F. NARTALL
JOHN BULLIVANT SMITH, Esq. (of Brixton) ...... Mr. NARTALL
AUGUSTE EUPHEMIA (his Wife) .... Miss L. GIMOND
FIFI } (their Daughters) ... { Miss PHYLLIS BEDELLS
POPPI }
LE COMTE DE CANTELOUP (A Vieux Marcheur).. Mr. TOM WALLS
BABETTE ("La Panthre") .... Miss BEATRIX COLLIER
A Nurse .... Miss M. PASTON
A Parson Officer .... Miss HILDA EDWARDES
ARLOSON .... Messrs. HUNTER and FORD
MIMI LA FLEURIE (A Street Singer) ...... Miss D. PAYER
MARI (a Blanchisseuse) .... Miss BELLE HILL
PERVENTS (a fashionable Modiste) ...... Miss ELSIE COLLIER
LA GRANADA (a popular Model) ...... Mme. ZANFRETTA
                                            AND
LA GLOIRE DE PARIS (in Scene 5) } ...... Mlle. LYDIA KYASHT
L'ARC-EN-CIEL (in Scene 5) }

And the Ladies and Gentlemen of the Corps de Ballet.

DANCES.

Scene 1.—Baker Boys and Midinettes Dance Pas Seul by Miss D. PAYER
Scene 3.—Sortorie......{ Mme. ZANFRETTA, Misses MARTELL
                         { TERRYBROOK, D. VANE, CUNNINGHAM
                         and Mr. FARREN
Scene 2.—Children and Nurses' Dance - { Pas Seul by Miss PHYLLIS
                                        BEDELLS
Duo Comique ...... Miss L. OSMOND and Mr. FRED FARREN
Grand Military Spectacle
Evolutions by the Zouaves } THE CORPS DE BALLET
Dance of Cantinieres and Officers }
March (Variations) .... Mlle. LYDIA KYASHT
                GRAND TABLEAU.
Scene 4.—Dames des Apaches ...... { Miss BEATRIX COLLIER and
                                     Mr. FRED FARREN
Scene 5.—Danse Tourbillon .... THE CORPS DE BALLET
Primantic Pageant .... LES BOURLOFFS
Polka Fantasy .... Mlle. LYDIA KYASHT
Pas de Trois ... { Miss L. OSMOND, Miss PHYLLIS BEDELLS
                  and Mr. FRED FARREN
DANSE RUSSE .... Mlle. LYDIA KYASHT
(Mlle. Kyasht's dances arranged by Mr. Alexander Genée.)
                GRAND FINALE.

9

THE BIOSCOPE. Special and Exclusive Pictures.

(Photographs by THE WARWICK TRADING CO., LONDON).

Italian Cavalry Manoeuvres. The Earthquake at Messina. A Review at Aldershot.

FINALE MARCH	...	"Ah! Si Vous Voulez"	... ... V. Scotto.

Manager	... ...	Mr. H. J. HITCHINS.
Acting-Manager	- -	Mr. A. ALDIN.

Stage Director—Mr. ALEXANDER BUTLER.   Musical Director—Mr. CUTHBERT CLARKE.

8

IN THE SUMMER of 1908 Walter Dickson sent for Mother to tell her
that he had decided I was getting 'too set' in the technique of the
Italian School and it was beginning to show in my work, which
was losing its spontaneity. The directors had therefore decided
to put me under Monsieur Alexander Genée, Adeline Genée's
uncle, and would pay for my lessons. Monsieur Genée lived in
Brighton but he came to London three times a week to give me my
lessons on the Empire stage. Was ever a child more fortunate?

A Day in Paris was our next big production. It was a ballet of
the lighter kind, and very expensively produced in five scenes,
with Wilhelm's *décor* and Cuthbert Clarke's music. Once again
Fred Farren, who also played the leading part as a Student from
Montmartre, disguised as a Man from Cook's, was responsible
for the dance arrangements. The ballet had the slightest of plots,
concerning the arrival of Mr and Mrs Smith and their two
daughters in Paris on a sightseeing tour. I was the younger
daughter. The whole thing had a striking success and ran for
nearly a year. In the Champs Élysées scene I had a skipping-rope
dance which gave me my first really big success. On the first
night I was quite bewildered, and did not know what to do when
the audience began to cheer me. Dear Fred Farren came to the
rescue and made me take call after call holding on to his hand.
Kyasht had a very fine *demi-caractère* solo arranged for her specially
by Alexander Genée and there was a splendid military spectacle
for the zouaves which brought the house down. Fred Farren's and
Beatrice Collier's *Danse des Apaches* became the rage of London—
it was actually the first time such a dance had been seen over here.

In the final scene, inside the Moulin Rouge, everybody was
given an opportunity. There was a *pas de trois* for Elise Clerc,
Fred Farren, and myself. Elise wore white, I black, and Fred
Farren was in black and white. But the crowning success here
was Lydia Kyasht's *Danse Russe*, which was a court dance adapted
for point work.

Next morning we had a call for cuts because the ballet was
rather too long. The press notices had been marvellous, and I
was beginning to think that I was already climbing the ladder to
the heights. Imagine the shock I had when, at the rehearsal,

Cuthbert Clarke came to me and said, 'Do you know your skipping-rope dance is cut?'

I thought it could not possibly be true and went to Fred Farren. With a twinkle in his eyes that I did not notice, he said: 'Oh yes, dear. It is.'

It was more than I could bear and I quietly slipped away to the back of the stalls and sobbed my heart out. Soon I heard them calling for me and when I did not answer they searched and found me, a crumpled heap of misery at the back of the dark theatre. They seemed very upset that I had taken their teasing seriously and explained that only a few bars of my solo had been cut to give me enough breath for an encore.

During the entire run of the show I danced an encore at every performance.

For the first time I saw my name on the sandwich-boards carried around London and on the sides of the buses. When I passed I used to feel self-conscious and very proud at the same time. In nearly all my press notices there was a reference to my having modelled myself upon Genée. One of my notices, which was quoted in the advertisements, was a family joke for many years: 'Phyllis Bedells is a dream of daintiness.' 'Here comes the dream of daintiness,' they'd say.

I had settled down to study hard under Monsieur Genée. I enjoyed my lessons with him and began to show more polish in my work. By the time I reached my fifteenth birthday I had begun to grow very fast and, I suppose, was fortunate to have a long contract to tide me over the awkward age when most girls find it difficult to obtain engagements.

I studied the piano under Mr Pinches, too. All the girls loved him. He lived in the country and came to rehearsal with his big pockets bulging with apples and nuts from his orchard; while he was playing, we put our hands into his pockets and took what we liked.

When I was doing my practice on the stage, he would sit down at the piano and, looking up suddenly, would say, 'Arrange something to this.' While he played music in five-four or nine-four time I was expected to improvise the dance steps. It was some time afterwards before I heard of Dalcroze and his method, which has been so useful in helping dancers to understand various time signatures I had only worked in the usual three-four, six-eight, or four-four rhythms, and I found it most refreshing to be introduced to these other rhythms. Mr Pinches had a special little way of attracting my attention. He would just play the first few bars of the old song 'Phyllis is my only joy' and sometimes, when he knew I was sad or disappointed, he would play it in a plaintive minor key.

Running at the same time as *A Day in Paris* was a one-act play, *After the Opera* by Malcolm Watson, then dramatic critic on the *Daily Telegraph*. His wife, Evelyn D'Alroy, played in it, and Owen Nares was her leading man. Often a short dramatic piece was put into the programme at the Empire to add weight to it. Tom Walls played a burglar on this occasion. He murdered Evelyn D'Alroy in the play and Owen Nares, her lover, was accused of the murder. Although I was so very young and he almost unknown then, I worshipped Owen Nares.

Elise Clerc left the Empire in the autumn to produce and dance in a ballet at the Alhambra. I missed her mixture of French and cockney humour very much. Her understudy, Lizzie Osmond, who had taken over her parts, came to join me in No. 6. Lizzie was very slender and, in those days, women were expected to have ample curves. It amused me to see that she had a bustle which she tied on under her skirt to give herself the necessary shape.

King Edward VII came often to the Empire. In my collection I have his programme for the performance of 18 January 1909. There was the complete ballet, *A Day in Paris*, which was preceded by a new one-act play by W. J. Locke, *A Blank Cheque*. C. V. France, Evelyn D'Alroy, and Margaret Lennox played in this. The programme ended with a bioscope. This was what we would now call a newsreel. But those were the early days of films and what we saw on the screen was poor, flickering stuff—grotesque, hurrying figures like marionettes.

It will be seen that the programmes were of generous proportions and that the public for ballet—a large and enthusiastic one even then—was amply catered for. But how did the ballet then compare with ours to-day? What of the choreography?

Choreography was a word we never used. Until Kyasht's arrival most of the ballets were produced by Fred Farren. Or, as the programmes sometimes put it, the dances were 'arranged by Fred Farren'.

Farren himself had very little of the pure ballet technique, but he had a decided flair for making individual dance arrangements and fitting these together into a plan of work. I would plot out my own dances to the music I was given, then take what I had done to him for criticism. He would add a touch of his own here and there and incorporate my material into the whole.

When I look back on those days it seems to me that Fred Farren's work was remarkably similar in quality and design to such contemporary ballets as *Douanes* and *Façade*, and that Kyasht's choreography was as fine as the best we see to-day. She brought us the classical style and, like the other Russians, she taught from her memory of what had been done in the great theatres of her homeland.

As for the music, it is true that sometimes it was selected from the works of widely different composers and the mixing of styles was only too evident. In this respect, however, the Diaghilev company was unable to escape criticism. In such works as *Cleopatra* similar music mixtures were offered. Cuthbert Clarke, the Empire's director of music, did compose the music for the majority of the ballets himself. The score of *The Débutante* was entirely his. Dora Bright wrote music for others.

The *décor* we would probably consider painfully realistic in these days. It corresponded to the theatrical taste of the times against which as yet only a few lone figures—notably, among them, Granville-Barker—were beginning to revolt.

9

It was then a habit of the more well-to-do to engage artistes for their evening parties; and in those days there was so much rivalry between hostesses that it was not difficult for me to obtain engagements of that kind. One of the first of these occasions that I remember was at a big party given by Lady Evelyn Guinness at her house in Grosvenor Place. The Prince and Princess of Wales—who were afterwards to become Their Majesties King George V and Queen Mary—honoured the affair with their presence.

Fred Farren and Beatrice Collier had also been engaged to do their apache dance, and Les Videos, a team of roller-skaters, completed what we would now call the cabaret. A small stage had been specially built in the ballroom and Their Royal Highnesses were of course seated in the centre of the front row. Les

Videos appeared first and, for their act, had powdered chalk sprinkled on the stage. When Fred Farren and Beatrice Collier came on to dance they fell about all the time. The chalk had made the floor extremely slippery. Luckily, in an apache dance, the effect is not marred by an occasional spill, however much it might hurt! When these two had finished, however, I refused to go on until the stage had been swept. I was only fifteen and I did not realize what a commotion I caused. Naturally I was nervous and my only concern was for my career which, I felt, would be ruined were I to fall. The entire performance had to be held up while two flunkeys in powdered wigs swept up the chalk and made a distressing display with their brushes beneath the Royal noses. I go hot and cold with embarrassment when I realize what a nuisance I must have been.

Another time I went with Mother to the Bourne End home of Mr and Mrs George Kessler, American millionaires, who were entertaining a large house-party for the week-end. We enjoyed our first experience of real luxury in the wonderful suite of rooms put at our disposal. After my last performance on Saturday we hurried on there. Mother often told me how ashamed she felt when the maid asked for our keys in order to do our unpacking for us. We had cheap Japanese baskets bound up with string. I was then blissfully unconscious of mother's chagrin at the maid's turning up her nose at this obvious sign of our poverty. My salary at the theatre was still only four pounds ten shillings a week; but, for this one engagement, I received a fee of twenty guineas. And I was treated by Mr and Mrs Kessler as if I had been a princess. After I had danced for the guests on Sunday evening there was a supper party, and I was made to feel that I was the guest of honour. I remember being immensely impressed by the long dining-table, the whole centre of which was inches deep in rose petals of a lovely shade of pink and with a heavenly perfume, and, above these, the long flames of the candles.

Across Leicester Square, behind the trees, the old Alhambra— a great Moorish palace of a place—was the Empire's rival house, and offered a similar programme of variety and ballet. Between the dancers at the two theatres a fierce rivalry existed, and I am afraid we at the Empire looked down rather on the Alhambra girls. I dare say this was because their theatre had never had a ballerina of Genée's status. Still, as often as I could, I used to slip across the square to see their productions, and still remember a delicious little Danish dancer named Britta, and La Belle Leonora who was in some of the same ballets. One of the productions, *On the Square*, was the work of Elise Clerc, who afterwards returned to us at the Empire. As well as producing this ballet she had an amusing dance in it in which she was partnered by Frank Lawton, who had made a name for himself as a whistler in *The Belle of New York*. His wife, Daisy Collier, was one of five beautiful sisters who were members of the Empire *corps de ballet* during my time there. Daisy had an attractive small son who is well known in the theatre world of to-day as Frank Lawton, and who certainly has the Collier good looks. There was a clever *pas de deux* danced by Carlotta Mossetti and Britta. Mossetti, a pupil of Rosi, was a great favourite there: she played the boys' parts, and her technique in 'male dancing' was extraordinarily good.

But some of the finest technique I had ever seen at this time was displayed by Katrina Geltzer and Tichomiroff, Russian dancers who were at the Alhambra a year or two later fulfilling a short engagement. Their placing was perfect. That they did not create more of a sensation was due, I think, to their both being rather thickset and lacking an appearance of lightness and delicacy.

It was July 1909 before Genée returned once more, and this time she danced the ballet from Meyerbeer's opera *Robert the Devil*, which was produced for her by her uncle.

The scene for this was set in a ruined convent at midnight. Noel Fleming was Robert and Genée the Spirit of Elena, the Abbess who haunts the convent. There was some beautiful work in the ballet, which was similar in style to Act II of *Giselle*, although, in many respects, more difficult for the ballerina.

I was still studying with Alexander Genée and he insisted upon teaching me the part his niece was playing because, he said, he hoped the management would allow me to take over the part when she had gone back to America. I found it very thrilling to be working with him on this. Several times I remember the great ballerina herself coming down to watch me. Once she asked how old I was; and I said, 'Fifteen, Madame—nearly sixteen.'

She said, 'I was a ballerina at sixteen.'

The management could not allow me to dance in *Robert the Devil*, however, as Lydia Kyasht was our *prima ballerina* and I was only second to her. I realize now that they behaved perfectly correctly. And anyway the training I received in the role from Alexander Genée must have been extremely good for me.

38

After twelve happy months the run of *A Day in Paris* was almost over, and we were at the final stages of rehearsals for our next ballet when Beatrice Collier had a serious accident to her foot, and a substitute for her had to be found. Monty Leveaux, who was responsible for bringing Lydia Kyasht to the Empire, brought Unity More along—to my everlasting joy.

Until then she had only appeared as an amateur, except for an engagement in Manchester in *Bluebell in Fairyland* in which she played the name part. She was put to dress with me in No. 6. A friendship was struck up between us which I treasure to this day. Unity was slightly my senior, and her nickname for me was Baby Darling. We had much in common, particularly our love of music, our love of the theatre, and the same sense of fun. We were never jealous of one another because our ambitions were wholly different. She longed to make a name for herself as a musical comedy star—which she did—and I yearned to become a great ballerina.

She had learned to dance with the famous Mrs Wordsworth, who was not at all pleased if any of her pupils went on the stage. Oddly enough, Theodore Gilmer, with whom I had studied, was Mrs Wordsworth's close rival—both taught in Queen's Gate, Kensington.

Unity More was with me in our next new ballet, *Round the World*, which opened in October 1909. The attempt to go round the world in a month in order to settle a wager between two rivals for the hand of a beautiful Argentinian heiress provided what story there was as well as being an admirable excuse for a succession of spectacular scenes. Kyasht herself was sensationally successful, I remember, dancing as a wild Russian gipsy in the Moscow scene. In this I played her younger brother and had to defend her against a brutal showman. So much did I get into the skin of the part that I shed real tears of rage at every performance. I think that part first awakened in me a longing to act and lose myself completely in what I was doing.

It is amusing to point the parallel between this Moscow scene and Fokine's production of *Petrouchka*, which London did not see for a long time afterwards. The music and the story were different, of course; but it had the same setting, the crowds were handled in very much the same way; there were cossacks and nursemaids—and even the street dancers and a performing bear.

The ballet ran successfully until the following March, when a

39

revised and shortened version, re-titled *East and West*, was put into an earlier place in the programme. Adolf Bolm, Lydia Kyasht's original partner, came to London to join her again. Since leaving the Imperial Russian Ballet in St Petersburg he had been dancing in Paris with the newly formed Diaghilev company.

I got very excited when my brother arrived on leave from the Navy. It seemed so long since I had seen him and so much had happened. One day after tea we went out to the shops to buy all sorts of things, and we were strolling casually back home carrying some flowers I had bought for Mother when we met her. She looked frantically at me and called out, 'Do you know the time!'

We discovered that my brother's watch had stopped and I was due to appear on the stage as a Japanese girl in less than half an hour. I just turned and flew as fast as my legs would carry me to Chalk Farm Station. It took twenty-five minutes to get to Leicester Square and to dash along Lisle Street to the Stage Door. The curtain was already up when I arrived. Luckily, donning my wig and kimono and dabbing rouge on my cheeks quickly effected the transformation. And I descended the stairs two at a time just as I heard the music for my dance beginning.

About this time an invitation came for me to play the first twin in *Peter Pan*, which was even then the regular Christmas entertainment. I had seen it several years running, with Pauline Chase as Peter Pan and Hilda Trevelyan as a most perfect Wendy. So when Dion Boucicault wrote, asking Mother and me to go to see him, I was ready to jump at the opportunity. He was really most kind but rather terrifying—a stumpy man who had piercing blue eyes. He would not let Mother talk at all but put all his questions to me, young as I was. He said he would ask the Empire's management to permit me to dance the pillow dance; but, unfortunately for me, they refused, and I was never able to do it.

Dion Boucicault, however, continued to be interested in me and asked Mother to be certain never to sign any contract or to commit me in any way without first letting him read through the conditions. For many years he gave us valuable advice whenever we found ourselves in a quandary. Our friendship with him and his wife, Irene Vanbrugh, lasted for the rest of their lives. Dion Boucicault died in 1929 but Irene lived until 1949. She was made a D.B.E. in 1941.

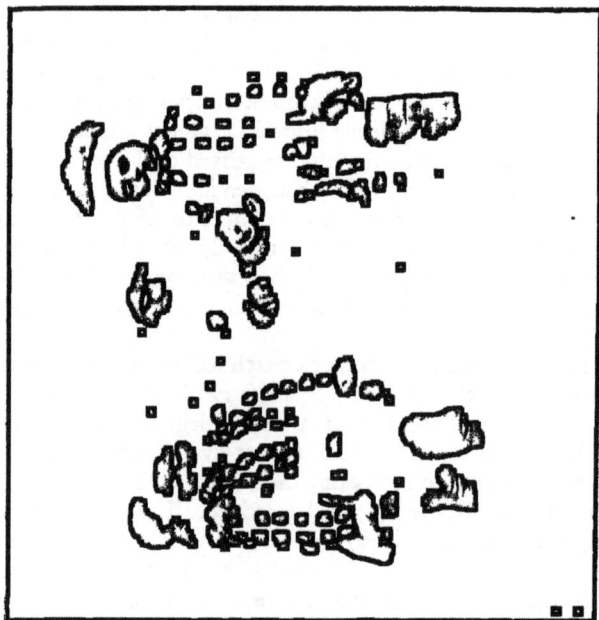

The author (*left*) as the second royal page in *Merrie England*, 1905, produced by her father for the Bristol Amateur Operatic Society. Her brother played the Queen's Fool.

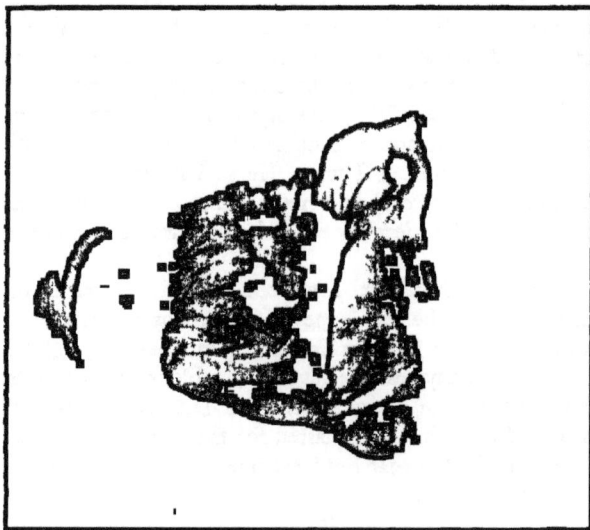

F. Jenkins

First appearance. With Paul Mill's concert party at Lowestoft, aged 8

Four of the dances in the author's repertoire while she was with Paul Mill at Lowestoft in 1906.
Top · Irish Jig and Coon   *Bottom*. Skirt Dance and Sunshade Dance.

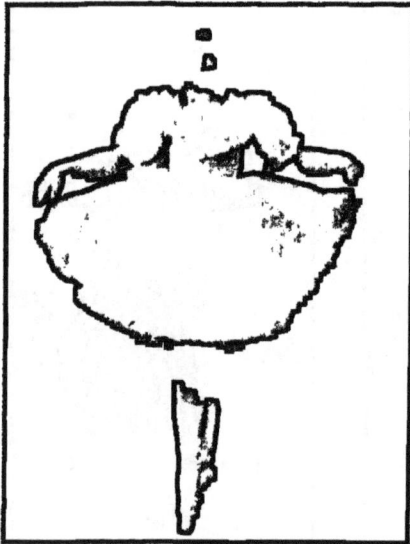

The portrait on the front of the leaflet prepared by Mrs Bedells in 1907, which helped in getting the first contract at the Empire Theatre

Adeline Genée, as the author first saw her in *Coppélia* at the Empire Theatre in 1906

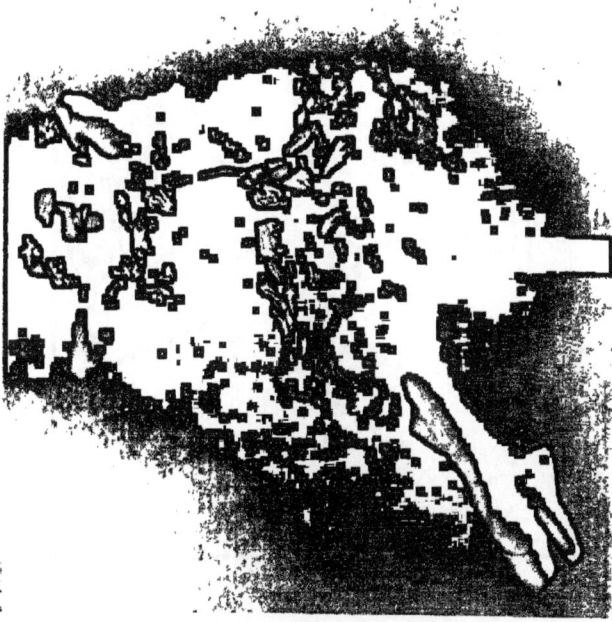

Left As First Oyster in *Alice in Wonderland*, at the Prince of Wales Theatre, Christmas 1906, and *(right)* as Cornflower in the same production.

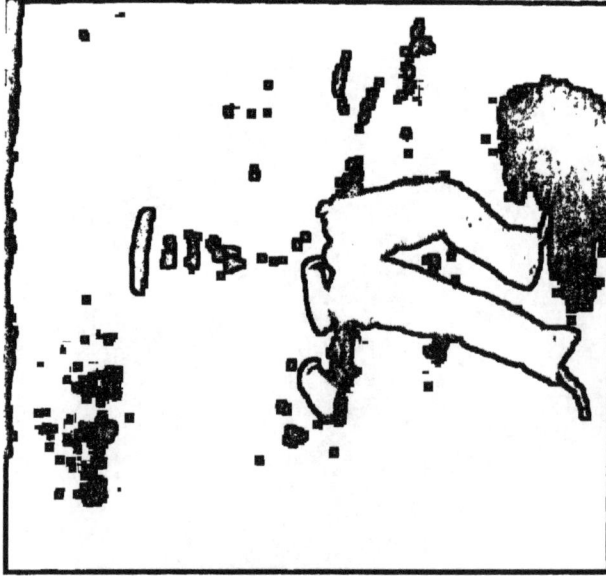

The Demon Dwarf and the Midshipman, two roles danced by Phyllis Bedells in *The Belle of the Ball* at the Empire Theatre in 1907.

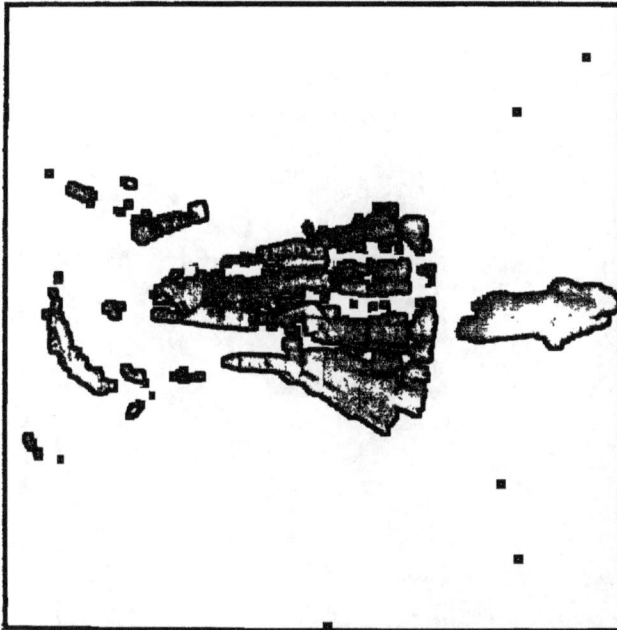

Ellis & Walery

The Skipping Rope Dance from *A Day in Paris*, 1908–9.

A snapshot taken at the stage door of the Empire Theatre during the run of this production.

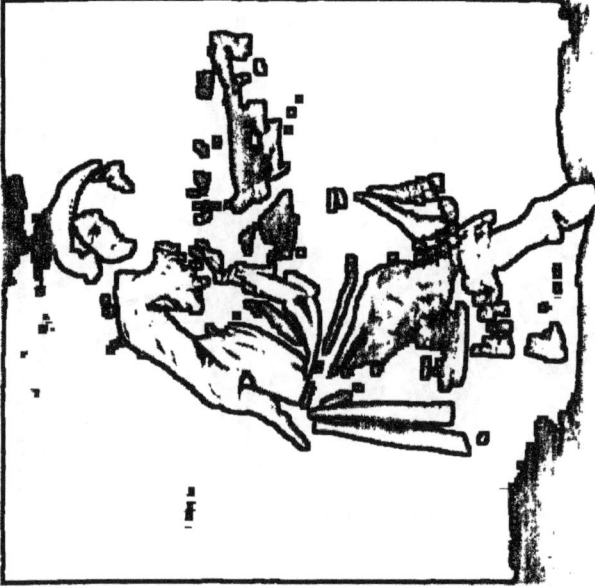

In *Ship - Ahoy* at the Empire Theatre, 1910.

Bassano

The author wearing practice dress, at the age of 16.

Edwin Neame

Foulsham & Banfield

As Red Riding Hood from *The Sleeping Beauty*, from a divertissement programme produced by Lydia Kyasht at the Empire Theatre, 1910   A photograph presented by Phyllis Bedells to her dresser.

In the theatre we heard a great deal about that first Paris season of the Diaghilev company, so that it was enormously exciting to go to matinées at the Coliseum and see some of the fine dancers from the company at last. Tamara Karsavina, Theodore and Alexis Kosloff, and Maria Baldina were supported by a small company of others. They had a success, particularly Karsavina; but I was a little disappointed not to see them in real ballet instead of in the *divertissements* which made up their programme. I remember a vigorous character dance being given by three male dancers. I think it was the Dance of the Tumblers from Rimsky-Korsakov's *The Snow Maiden*, or it may well have been what I now know as The Three Ivans from *The Sleeping Beauty*.

Beatrice Collier had now fully recovered from her accident and returned to dance in *East and West*. Then, in the May of 1910, Kyasht, Bolm, and I danced a *divertissement* with the *coryphées* of the Empire ballet. I was given the Red Riding-Hood duet to do from *The Sleeping Beauty*, with Bert Ford as the Wolf. I also had a solo dance, the Lily of the Valley.

The very day of the dress rehearsal I had a sharp attack of ptomaine poisoning. Mother brought me all the way from Belsize Park in a hansom cab, and I hung limply over the apron front of it and kept fainting all the way to the theatre. When I ought to have been making up I was found lying full length on the floor of No. 6 in another dead faint. As I opened my eyes I saw my dresser was standing over me and holding up my beautiful Lily of the Valley dress. It was like magic. I forced myself to get up, and managed to go through the dress rehearsal without anyone, except my dresser, suspecting how ill I was. For I was determined not to allow my place to be taken by anyone else. Anyway, I had no understudy.

Next day, luckily, I felt fully recovered.

Now that Adolf Bolm was back with the company the management decided to put me to study under him. For a full year I had been a pupil of Alexander Genée; and now, after studying the technique of the Danish School, I was to learn the Russian method. Bolm was a wonderfully helpful teacher.

Unity More also had to join me in my lessons, but she was not nearly so serious about her studies as I. It always amazed me that Bolm would allow her to 'get by' without really working hard. If for a single moment *my* attention strayed he appeared to be very cross. But Unity always had so much charm and such an impish manner that everyone loved her. Even now, we often laugh about it.

I suppose it was true that both she and I spent too much of our time in the theatre. The Stage Director, Spencer Barry, who was a keen golfer, told us that we ought to learn to play, as it would get us out in the fresh air, at least at week-ends. He offered to select our clubs for us and to give us our first lessons. I had five very good clubs—a driver, brassie, iron, mashie, and putter. In the early evenings before the show began we went on to the stage and he taught us the Vardon grip and the correct way to use the different clubs. A huge coconut mat was spread out and we had to strike at a captive ball. Later on I took lessons from a professional whom Mr Barry had recommended. It was not often I could get away for long enough to play a proper game, but years afterwards I did play often, and my early lessons stood me in good stead.

I still possess the original five clubs. They look curiously antique now. . . .

IO

In May 1910, Pavlova and Mordkin made their first appearance at the Palace Theatre. Mother was in a very excited state when I arrived home after my performance. She had been to the Palace and had come away completely enchanted by Pavlova. We sat up very late, while mother tried to put into words what she had felt. I was impatient for the chance to see for myself. We were fortunate in having a friend who told Alfred Butt, the Managing Director of the Palace, about my longing to see the great dancer, and he kindly arranged for me to stand at the back of the dress circle and watch Pavlova and Mordkin with their small company every evening. It happened that my own appearances at the Empire were earlier in the evenings than usual and I was able to change very hurriedly and go along to the Palace just before Pavlova began to dance. When I came in, one of the variety turns would be on—that excellent ventriloquist Arthur Prince or, it might be, Albert Whelan. I soon came to know all of their acts by heart as I stood there, waiting.

That first season the programme was Valse Caprice (Rubenstein)—a mischievous, elflike *pas de deux*, the Chopin C Sharp Minor Waltz *pas de deux* from *Les Sylphides*, and Mordkin's Bow and Arrow Dance which suited his fine masculine build so well. Then came The Swan to Saint-Saëns's music, for which Pavlova will always be remembered. A hush fell over her audience as she danced alone on the great stage. To end there was an Autumn Bacchanale by Glazunov.

There never was a dancer who could change her moods so wonderfully. Even then, before I came to know her as I did later, she was to me a creature all temperament. As you watched her dancing The Swan involuntarily your eyes brimmed with tears until you found yourself unashamedly weeping. In a moment, it seemed, she would change to the bright mischief of the Valse Caprice. Her Papillon and Dragonfly were so true to nature as to seem magical and uncanny. And with the greatest ease in the world she caught perfectly the romantic mood of the Sylphide.

In complete contrast to Genée's studied perfection she was the most versatile of dancers. I thank God that I saw her then, when she was at her very best.

The small company she had gathered around her danced Liszt's *Hungarian Rhapsody*, No. 2, and a Polish mazurka by Glinka, both of which were very fine and, to me, a revelation of what character dancing could be.

At the Empire a revised version of the first act of *The Débutante* was being prepared. It was the ballet I had first seen Genée dance in 1906, and in which I had made my own début in 1907. It was re-titled *The Dancing Master*, the main role being played once again by Fred Farren. Kyasht had been given Genee's role of the Débutante; her lover—originally played by the *travestie artiste* Dorothy Craske—was being played by Adolf Bolm, and I was the Head Pupil. Beatrice Collier, the mime, was the quick-tempered ballerina who threw up her part at the last moment, and Flo Martell had the very amusing comedy part of the Dancing Master's elderly wife who coveted the *prima ballerina's* role.

We opened on 25 July 1910, and the revival drew large audiences. *The Dancing Master* was on from 10.25 until 11.10 p.m. It was preceded by another revue, *Hello, People!* on from 9.20 to 10.0 p.m. George Grossmith Junior wrote it, and the star was Valli Valli, whose impersonations were brilliant. I danced as a Pierrot, but the dance was in fact an impersonation of Gertie

43

Monday Night. Aug. 8. 1910

Just a line, in great haste, my dear little "Débutante" to send you my very hearty Congratulations on your success to-night ~ I have watched your career with so much interest that I felt quite a personal anxiety

The letter received by Phyllis Bedells from C. Wilhelm on her seventeenth

Millar's Moonstruck number in *Our Miss Gibbs*, then running at the Gaiety. Of course I did not sing her song; but I wore a similar costume and danced in a flickering light to her music. It was fun for me, and provided an effective contrast to my classical work in *The Dancing Master*.

Soon after *The Dancing Master* opened, Adolf Bolm left us again to rejoin the Diaghilev company in Paris, and his part was taken over by Rosi who, until then, had been dancing at the Alhambra. And soon after that Kyasht left us, too, to go to Russia on a six weeks' holiday, and I was given what was the greatest chance of my young life—the part of the Débutante. Although I was not Kyasht's understudy, officially, my enthusiasm and love for my job had led me to make a careful study of her part for the sake of the sheer enjoyment I got from working at a role which had been Genée's four years earlier. I cannot describe my feelings when I

44

*this Evening that all sh^d
go well & that your per-
formance of a character so
closely associated with one
of Mlle Genée's greatest successes
might fully establish a
record for yourself, & reward
you for all your perseverance
& hard work. Go on working,
dear Phyllis, & prosper — &
give us all more of the pleasure
we felt to-night. Cordially y^rs,
C. Wilhelm*

birthday after her first performance as the Débutante in *The Dancing Master*

was told that I was to be given the part to dance on 8 August 1910—the day before my seventeenth birthday. By the skin of my teeth I managed to be a ballerina while I was still sixteen years old. I remembered what Genée had told me. 'I was a ballerina at sixteen,' she had said.

All the company and stage staff were simply wonderful. I had one full rehearsal with the orchestra, and for the first time in my life I danced a supported *pas de deux*. In my first lift I sprang up so exultantly that I completely left my partner's hands. Rosi gasped; and I heard him say, 'Oh, what a feather!' Luckily he was able to catch me again. I was much less plump than Kyasht and had always had a good, natural elevation.

I was in the seventh heaven and was actually dressing in the much-coveted No. 1 dressing-room. What a wonderful birthday present that was! All my dreams were coming true.

45

During the early days of the run of *The Dancing Master*, Walter Dickson sent for Mother and offered her a new contract for me for a further three years at a salary of £6 10s a week for the first year, rising to £7 10s, and then to £8 10s. We were able to realize another of our ambitions, and found a dear little house, No. 11 Rotherwick Road, Golders Green, just behind the tube station. As yet there were only eight houses built. None of them had been sold, and the road was still unmade, so the owners of the estate decided to let one of the houses at £110 a year and we became the fortunate tenants. The house had two good reception rooms, a kitchen, and four bedrooms, one a very large one which we fitted up as a studio with practice bars and a large mirror. We had a garden of our own which led directly on to the tennis courts, and a rose garden belonging to the estate.

Lydia Kyasht also rented a house in Golders Green when she returned from her holiday in Russia. I often went over to practise with her in the mornings: she was a darling to me and always ready to help and advise. It was from her that I first heard about Nicolini ballet shoes, which I have worn ever since. Lydia always wanted me to stay on after our practice and we used to eat lots of sweet, sticky cakes and drink Russian tea. We came to be good friends and, I am glad to say, we still are.

In 1910 I first saw *Le Lac des Cygnes* at the Hippodrome with the great Russian ballerina, Preobrajenska, who was supported by Georges Kyasht, Lydia's brother, and Ludmilla Schollar. My memory of it is rather hazy as I was only able to see one performance. I remember being very impressed by their technique but not by the production as a whole. I felt that Preobrajenska herself lacked charm and beauty.

And about this time I went to my first wedding. It was the wedding of Genée and Frank Isitt at All Saints, Margaret Street. The lovely church was crowded with her friends and admirers; and the prayers we offered for their happiness were certainly answered, for a more devoted married couple I have never known.

Their nephew, Goodwyn Isitt, had saved me from an unpleasant experience some time before. Then quite unknown to us, he called upon my mother at our flat with his arm in a sling. He told her that while in the parterre at the Empire on the previous evening he had overheard two inebriated young-men-about-town making a bet. One declared he would kiss me before the night was through. Goodwyn Isitt followed them and saw them wait

46

until I left the Empire's stage door, and then begin to follow me as I made my way along Lisle Street to the Underground at Leicester Square. My walk home was along an ill-lit and quiet crescent which had gardens in front of the houses. Before I reached our front door the two young men seemed to be gaining on me and Goodwyn, who was also following, tackled them. There was a fight, in the course of which his arm was broken.

For some time after that Mother escorted me to and from the theatre. Goodwyn became a very welcome visitor to our home. We used to tease Nell Carter, who lived with us, saying that she was the reason for his frequent calls.

In a new ballet called *Ship Ahoy* I was Unity More's sister and always up to mischief. When we were sitting on the rail of a ship at sea I fell backwards into the water and had to be rescued by Fred Farren. Both of us reappeared in clothes cleverly camouflaged to give the illusion of being wet through.

It was during the run of this show that there was an innovation which I hope will never be repeated. Perhaps because it was a light, topical sort of production, it lent itself to the experiment: on the night of the General Election the captain's bridge was arranged to show the latest election results as they were received. We were horrified. In the middle of a dance we would hear a sudden cheer go up from the audience or a long wail as seats were gained or lost. However, the management seemed to feel that the importance of the event justified such a thing.

II

♦♦♦

WHEN I was just seventeen I had my first serious admirer. Night after night for weeks glorious flowers came for me from Felton in Hanover Square. Our little home was filled with red roses, daffodils, white lilac—all out of season—and by Christmas poinsettias were coming too. At first it was embarrassing, as I did not know who could be sending them. Then one day, through a mutual friend, Mother was introduced to Niel Ove Nielsen, a Dane who was then living at the Carlton Hotel, and she discovered he was my unknown admirer. The flowers kept arriving, until Mother told him that it was not a good thing. After that they only came on Saturdays, first accompanied by a book of fairy tales, and then by Dickens, and other classics. In time Niel's presents gave me a fine collection, and I began to acquire a taste for literature and an understanding of the illustrator's art—for many of the books he sent were in beautifully produced editions. All this time I still had a child's outlook on life. I still wore my hair in curls, tied back with a big black ribbon. Niel often came to tea with us; but I was never allowed to go out with him alone. Sometimes he would take a box at a theatre for a matinée and Mother would come as well. Once, I remember, we saw Gertie Millar in *The Quaker Girl* at the Adelphi.

The 1910 Christmas was our first at Golders Green and we decided to give a party. We asked the vicar at Child's Hill if he would send us six boys and six girls from the poor of his parish on Christmas Day.

The dining-room table simply groaned with all the good things to eat and looked very festive with its crackers and holly. As soon as we had seated the children and given them a cup of tea we told them to help themselves and to ring if they wanted us. There was an immediate change in them. From being wide-eyed and shy—perhaps they had felt a little out of their element—they warmed up and became almost too noisy. After they had eaten all they could we took them into our big sitting-room and one of the little girls asked if she might recite. She stood with her back to a blazing fire and in a monotonous cockney voice plodded solidly through *King Henry of Navarre*. She must have been nearly roasting, for the perspiration was streaming down her face; but, undaunted, she went on to the end.

Niel would insist upon giving the children Christmas presents, and a huge crate of toys from Hamleys had arrived for them. One child chose a big box of beads which, in her excitement, she dropped. There must have been hundreds of beads scattered over the floor, but she refused to let any of them be lost. All of us, groping on hands and knees, had to help to recover her treasures.

They all went back to Child's Hill with their pockets bulging with oranges, nuts, and cake for their brothers and sisters.

I played my first part in a film in the spring of 1911. It was directed by a Mr Fitzhammon—for Pathé, I think. I had the *ingénue* lead in one of a series called *The Children of the Forest*. Briefly, the story concerned the daughter of a rich man who had

48

disappeared while riding her bicycle in Epping Forest. She was found by some children and returned to her doting father who rewarded the children handsomely. I believe I was chosen for the part because I couldn't ride a bicycle—I had never been allowed to learn because we knew it was bad for a ballet dancer. 'Fitz' said that no one who can ride a bicycle can fall off naturally. I remember being held up at all sides until the handle of the camera began to be turned—cameras were turned by hand in those early days—then I was given a push and came into view wobbling along the road, apparently feeling faint. The climax of my scene came when after being let go at the top of a slope I came tumbling down and fell with a mighty crash in full view of the camera.

I was supposed to have broken my leg and to lie there helplessly all night until found next day. The story ended happily enough; but I know I was black and blue with falling off that bicycle before it was just as 'Fitz' wanted it to be. I ruined a very pretty frock and several pairs of silk stockings, which I had to provide for myself. I think I was paid two pounds a day!

Another part I played for 'Fitz' shortly afterwards was a half-witted farm girl. It was a slapstick comedy, and I enjoyed it. I still feel very proud that I had something to do with those very early days of film-making. I only wish I knew if any of the films are still in existence and I could see them again.

Delibes's *Sylvia* was produced on 18 May 1911. Originally intended to be in three acts, it had been adapted so that it could be performed without scene changes. Because the continuity was therefore unbroken I think it probably gained from this treatment. The ballet has some of the loveliest of Delibes's music. Kyasht played the name part. Unity was Eros. She had a very tantalizing ten minutes posing as a statue before she was permitted to move. Fred Farren was Pan, I played Ianthe, and Flo Martell Artemis. I remember Flo Martell making a magnificent entrance down the hillside, leading two handsome borzoi dogs. Audiences liked that kind of realism in those days.

It was usual on Boat Race Night for the Oxford and Cambridge crews and flocks of their supporters to come into the Empire after a very good dinner, and much the same thing would happen on the night of their annual Rugger match. On those evenings there was pandemonium in the theatre: often the noise was such that we on the stage were unable to hear the orchestra. Our musical director, in despair, had to follow us as we danced, and take his time from us. The company took it all in very good part; and, from the first, I enjoyed the fun and let the audience see that I did. As a result I became extremely popular on these occasions.

But it caused ill-feeling between Lydia Kyasht and myself. During a performance of *Sylvia* Lydia disapproved of the audience's behaviour, and showed it only too plainly in her icy manner. That was fatal! At the end of one of her solos I had to come on carrying a tribute of fruit which I held at arm's length above my head before kneeling and laying it at her feet. As I was doing this someone in the stalls shouted 'Have a banana!'— a popular catch-phrase of the day. It struck me as being apt, and somehow extremely funny. I collapsed with laughter and so did the *corps de ballet*; and then, in front of the audience, Lydia stamped her foot at me and cried angrily, 'Phyllis, you encourage dem!'

I tried afterwards to apologize to her, but for more than a week she refused to speak to me. Poor darling, I can understand that such a thing would never have been allowed in the Imperial Russian Ballet; but then Russia did not have our tradition of Varsity Nights.

In June that year Genée began a season at the Coliseum with a miniature ballet, *Butterflies and Roses*, and had several of the Empire *coryphées* supporting her. I confess that this production did not appeal to me very strongly, except that I was able once again to study her wonderful technique. Thanks to Sir Oswald Stoll, however, this was only the first of several seasons, and later Genée was to appear in ballets which gave her much better opportunities.

I was still only seventeen, and still very much a child when I had, altogether unexpectedly, a most shattering experience. Niel Nielsen asked me to marry him. I discovered afterwards that for months he had been asking Mother's permission to speak to me, and she had been telling him that I was too young. Eventually she had agreed that it would be better if he found out how I felt about him.

I was terribly upset. For a time I quite disliked Niel because he had forced me to grow up all at once. Poor man, he little realized that I regarded him as a rather elderly friend of my mother's—though he was only thirty at the time. He offered to give me everything that most girls long for: riches, the chance to travel, and all the good things of life.

'I shall not marry until I am quite old: not until I am thirty,' I said in a very haughty way.

For years he went on trying to win me. He sent a magnificent three-stoned diamond ring, which I promptly returned to him by special messenger. Nevertheless the lovely ring went to and fro between us a number of times before he could be convinced that I would not accept it.

One night, as I was leaving the theatre, the stage-doorkeeper said, 'Your car is at the door, Miss Bedells.'

There I found a brand new limousine with a liveried chauffeur who informed me that he was at my service and that the car was mine. I flatly refused to enter it and strutted along Lisle Street to the Underground as usual. I felt furious with Niel for having dared to do such a thing. He, for his part, seemed dumbfounded that even so extravagant a gift could not affect my determination to have nothing to do with him until he stopped throwing such temptations in my way. However, I did accept from him a bronze of a sleeping boy violinist, called *Sans Souci* by H. Tharel, which is still one of the loveliest things I possess. It was a Christmas present and really I could not bear to part with it once I had seen it.

12

WHEN the Diaghilev Ballet made its first appearance at Covent Garden with the full company it was maddening not to be able to see them as there were no matinée performances. All London was raving about their success, and eventually I had to go to the Empire directors and say that as part of my education I must be given the opportunity to see them. Very reluctantly it was agreed that I take one night off which, unless one was ill, was an almost unheard-of thing. I booked a seat in the circle—just one. I could not afford to pay for another seat on my small salary.

My father took me to the theatre and collected me when the performance ended. For the first time in my life I heard Grand Opera sung. The ballet programme followed the performance of *I Pagliacci*, with Emmy Destinn, Sammarco, and Robert Martin. Then the curtain rose on *Carnaval*, with Karsavina dancing Columbine; Nijinsky, Harlequin; Vera Fokina, Chiarina; Schollar as Estrella; Nijinska, Nijinsky's sister, as Papillon; Adolf Bolm, Pierrot; and Cecchetti, Pantalon. And afterwards there were the *Prince Igor* dances.

As long as I live I shall not forget that night. I could hardly keep still in my seat. Because people who were sitting in neighbouring seats would keep chatting away in a blasé manner I worked myself into a state of fury. It seemed impossible to believe that anyone could behave like that while the magic of those artists filled me with such delight. Several times, young as I was, I asked them to be quiet.

We had so much to learn from Diaghilev in those days. His great genius lay in his ability to co-ordinate the work of such choreographers and painters as Fokine and Bakst, to select the right music from Schumann, Rimsky-Korsakov, and others, and by his energy and enthusiasm to draw out from his dancers the best that was in them.

There was soon a demand for matinées at Covent Garden and I was able to go to these to see the other ballets: *Le Pavillon d'Armide, Le Spectre de la Rose, Cleopatra, Schéhérazade, Thamar, Les Sylphides, Le Lac des Cygnes, Giselle, L'Oiseau de Feu* . . .

I count myself fortunate indeed to have been young enough to have seen those wonderful performances and yet to have been grown up enough in my knowledge of dancing to have been able to approach what I saw with understanding. Diaghilev's dancers brought the colour and excitement of the Slavonic temperament to London, and set us on fire with an enthusiasm we had never before experienced. But versatile as the great and beautiful Karsavina was in the roles she undertook, I felt it was impossible to compare her with either Pavlova or Genée. Each, I suppose, stood alone without in any way rivalling the other.

I cannot write about Nijinsky. It is useless. Then he was at the very height of his powers. I was breathless as I sat there in my seat and watched his dancing.

Cecchetti I met through Adolf Bolm. He was not only Diaghilev's premier mime but was the chief instructor to his entire company; and Bolm had been able to persuade him to take me as a private pupil. I had my lesson with him daily at nine o'clock in the morning. It meant I was called at half past six in order to get there from Golders Green in time.

He had no other private pupils, and for the next three seasons while the Diaghilev company was in London I studied with him all the time. For those priceless lessons I paid him a pound a week! It showed how one artist will help another. He knew my salary was small and wished to encourage me. We got on famously together. He used no music, but he had a quiet whistle, and tapped with his little cane to keep time. The lessons were held in some odd places, in the Swiss Waiters' Club in Soho and in a drill hall. Often Karsavina had her lesson following mine; and, if there had been a rehearsal to prevent her working at ten o'clock, she would join me, and we would work together under the *maestro*. When I was able I would stay on and watch Fokine take a rehearsal. This, too, was of inestimable value to me at that stage of my career.

Lydia Kyasht had her usual six weeks' holiday and went to Russia and, while she was away, I danced the part of Sylvia. Fred Farren was away at the same time, and his part of Pan was taken by Edward Kurylo who had recently joined us and brought with him a young pupil of his, Stanislas Idzikowsky from Poland. This youngster later became Cecchetti's own favourite pupil and an exponent of several of Nijinsky's roles with the Diaghilev Ballet. Unity More still played Eros.

Looking at an old programme I find that while I was still dancing in *Sylvia* in October 1911, one of the turns in the variety show was George Robey and another was Ivy St Helier. With both I became firm friends. Ivy was dressing in No. 6 with Unity and myself. *Sylvia* was on early and then, after the variety, came *New York*. Kyasht had returned from her holiday and appeared in *New York* with Unity, Fred Farren, Ida Crispi, Carlotta Mossetti, and me. When Mossetti left Idzikowsky and I danced a Dutch duet as emigrants. Ivy, Unity, and I often went back to sleep at each others' houses. Whenever we could manage a little time off we made the most of it and thoroughly enjoyed ourselves together.

When the Three Arts Club was started in 1911, under the presidency of Her Royal Highness Princess Marie Louise, I was invited to become one of its first honorary members. Sir Herbert Morgan was our chairman and Lena Ashwell a prime mover in getting the club established. We had premises in Northumberland Street off Marylebone Road, with bedrooms and cubicles that could be let at low rents to students of the Arts. Downstairs the comfortably furnished lounge was used for meetings and concerts and in the basement there was a large dining-room. It soon became a favourite meeting place.

The first of those marvellous Three Arts Club Balls was held at the Albert Hall that December. What a night that was! I can well remember Arthur Bouchier, dressed as Santa Claus, being pulled round the ballroom by twelve fairies—I was one of the twelve! *Snow* fell from somewhere up in the enormous roof and a dozen Yeomen of the Guard had to clear a way for us through the crowds. There were thousands there and all in fancy dresses. Christmas presents, in the form of souvenirs of the occasion, were distributed. Almost every star of the theatre was there. I saw Sir George and Lady Alexander, Sir Herbert and Lady Tree, Eva Moore, Lilian Braithwaite, Dennis Eadie, Sir Alfred Sutro, Guy Standing, Frank Curzon, Lena Ashwell, Lily Brayton, Marie Lohr, Madame Kirkby Lunn, and many many more. The Three Arts Club had started with a flourish. I have been on its Board of Management for several years and I am glad to say the good work still goes on under the new title 'The Three Arts Centre.'

By the winter of 1911 life was becoming more and more strenuous. My evenings were taken up dancing the title role in *Sylvia*, then dashing across in a cab, wearing my full make-up, to the Lyric to appear in the ballet in *Nightbirds*—an English version of *Die Fledermaus* in which Constance Drever, C. H. Workman, and many other famous artists were appearing. After that I had to fly back to the Empire to dance in *New York*, in which I had two particularly strenuous numbers. And all this time I was getting up at six-thirty in the morning so as to be with Cecchetti by nine o'clock for my lesson. The dear old man pretended to be very stern with me if I dared to appear sleepy or tired. Once when I told him I had only six hours in bed he assured me that it was all anybody needed. He never slept that long himself.

But this was a time when I made many new friends. As, after I had dressed for my Empire appearance, I only needed to change my shoes and powder my nose, I used a dressing-room at the Lyric which was occupied by three or four other girls. I became very attached to Peggy Bethel (Mrs Charles Bartlett) who was one of these. She introduced me to Paul Rubens and to Sir Charles and Lady Crutchley and their son, G. E. V. Crutchley. I was old enough to go to small supper parties, and occasionally went with my new friends to the Carlton Grill.

Through the charity performances in which I was always being asked to appear I met more people. Each year I danced at the smoking concerts in aid of the Middlesex Hospital Cancer

Research Fund, which were generally held at the Queen's Hall. It was at one of these I met Marie Lloyd. Her public adored her and her cockney humour and big generous-hearted personality. My dance followed her song so we only had time for a word or two together, but her cheery 'Good luck, dearie' warmed my heart.

In 1911 I had a charming young admirer who had been on tour with F. R. Benson's famous company. He was Dennis Neilson-Terry, the son of Julia Nielson and Fred Terry. I lost my heart to him and he to me. It was my first love affair. He was then seventeen and I eighteen. Mother allowed him to visit at Golders Green; and one day, in the Underground, he proposed to me and I accepted him.

'But,' I said, 'we must wait five years before we make it known because we both have our careers to think of and we are far too young to marry.'

He gave me the silver ring he was wearing, as a secret engagement ring.

Another dear friend of whom I saw a good deal was Henry Ainley. His mother and father were known to me as 'Mummy and Daddy A', and my mother and father were known to Harry as 'Mummy and Daddy B'. In September 1912 he and Dennis were together in the Granville-Barker production of *The Winter's Tale* at the Savoy. Harry played Leontes, Perdita was played by Cathleen Nesbitt, and Dennis was Florizel. How I envied Cathleen her part when Dennis was playing opposite to her, especially so when he spoke the lovely lines:

> *when you do dance, I*
> *wish you*
> *A wave o' the sea, that you might ever do*
> *Nothing but that; move still, still so,*
> *And own no other function. . . .*
>
> *But come; our dance, I*
> *pray.*
> *Your hand, my Perdita: so turtles pair*
> *That never mean to part.*

When Mother and I went to stay for a week-end at Capel Dennis persuaded us to come to lunch with his mother whom I had not then met. We all had lunch in a private room at an hotel in Eastbourne. I was terribly nervous because Dennis had told me his mother knew how fond we were of each other. But she was absolutely charming. She seemed to approve of me: so all was well.

Ivy St Helier had a part in the new revue which was put into the Empire's programme in February 1912. This was *Everybody's Doing It*, and it must have been one of the most popular revues ever seen. Robert Hale in his Hunting Scene was exceedingly amusing. How the young-men-about-town—and the old ones, too, for that matter—enjoyed yelling 'Yoicks' and 'Tally Ho' and making other raucous noises to the accompaniment of the hunting horns! The show was the rage of London and ran for over a year. Ivy was with us in our dressing-room again, and we were still the same merry and rather impoverished trio, bursting with ambition.

We were discussing in the dressing-room one day if we dared go by ourselves and take tea at the Carlton Hotel. Unity said she thought it only cost two shillings: I thought it was two and six. Mrs Smith, our dresser, exclaimed, 'Arf a crown! I should want an 'igh tea for that.' We giggled to think of her sitting down to her 'igh tea in the Palm Court at the Carlton.

I am reminded of the occasion when Unity and I had gone to lunch at the Queen's Hotel. Never before had we eaten there at our own expense and had no idea of the cost of a meal. When we had finished eating I grandly asked the waiter for the bill. To my horror it was much more than either of us had expected. I whispered to Unity to give me her purse, and she passed it to me under the table. When I emptied it and mine as well into my lap I was enormously relieved to find that, between us, we had exactly the right amount with one halfpenny over for the tip! Fred Farren was lunching at a nearby table and must have seen that something was wrong. He was kind enough to come over and ask if he could help. But we thanked him politely and said it was quite all right; and, after haughtily telling the waiter he could keep the change, we made our exit—or was it our escape? I go hot all over when I think of it.

13

WHEN Pavlova moved into Ivy House in May 1912, she was persuaded to take a few picked pupils, among whom I was fortunate enough to be included. Hilda Bewicke was another lucky one. Muriel Popper, Helen May, Beatrice Griffiths, little June Tripp, and five others worked with us in the lovely hall of the house. In my mind's eye I retain a vision of Pavlova as she appeared on the balcony which surrounded the place, leaning with her hands on the balustrade and smiling a welcome to us eager pupils who were waiting below for class to begin.

That summer she gave a wonderful garden party as a house-warming. It was a sunny day, and a performance was given on the lawn which led down to the lake where she kept several swans. Novikoff was now Pavlova's partner—she had quarrelled with Mordkin. She and he danced for us. Several children, including little June, who was well known later on, did a charmingly simple *corps de ballet* number which Pavlova had arranged. I had a new dance I had invented specially for the occasion to the music of Dvořák's *Humoresque*. The full orchestra from the Palace came, and Herman Finck conducted. It was a truly marvellous party.

The garden was crowded with people. I remember being very thrilled to find myself sitting at a table outside with dear Cyril Maude. I still had on the pierrot costume I had worn for my dance with short knickers and black stockings. He, charming as always, fed me with delicious ices and sweet cakes.

In the days when I was studying with Pavlova her husband, Monsieur Dandré, was often away, I believe in Russia or else-where, planning the various tours which would follow her London seasons. I did not see a great deal of him. As I progressed in my work I think that Pavlova and I became very fond of each other. I qualify this because hers was such an exuberant and warm-hearted personality and she had the gift of making you feel that she loved you more than any of the others. I like to think she did. She would frequently invite me to stay after class was over and practise with her. At practice her technique was as clean as could be; but on the stage she could do unorthodox things technically and carry even the most critical audience with her. At no time did she become the mere slave of her technique.

Afterwards we would lunch together in her exquisitely furnished dining-room, and for such an ethereal person her appetite amazed me. When it was fine weather we would go and rest in swing hammocks in the garden for the remainder of the afternoon; then she would drive me to the theatre in her car. What bliss it was! I think I must have been the proudest and yet most humble of her adorers.

And there were times when she invited herself to tea at my house. A single incident will show how charming she could be. We had a few very nice standard rose-trees in our garden. Pavlova generally wore a long lace or tulle scarf which hung in loops from her elbows; and one day, having paid me a surprise visit, she ran into the garden where I was resting, and her scarf accidentally caught on one of the rose-trees and snapped it off where it had been grafted. She was quite heart-broken and insisted upon my fetching cotton wool and a bandage, with which she carefully bound up the broken rose and, with tears running down her cheeks, kissed it, and apologized to it. It grew again and was none the worse for the mishap.

We had started having one matinée every week at the Empire; Kyasht had produced a miniature ballet for herself called *The Water Nymph*, in which I was not given a part. But one day during my class at Pavlova's, a message came that I must go at once to the Empire as Kyasht had hurt her knee and could not appear. I had not studied this part at all except by watching from the wings as Kyasht danced it. There was hardly any time to rehearse, but somehow I managed to get through the performance successfully, and at the end I was presented with a huge basket of hydrangeas, blue ones and bigger than myself. I found that it had been sent by Pavlova.

My brother happened to be on leave again at the time and told me that as he sat in his stall he saw Pavlova in front of him applauding enthusiastically. She ran up the gangway before the house-lights came up, hurrying off to the Palace with little time to spare for her own matinée.

After that performance I made another friend. Flowers and congratulations came from Lionel MacKinder, who was then appearing in *Everybody's Doing It*, but whom I had not met previously. Later on he was very kind to me. He and his delightful wife, Gracie Leigh, who was having such a success in *Miss Hook of Holland*, used often to invite me to their house. They were the most charming and devoted of couples. Our friendship ripened quickly, and lasted until he was killed in the 1914–18 war. I believe he fibbed about his age when he joined up as a 'Tommy', and was the first actor in that war to give his life for his country.

Every week-end he bought three books, one for Gracie, one for himself, and one for me. I still have the set of Kipling he gave me when I went on holiday—to keep me out of mischief, he said, and to make me rest. At that time I only had two weeks' holiday a year and Uncle Mac, as I called him, was very concerned about my needing a complete rest and change.

I had an unexpected visit from a charming girl of my own age in the summer of 1912. She was Daphne Gamage, daughter of A. W. Gamage, the founder of the famous shop, who then lived with his delightful family in the Manor House, Finchley. Daphne asked if I would join her cricket eleven to play against the choir of St Jude's Church. I said I would—although I had never played cricket in my life. The match was an amusing one. I was out first ball. However, I distinguished myself by bowling out three of the choir. I bowled underhand in the most amateurish way and they simply could not time my balls.

Afterwards I was invited back to the Manor House. The whole Gamage family soon became good friends of mine. I loved the atmosphere of their home: it was a beautiful Georgian house, and the family who lived in it were simple and kindly people. I was always sorry that poor Mr Gamage was far from well and on a strict diet, and so unable to enjoy the delicious meals which were provided.

For several years Leslie and Daphne Gamage would call for me after my performances with a friend of theirs, and we would go to dance for an hour or so at the Boston Club where they were members. It was with them I first came to enjoy ballroom dancing, although it took Leslie a long time to persuade me that I must follow my partner and not try to lead him. But he was very patient and an excellent teacher.

Later on Daphne took dancing lessons with me. She was one of my first pupils and, although she did not want to dance professionally, she was keen to learn a correct technique. I passed on to her much of Cecchetti's instruction, which I was still acquiring

59

myself. I had notes of my first lessons with him in October 1911, and still more notes covering the period of June 1912 and onwards.

I find that my spelling of the French names of the steps was most peculiar. But when I read those notes I can still recapture the old magic. I have also kept the notes I made of my first lessons with Pavlova in 1912.

I worked on all these with Daphne, and gradually I took on one or two more private pupils. One of them was Rhoma Mann, the little daughter of Charlton Mann, then General Manager of the Adelphi Theatre. She was very promising, and had an exquisite grace and charm about her. Then when Pavlova had to leave London on her tours she asked me to teach some of her pupils for her while she was away. I gladly agreed to do this, and was very proud that she had such faith in me. I see from the notebooks in which I planned each class that I called these pupils 'Pavlova's kiddies'! I found that thanks to my early grounding at Gilmer's I could teach well. I was able to impart what knowledge I had, which is not at all the same thing as being able to dance oneself.

Well on into 1913 I was taking on more and more pupils, among whom were Babs, Fred Farren's daughter, Dorothy Turner, who later took over my part in a de Courville revue in 1919, Eileen Hunter, Phyllis Symondson, and Marjorie Moss, who became my understudy at the Empire and later, teaming with Georges Fontana, was to be the world-famous exhibition ballroom dancer.

14

◆◆

WHAT RICHES the theatre had to offer us in 1912! Genée, to my delight, reappeared in a graceful eighteenth-century ballet as La Camargo. This had music by Dora Bright and really exquisite costumes designed by C. Wilhelm. Genée was given an opportunity to act as well as to dance as divinely as ever. Her miming —except for a slight tendency to use her lips as if speaking aloud, instead of letting her hands and the expression of her face speak her feelings—was perfect.

Kyasht was at the Empire in a ballet called *First Love*, and partnered by Alexander Volinine. Another Diaghilev season had opened at Covent Garden and a number of new ballets had been added to the repertoire. And Pavlova was at the Palace. The London public can seldom have had so much good ballet to enjoy.

While all this was happening I was ardently running off to my classes, first with Pavlova and then again with Cecchetti.

In November a season under Granville-Barker's authoritative direction opened at the Savoy. Harry Ainley was tremendously successful as Malvolio in *Twelfth Night*. The rest of the company were all people who were, or were to become, famous on the stage: Cathleen Nesbitt, Laura Cowie, Léon Quartermaine, Hayden Coffin, Arthur Wontner, Arthur Whitby, and Athene Seyler amongst others. I went to every matinée I could manage. I felt that this was a major experience. I do not believe I have seen Shakespeare so well done since.

In the autumn Kyasht went to Russia again, but I was not given anything very exciting to do at the Empire. I was appearing in the revue and at the same time rehearsing hard for a new, colossal, and immensely ill-fated production. The famous 'Follies' had been engaged and were to join forces with the Empire Ballet in a magnificent pantomime to be called *Aladdin*. An incredible amount of money was spent on the show. Rehearsals went on for ten weeks. We opened on 11 December and closed after ten performances.

This was the cast:

ALADDIN	*Douglas MacLaren*
WIDOW TWANKEY	*H. G. Pelissier*
UNCLE ABANAZAR	*Morris Harvey*
SLAVE OF THE LAMP	*Lewis Sydney*
SLAVE OF THE RING	*Phyllis Bedells*
PRINCESS BADROULBOUDOUR	*Fay Compton*

I think the main trouble was that H. G. Pelissier was not his usual self—it was just before his last illness. All through rehearsals—which were chaotic—he behaved like a spoiled child. There were interminable rows.

My own big chance was in the Cave Scene, and I was told to go off and arrange my work to my own satisfaction. I rehearsed a ballet and *pas de deux* which I taught to Douglas MacLaren, who was supporting me, putting everything I knew into it. Having so long to rehearse made it possible for me to perfect it.

But on the first night poor Pelissier was unable to remember his

61

part and had to take the script with him on to the stage and read it. This, as can be imagined, scarcely helped him to give a good performance. All of us in the company were very unhappy and must have shown we were. For the first time in my life, from an Empire audience I heard hissing and booing, which rose to a crescendo when Pelissier went before the curtain. And then he did an unforgivable thing: he poked out his tongue at the public. Afterwards he just sat down and wept like a child. Such a disgrace was enough to break anyone's heart—he and his Follies had been right to the top of the ladder and, for many years, were the most popular group of artists in London.

The revue *Everybody's Doing It* ran on into the next year. The 'fantastic oriental scena' I was given to do in it was substantially my scene from *Aladdin* over which I had worked so hard. I was glad to have the opportunity of doing it again, even if, as I suspected, it was only a way to keep me busy until the next production was ready.

As I have said, I was studying hard at this time. I was working hard, too, and enjoying to the full the life of dancing I had chosen for myself—so much so that I cannot often have thought seriously about it. Naturally, from time to time I was gratified to read in the press notices the words which confirmed me in my desire to go on.

I received my measure of praise.

The Times critic, writing of my dancing as a Ray of the Sun in *The Reaper's Dream*, which was produced at the Empire early in 1913, said, 'She has a touch of the merriment of Genée about her; and since she knows the secret of dancing as if she thoroughly enjoyed it, she communicates her joy . . .'

Did I ever ask myself if I would become a great dancer? I must have done so—a hundred times. The critic of the *Pall Mall Gazette*, I remember, asked just that question.

'Will Miss Phyllis Bedells become a great dancer? It rests with her,' he wrote. 'She has all the *élan* and sense of spiritual rhythm without which the most finished of experts is a mere clockwork toy. But at present there are gaps in her technique: sometimes in her pirouettes you are aware that she has two feet when you should believe she has hardly need of one: sometimes she treats—not unpleasantly, I admit—the delicate art of ballet in a boisterous schoolgirl way. Perhaps it is part of her charm that she impresses us as a very youthful and gifted amateur. Yes, it is part of her charm now, because she really is so very young, so very reckless and gay; but when she is older she will need unfaltering technique to keep her from stumbling. And so for all her success she must still regard herself as a pupil. If she must remain a ballet dancer, then the tricks of her trade must become so automatic that she forgets them—as Adeline Genée forgot them. But she is an artist fine enough to go beyond the tiptoe ballet—a form of dancing long since archaic and bound soon to disappear. Let her learn, if she can find anybody to teach her, "the expressive mode of dancing" which is destined in the long run to triumph over all other modes. . . .'

For the ballet dancer, as for all other artists, there must always be something to learn I wanted to learn. The friends with whom I was growing up felt as I did. We wanted the stars. We longed to excel. . . .

In March 1913 Henry Ainley played Ilam Carve in Granville-Barker's production of Arnold Bennett's play, *The Great Adventure*, at the Kingsway. He invited Mother and me to the dress rehearsal and asked us to take notes on his performance. Afterwards he came back with us to Golders Green and stayed until the small hours of the morning while we went through our notes with him. I managed to go to the opening night of the play, but only saw the first and last acts because I had to rush away to the Empire for my own performance in between. It was one first night I shall never forget, and certainly one of the biggest successes of Harry's career. I went so often to matinées during the run that the stage box was known as 'the Bedells' box'. Harry always saw that there were chocolates, a posy of flowers, and tea sent in to me. He, Mother, and I had a signature tune—the tune of an old Christmas carol. Whenever I was in front Harry would discover some opportunity or other to whistle a little of it during his performance. It was his way of letting me know that he knew I was there. To have glanced up towards the box where I was sitting would have been to break one of the unwritten rules of the theatre. I have a vivid memory of the supper party celebrating *The Great Adventure's* first anniversary, which was attended by many of the famous as well as by everybody connected with the play.

I began to find all the teaching I had been doing rather tiring. When, in May, Pavlova returned to London and I resumed my lessons with her, I decided to do less of it and give myself more time to spend happily with her at Ivy House in the afternoons. However, I kept on one or two of my special pupils: Marjorie (Mollie) Moss, Dorothy Turner, Nora Swinburne (Johnson)—now the well-known actress—and Dorothy Watkins.

In August 1913 P. Michael Faraday engaged me to arrange the dances in a new operetta, *Love and Laughter*, at the Lyric, with Oscar Straus's music. This was an entirely new experience and perhaps the most enjoyable part of it was giving Yvonne Arnaud a private lesson every day so that she would know enough of dancing and deportment for the musical numbers. She had never previously danced. We had the greatest fun working together Her bubbling sense of humour and her delicious squeaks of merriment I found irresistible. She had just had a great success in *The Girl in the Taxi*, Michael Faraday's last show at the Lyric, and both he and I were very keen that Yvonne should dance well so that she might be helped towards further successes. Although, of course, no one can expect to 'make' a dancer in six weeks.

My job was to coach her in simple steps and movements and arrange her dances so that they did not seriously affect her breathing when she was singing. It was my chief difficulty, too, with the rest of the cast. I soon found out that one cannot be too ambitious when teaching singers to dance.

They were a wonderfully co-operative cast—Evelyn D'Alroy, Amy Augarde, Bertram Wallis, Claude Fleming, Tom A. Shale, A. W. Baskcomb, Frederick Volpe, and Nelson Keys, who became my special friend. He did not have a very big part in the show. During the rehearsals, when we were not busy, he and I sat together in the stalls and he used to give extraordinarily good imitations of various actors—by far his best was Henry Ainley. Naturally that delighted me.

Kyasht returned from her holiday in the late summer and arranged for us to give a programme of *divertissements* while we were rehearsing our next big production. I had a spirited gipsy dance in this programme, which I thoroughly enjoyed doing, and my own Humoresque—the one I had arranged specially for Pavlova's garden party. This appeared to be very popular with the public; and, in later years, when Volinine danced with Pavlova, he did an almost identical version of it.

Michael Faraday asked me to arrange the dances and musical numbers for another of his shows, *The Laughing Husband*, translated from the German and set to music by Edmund Eysler. This

64

opened at the New Theatre in October 1913. I remember sitting with Michael Faraday during rehearsals and both of us weeping copiously as C. H. Workman, that grand old Savoyard, sang his drinking song. In the play his heart was breaking because his wife had been false to him.

I decided to spend some of the money I had been paid for my work on these two Faraday productions on buying a really good grand piano. Mr Pinches at the Empire helped me choose it. We visited the Bechstein Hall, the Steinway Hall, the Aeolian Hall, as well as a piano exhibition where examples of the finest makes were assembled. Nevertheless, it took us three months to find the ideal instrument!

·15

◆-◆

I HAD been working daily with Pavlova at Ivy House during that summer and early autumn. One September day she said to me, 'Phyllis, I want you to come with me round the world. I will promise to give you the leading part in one ballet in every programme; and I want you to learn some of my dances so that if I am very tired you can dance them instead of me.'

I cannot describe what a wonderful moment that was for me. At once I told her that if I could I would join her. I was absolutely thrilled at the prospect. We hugged each other and began to talk with delight about working and travelling together.

Next day I went to see the Empire directors and told them of Pavlova's offer and how much I wanted to go with her. They told me that it was quite out of the question, as they held an option on my services and that my contract—which was due to end shortly—would be renewed for a further two years. But what was more exciting, they told me, too, that Lydia Kyasht would be leaving and I was to be *première danseuse*. No. 1 dressing-room was to be mine. Walter Dickson said I would receive twenty pounds a week for the first year and thirty pounds for the second and would be given an all-the-year round guarantee and 'all found'.

What could I say? My great ambition was at last to be realized, but at the expense of having to refuse Pavlova's offer.

When I told her about it we both broke down and cried; but,

at the same time, she congratulated me on being the first English girl to be given so exalted a position. I did feel very deeply the honour of following Genée and Kyasht.

September and October had been very busy months because, in addition to working on *The Laughing Husband*, I was in the thick of rehearsals for our new ballet, quite the loveliest of all Kyasht's productions, *Titania*—an adaptation of *A Midsummer Night's Dream* to Mendelssohn's music.

I opened the ballet, dancing in the moonlight to the music of the overture, awakening the fairies by scattering them with dew. This was really silver paper cut up very fine, carried in an upturned bluebell. Unity More ended the ballet by coming in front of the curtain and speaking Puck's lines—'If we shadows have offended . . .'

Dennis (Neilson-Terry) was playing the leading part in *The Witch* at the St James's with Lillah McCarthy in the title role. It was a very terrible play and Mother, whom I had taken with me to see it, was shocked that Dennis should play such a passionate part while he was still so young.

The following day when he came to see us at Golders Green, very eager to know whether we thought he had done well, Mother told him, 'Far too well', and she went on, 'What I want to know is how you got the experience to understand what you were doing?'

Poor Dennis flushed scarlet, and was obviously very upset by Mother's question. Suddenly he rushed after her as she was going into the next room and cried, 'If I had to commit a murder on the stage, would that mean I would have to be a murderer to do it?'

Mother capitulated.

We all laughed. But I am sure Mother's remark was made because she was anxious about my future happiness, for she knew how much I was in love with Dennis. . . .

During the run of *Titania*, Unity More, after having been with us for several years, left the Empire to go to Daly's, and Ivy St Helier took over the part of Puck, which she played charmingly. Another member of the cast, Joukoff, who had been playing Oberon, left also and his part was taken by Alexander Gavrilow, who had been with Diaghilev at Drury Lane.

Then came the end of Kyasht's contract, and on 20 December 1913 I was Titania and queen in my own right.

Quite frankly, I was terribly nervous.

66

The press was making a big fuss, and, as I was going to the theatre that night, the *Evening News* placards blazoned the news: PHYLLIS BEDELLS—*première danseuse*. On the front page there was a large photograph and nearly a full column about me. *The Times* carried a long article, and, for weeks there were articles and photographs of me in most of the newspapers.

As well as dancing the title role in *Titania* I made two appearances in the revue which was in the same programme—*Nuts and Wine* for which P. G. Wodehouse had written some of the material. I was supposed to be Pavlova in one of the solos, which I danced to music composed specially for me by Frank E. Tours who was our new musical director. Naturally I did not attempt an imitation, but arranged a strong technical classical ballet variation with a brilliant coda to end it. This brought the house down and no one was more surprised than I when, next day, the press gave it most remarkable notices. The other number in the revue was a modern duet, which I danced with an American, Julian Alfred, who produced the show. He was an excellent light tap dancer. Both he and Melville Gideon, who had written the music, were surprised at my ability to adapt myself to their modern style. I enjoyed doing this number, but confess to feeling slightly uneasy about it at the same time.

A critic in the *Standard* had the same feeling. 'It seems a mistake,' he wrote, 'after showing Miss Bedell's grace and skill in a conventional gauze skirt, to bring her on again in ordinary costume to do tango or ragtime steps, or whatever they are. A *première danseuse* should surely be hedged round with more ceremony than is possible in this sort of frolic, or else we are in danger of mistaking her for an ordinary member of the cast.'

The third Three Arts Ball was held at Covent Garden on 22 January 1914. Just before this, or just afterwards, Sir Herbert Morgan gave one of his delightful dinner parties at the Club. We were not a large party, and after dinner we retired to a small sitting-room where there was a piano. Her Royal Highness Princess Marie Louise was among the guests, several of whom sang or played for us.

Suddenly the Princess insisted that I dance. I tried to explain how impossible it was because I was wearing a hobble skirt and high-heeled shoes; whereupon she sent for a pair of scissors and cut my dress from the hem to the knee and told me to kick my shoes off. I did not like to refuse or make a fuss: so, in that cramped space, I performed an impromptu dance to one of Chopin's nocturnes. Her Royal Highness seemed quite delighted and was charming to me. When I reached home, however, Mother was very annoyed to see that my dress had been spoilt. It *was* a lovely dress, too—one of my first real evening dresses, made of cerise charmeuse with the edges of the sleeves and the hem of the skirt trimmed with skunk!

All the time I was growing up in the Empire Ballet several schools of stage dancing in London were specializing in training child dancers. Steadmans, the Ware School, and Lila Field's were a few of them. In 1913 Lila Field had formed her own little company, which appeared at the Palladium and on tour, and she had as her *première danseuse* Ninette de Valois. One day, Ninette's mother, Mrs Stannus, brought her little girl over to tea with us at Golders Green. How far we were from realizing what a great influence in the world of the ballet Edris Stannus would become! I was sorry she had changed her name to a foreign-sounding one. Even then I felt strongly that we would never break down the belief that British girls could not dance until we stopped pretending we were foreigners. In my intense way, too, I disapproved of Ninette's dancing the Dying Swan. To me it was almost sacrilege. Only Pavlova, who had created it, ought to dance it. But there was a craze for performing that solo. Every child who could put on a pair of 'toe-shoes'—as they would call them—seemed to think she could attempt it.

To my great joy *The Dancing Master* was revived and I had Genée's and Kyasht's part of the Débutante. Now I was twenty and felt I was better able to do it justice. The part of the Dancing Master which Fred Farren had created was taken over by Espinosa who had also revised the choreography. The revival, which opened on 13 February 1914, proved a big success. I had all the *pas de deux* work with Espinosa, while the part of Armand, his son, was taken by a female, Hilda Edwardes, as in the original production. Espinosa did more actual dancing than Fred Farren had done, but somehow I always preferred the latter's interpretation of the eccentric Dancing Master's part. However, as I have said, we had a success. Once again I rode on buses which had my name in huge letters along their sides.

A condensed version of *Nuts and Wine* was put on with *The Dancing Master*, and the management insisted that I continue to dance my very difficult Pavlova solo. I was kept hard at work.

68

Then I had my first quarrel with my mother; and, oh, how right she was! Every Sunday there were flying displays at Hendon, and one day a charming young man called to see me at the Empire, 'on business', he said. He was only about twenty, but already a star performer in his plane. He asked if I would consent to fly with him at Hendon on the following Sunday and said that, if I would, it would be good publicity for him and I would probably find it amusing. Of course I was excited by the prospect, and agreed. But when I got home that night and told Mother she was absolutely horrified and forbade me to go. I got upset and said, 'I have never yet gone against your wishes, but I am determined to fly. I mightn't ever have such an opportunity again.'

For two or three days we continued to argue about it. I was adamant. Sunday arrived; and it was bitterly cold. I dressed in two of everything, with lots of woollies and scarves. Just as I was about to leave the house Mother lost all control and became hysterical. It was awful. She seemed to be beside herself with anxiety, and kept shouting, 'You'll be killed. You'll be killed.' In the end, in order to quieten her, I had to relent, and promised I would not fly that day. But I insisted she must get used to the idea as I intended to make another date.

Young Lee Temple and his manager and mechanic, who obviously adored him, were waiting for me at the aerodrome when I arrived and showed me over the hangars, explaining how the planes worked; then press photographers took pictures of Lee Temple and me climbing into his two-seater plane.

Lee said, 'Are you ready?'

But I said, 'I'm not coming.'

'Have you got cold feet?'

'No,' I said, and told him of the promise I had made.

'If you come up now,' he said, 'she'll never know until it's all over.'

'No,' I told him. 'I can't break my word. I'll come up with you next Sunday.'

He explained that, according to his contract, he must go up for an exhibition flight, but that it wouldn't take long and we could have tea together afterwards at the club. I climbed out of the plane and stood with his manager and mechanic, warming myself at the brazier burning outside the hangar as we watched the brilliant airman loop the loop and fly upside down—both quite difficult stunts in those days. All of a sudden, when he appeared to be flying quite normally, we saw the plane drop like a stone and crash.

I cannot tell the horror of it. I was taken into a waiting-room while the ambulance and the young man's manager sped across to the wrecked plane. The public had been asked to leave the aerodrome; and I waited with sickening fear for news. When Lee's manager returned tears were streaming down his face. Lee Temple was dead.

They took me home in a car. As I came out of my daze I began to realize that it was only my mother's interference that had saved my own life. It came out at the inquest that the poor boy had lost consciousness and fallen on to the joystick, which had caused the plane to dive steeply. Apparently he had just recovered from an attack of influenza and ought not to have flown so soon. It was a terribly sad time. I begged the press not to publish the photographs, and they were good enough to agree. I felt that there might be sensational headlines, 'Ballet dancer's escape from death', or something of the sort; and for the sake of his family—who all came to Golders Green after the inquest and were very kind to me—it was the least that I could do.

It was a long time before I fully got over the shock. When I was dancing I would suddenly have a mental picture of that dreadful accident, see the plane falling out of the sky like a stone. It was horrible, horrible. . . . I vowed that I would never fly. And it was 1948 before I did go up for the first time.

16

In March 1914, the management of the Empire was changed and so, to some extent, was the policy. Walter Dickson retired and Alfred Butt of the Palace took over the managing directorships of both theatres. Charles B. Cochran became the Empire's general manager. *Nuts and Wine* was withdrawn at the beginning of April and a new short revue, *A Mixed Grill*, put on in which Jack Buchanan appeared, and Ida Crispi and Fred Farren had an eccentric dance which had some success. As a whole, however, the show was not particularly well received.

It seemed odd to me to have Fred Farren appearing in the same programme as *The Dancing Master* and not playing his old part. I felt that somehow my world was changing.

A letter appeared at that time in all the London newspapers:

Sir. The news that the great Danish *danseuse*, Mlle Adeline Genée, begins with her season at the London Coliseum next month a series of performances prior to her final retirement from the stage, will be received with sadness by all who have been fascinated by her beautiful personality and delighted with her exquisite dancing. We, as representing only a tiny handful of her sister artists who give way to no one in their admiration of Mlle Genée's art, venture to suggest that such an occasion should not be passed over without some recognition of the hours of delight which she has given to all lovers of dancing.

From the moment when she, a young Danish *danseuse*, made her first appearance in London, Mlle Genée has endeared herself to the heart of the British public, and her career has been marked by a series of artistic triumphs.

May we therefore hope that those who love the art of dancing will help us in offering Mlle Genée some small token of our affection and admiration for her which she would afterwards treasure as a keep-sake, reminding her of the affectionate esteem by which she was held in this country. Contributions, however small, will be most gratefully received by Mr Alfred Barnard, the 'Era' Office, Tavistock Street, Covent Garden, W.C., who has most kindly given his services as honorary treasurer.

> *Pavlova,*
> *Karsavina,*
> *Kyasht,*
> *Karina,*
> *Phyllis Bedells.*

Genée opened in April 1914 with one of the most exquisite ballets I have ever seen, *La Danse*. In this she was at her best, representing the great dancers in history from Prévost to Taglioni. For the present generation's sake I wish someone would revive that ballet, and also *Camargo*, in which Genée danced as well. I doubt, however, if anyone could give as good a performance as hers. The season ended on 9 May.

George Woodhouse was giving me piano lessons twice a week at the Bechstein—now the Wigmore—Hall. I am afraid I never gave enough time to practising, being able to manage only about an hour and a half daily. Poor George Woodhouse was sometimes in despair, and said if only he could cut me in two and let the Empire have my legs and give himself my hands, he would make a great pianist of me. Evidently he did not realize that a dancer's arms and hands and head are important parts of her equipment. We struggled along; and I have always been grateful to him for his patience and for helping me to develop my appreciation of music.

In June, Alfred Butt and C. B. Cochran decided to make another attempt to catch the public's fancy. They mounted an enormous revue called *The Merry-go-Round*. There was an internationally famous cast: Alexandra Balaschowa and Michael Mordkin from Russia, Nora Bayes, Wellington Cross, Lois Josephine, Smith and Doyle, and Harry Cross—all celebrated American musical comedy artists—and Messieurs H. Morten and René Koval, and Madame Marie Massart from Paris. The British members of the cast were Harry Roxbury, James Godden, Hugh E. Wright, Nell Emerald, A. H. Majilton, and myself. No expense was spared on this sumptuous production. Yet the press next day gave it very mixed notices.

With A. H. Majilton I had an exceedingly dramatic *Danse des Sans Culottes* set in the Palais Royal of 1796. It was a glorified version of the apache dance of 1908, for at the end of it I was flung violently down a flight of steps and rolled over and over until I reached the footlights.

It was common gossip in the theatre that Mordkin and Balaschowa were paid two hundred and fifty pounds a week for their appearances. I was under contract at only twenty pounds a week: yet we shared the honours of what little success the revue had. Its life was short, however, and on 17 July I was transferred to the Palace to dance in the Carnaval de Venise scene in *The Passing Show*. My dances were arranged by Cecchetti to music composed specially by Herman Finck.

After having studied for four years, off and on, with Cecchetti I naturally felt pleased when Alfred Butt told me he was to arrange the suite of dances for us. Quite frankly I do not think he was very successful. He was not experienced in the kind of choreography suited to revue, nor did he seem able to catch the spirit of the scene at all.

I regretted I had not arranged my numbers myself as I had done so many times in the past. That interlude, however, lasted for only six weeks, while the rehearsals for the Empire's new ballet were going on.

At the Palace I dressed with Gwendolen Brogden, although we each had our own dresser. She had 'Morey' and I had dear Mrs

Smith from the Empire. There was an amusing rivalry between the dressers. Gwennie was then at the height of her popularity and singing 'I'll make a man of every one of you', which was all the rage.

'Always visitors in the dressing-room', Mrs Smith kept muttering. 'How does she expect us to dress?'

For some time I had frequently lunched with Lady St Helier at her lovely house in Portland Place. She was extremely interesting, a kind friend, and a wonderful hostess. Through these luncheons I came into touch with her daughter, the charming Mrs Henry Allhusen, who then lived at Stoke Court, Stoke Poges, in Buckinghamshire. Dorothy Allhusen often used to invite me to her home at week-ends. I particularly remember one house party. Among the twenty guests were Lord Peel, Lord Alec Thynne, Sir Owen Seaman, the editor of *Punch*, and Major Bobby White who was soon to raise a fine force of London volunteers. Laura Cowie and I had gone down after the performance on Saturday night. It was 1 August. Next day the atmosphere was electric. Every hour someone would be telephoning from the Carlton Club with the latest news of the fateful cabinet meeting which was in progress. Our house party spent a strangely excited day wondering if there would be war or not. Belgium had been invaded. I was listening to the others putting the arguments for and against, and feeling it all very deeply, as I was naturally anxious about my brother in the Navy.

To hide our anxiety, I suppose, we played foolish games like a lot of children. I was the youngest member of the party and a light-weight. I can remember being tossed like a ball from one to another up over the net on the tennis court. It was a hot and quite crazy game for such an exhausting day. But by the evening, before we dined, we were on our hands and knees on the floor of the library, poring over a map of Europe, while those men who knew about military strategy—and there were several there who did—discussed what was likely to happen if the worst came about.

On Monday—it was 3 August—I got back to the Palace just in time for my show. There was not much time to practise. The people in London seemed to be on fire with a warlike spirit. A few days later, Gerald Crutchley came to tell me he had been given a commission in the Scots Guards and from then on, one after another, all my young men friends joined up, including, as I have said, dear 'Uncle Mac' (Lionel MacKinder). I soon became used to seeing men in khaki uniforms, and posters all over the place. The head of Lord Kitchener stared sternly from the walls; his finger pointed straight at you: 'Your King and Country Need You.' Another war-time slogan was: 'Business as usual', which de Courville adopted as the title of his new revue at the Hippodrome in which Unity More was to have a big success.

Immediately after the declaration of war, Mr Butt told me that he was putting on a topical ballet written specially to reconstruct the events which had led up to the war, and which would reflect the patriotic feeling of the time. It was incredible how quickly this was got ready.

The ballet, *Europe*, opened on 7 September, and it had a good run. It seemed to be just what the public wanted. I confess I would have preferred more beauty and less patriotic fervour. In the second scene there was a set-piece showing a huge map of Europe, built most solidly with a rostrum and steps behind it. We made our various entrances through doors cut in the map where our respective countries were. As Mademoiselle Paris, I represented France.

My love affair with Dennis Neilson-Terry was now coming to an end. We had somehow drifted apart. I realized we could not be happy together. But I always had a soft spot in my heart for him. He, too, joined the army in 1914 and we occasionally wrote to each other.

Leslie Gamage, another dear friend who joined the army, often wrote to me; and, when he came on leave, I saw a lot of him. I wore his regimental badge.

Gerald Crutchley introduced me to a friend of his, Betty Spottiswoode, who was the daughter of Hugh Spottiswoode, one of the King's printers. She and I found much in common. She brought her brother, Andrew, to tea with me at Golders Green. He was then at Eton and brought with him a young friend of theirs, Ian MacDonald, who was at Charterhouse. That began another friendship which was to last for many, many years. The Crutchleys, the Spottiswoodes, and the MacDonalds each made me very welcome in their homes, and Unity More, too, often joined us in the jolly times we spent together. Ian, who was very tall and good-looking, was only seventeen years old when he joined the Grenadier Guards after leaving Charterhouse. He was badly gassed in 1918 and eventually invalided out of the army.

Another friend of those days was Eric Blore who, I thought,

74

was a fine comedian. He had first appeared at the Empire in *All the Winners* in 1913, and then he was with me in *Nuts and Wine*. He and my mother were devoted, and he was frequently a visitor at our house, when he gave us ample opportunity to enjoy his dry sense of humour. Much against his own inclination he joined the army in 1915; but Mother had rather talked him into it. On the day he received his 'Tommy's' uniform he came to see us and said to Mother, 'Look what you've done!'

I had never seen anything fit worse. We were helpless with laughter at the sight of him; but then he had never had a very good figure. He was inclined to stoop and poke his head forward, which was not conducive to making a smart appearance in the anything-but-well-cut uniform of those days. Eric was certainly not meant to be a soldier. While he was away he wrote many long descriptive letters to Mother which were so funny that they had to be sent to our various friends and to my brother at sea for their common enjoyment. At first Eric served in kite balloons but later the authorities found him most useful running the 38th Divisional Concert Party, which he did until 1919. Since then he has had a very successful stage and film career both in London and Hollywood. In 1924 he was godfather to my daughter, Jean.

Granville-Barker produced Thomas Hardy's *The Dynasts* at the Kingsway in November 1914. The epic drama of the Napoleonic Wars was, in my opinion, a masterpiece of production. Henry Ainley read long and beautiful passages, seated in the orchestra pit, and there were two figures on each side of the stage acting as chorus. Many of the most famous actors and actresses of the day were in that production, proud to be playing even small parts in something so important.

Mother and I went to see it many times, and we bought a copy of the play, which Harry would read to us when he had driven me back to Golders Green after the performance. He would also read the poems of W. B. Yeats and Rupert Brooke. We often sat up late, listening with delight to his wonderfully musical voice. He had joined the special constabulary and was often on duty, directing traffic; but he told us that he looked upon our home as a refuge 'far from the madding crowd', offering him rest and refreshment.

That October another patriotic revue was produced at the Empire, *By Jingo*. My scene in it was called The Tricolour. I was La Belle France; and there were dances, or rather massed drilling, for the chorus of *cuirassiers, chasseurs, zouaves,* and members of the *Garde Républicaine,* together with *vivandières.* The whole affair ended by my crowning the flags of the Allies with laurels. *Europe* was running at the same time. Our management was clearly determined to cater for the popular audiences of those stirring times.

17

◆◆◆

DURING the run of *By Jingo!* Mabel Russell, one of the stars of the show, was given a big party by Sir Guy Chetwynd at the Savoy Hotel, where a suite of rooms had been engaged for the occasion. Over fifty guests were present, and Mabel, who dressed in No. 2 dressing-room next to mine, begged me to bring Henry Ainley. He seldom went to parties, but I managed to persuade him to come. At supper I sat between him and Basil Hallam. On Basil's left sat Gaby Deslys and on her left Sir Thomas (later Lord) Dewar.

Harry said to me, 'Look around this table and tell me who you think is the nicest looking man.'

I took what he said quite seriously, and it was a long time before I answered. 'The young officer at the far end of the table', I heard myself say. 'The one with crutches, and a bandage round his neck.'

Harry nodded and appeared to agree with me. When all the speeches were over and we were moving into the adjoining ball-room Nelson Keys stopped me and introduced the young officer —Lieutenant Ian Macbean.

Later on, while I was dancing the Argentine tango with Basil Hallam I saw him again, sitting with Gaby Deslys. However, shortly afterwards Harry and I slipped away. We neither of us wanted a very late night; but I kept on thinking of the sad-faced young officer.

On 2 February 1915, I had one of the most delightful of my experiences. The occasion was an all-star matinée at Covent Garden in aid of the Actors' Benevolent Fund. Their Majesties King George V and Queen Mary and Princess Mary were there and the great opera house was crowded from floor to ceiling.

76

Madame Kirkby Lunn opened the performance by singing the National Anthem, and then followed *The School for Scandal* with Irene Vanbrugh playing Lady Teazle; Sir Herbert Tree, Sir Peter; Henry Ainley, Joseph Surface; Fred Terry, Charles; and H. V. Esmond, Sir Benjamin Backbite. Lady Tree was Mrs Candour, and Marjorie Maude, Maria. Many well-known actors and actresses danced in the minuet, led by Adeline Genée and myself. We had been rehearsed by the famous old teacher, Louis d'Egville. It was an extraordinary evening: the four servants in the play were played by Sir George Alexander, Arthur Bourchier, H. B. Irving, and Weedon Grossmith. Donald Calthrop partnered me in the minuet.

Our dancing received an ovation. It must have been a pretty sight, all powder and patches, silks, flashing swords, and quilted gowns. Nothing, it was remarked, seemed to give greater pleasure to the occupants of the royal box than this reminder of a bygone day.

Granville-Barker had revived *Fanny's First Play* at the Kingsway and Henry Ainley had another great success in it as Juggins the butler. Ivy St Helier was playing, too, as Dora Delaney. She made the most of her opportunities and wore the most frightful clothes as 'darling Dora'.

One evening Harry took me to meet a very dear friend, Mrs Frank Dawes. She was the hostess of our little party at Driver's. It was the first time I had tasted oysters—and I didn't like them. Dear 'Dawsie', as she was called by the countless musical and theatre folk who knew her, became one of my closest friends. Harry's nickname for me was 'Fizz', because he said I affected him like champagne. When, at that first meeting, Dawsie began calling me Fizz, too, he said, 'That's my private name: you can't have it.'

'Very well,' she said, 'I shall have one of my own.'

From then on she called me 'Fizzle'. She lived in a beautiful flat on the top floor of 11a Portland Place, and for many years there was always a welcome for me there.

Mollie Moss, my own pupil, had joined the Empire *corps de ballet*, and danced for the first time in the new half-hour ballet, *The Vine*, produced on 22 March 1915, for which Fred Farren once again did the choreography. I asked the management to make Mollie my understudy and I taught her my dances; so that I would be able to go away to Newquay again for a holiday in the summer. Mollie told me, when I returned, how glad she was to see me again. She had been terribly nervous all the time; and I think that perhaps she lacked enough dramatic power for the part, which was an exacting one. Little June was dancing as the Spirit of the Mountain Stream in the same ballet. She, of course, had attended Pavlova's classes with me at Ivy House in 1913. Now just fourteen and with flaxen curls and a simple charm she made an excellent foil for me. I was the Spirit of the Vine and thoroughly enjoying, for once, being an evil spirit. I had had my long curls cut off for the part. At first I had worn a wig, but found it too hot. My hair refused to flop about as it should have done. Just the same it was an awful feeling when the hairdresser started to work with his scissors.

Once again Mother and I were asked to come to the final rehearsals of Harry Ainley's play and 'bring our notebooks for criticisms'. We had a lovely time; but there was not much fault we could find, for the play was *Quinney's* at the Theatre Royal, Haymarket. What an enjoyable show it was! Harry was Jo Quinney; Sydney Fairbrother, Susan; and Godfrey Tearle, James. For his lovable characterization Harry could use his native Yorkshire accent. His doing so made the play doubly amusing for me as, off-stage, he and I generally spoke Yorkshire— and I always did when visiting his father and mother.

About this time I tried to fulfil a long-standing promise I had made to my brother. He was organizing a big ship's concert which was to be given in a hall alongside his ship at Harwich. He had always wanted me to dance for him. So I asked for the night off and it was granted. Mother and I travelled up with an enormous basket full of my dresses.

Stuart felt that it was going to be a great occasion. The hall was overcrowded when we began: some of the sailors sat on a beam up near the roof, over the heads of the rest of the audience. I was all ready for my first dance and standing at the side of the stage during the opening item, a rollicking chorus song, 'Go to sea, my lads, go to sea', which was being sung by my brother and his concert party dressed in pierrot costumes. Suddenly there was an awful crash. The beam upon which the sailors had been sitting, gaily joining in the chorus and swinging their legs, had fallen on the audience below.

A terrifying hush followed. The curtain was rung down at once. Words of command were briskly given and obeyed; and

78

ALFRED BUTT

presents

6 "WATCH YOUR STEP"

Written by H. B. SMITH   Music and Lyrics by IRVING BERLIN

English Book by HARRY GRATTAN

Staged by R. H. BURNSIDE

Scenery by R. C. McCleery, Philip Howden, John Bull, Bruce Smith

Costumes Designed by Helen Dryden

Dresses by Mme. Suzanne, Allix, B. J. Simmons & Co., Michard Soeur, Morris Angel & Son, Miss Hastings

Miss Ethel Levey's Dresses and Hats designed and made by Lucile, Ltd., Mme. Giddy and Reville & Rossiter, Ltd.

Gentlemen's Evening Dress Suits by Jones & Bowram

Gentlemen's Hats by Henry Heath, Ltd.

Hats by Maison Lewis   Shoes by A. L. Gamba and H. & M. Rayne

Hosiery by B. Burnet & Co. and Husbands, Ltd.

————

The Cast includes:

GEORGE GRAVES	ETHEL LEVEY	JOSEPH COYNE
DOROTHY MINTO	LUPINO LANE	BLANCHE TOMLIN
REGINALD CROMPTON	CHARLES GARRY	IVAN BERLYN
IVY SHILLING	PHYLLIS BEDELLS Première Danseuse	CHARLES STONE

the audience quietly marched out of the wrecked building while ambulances and stretchers were brought for the injured.

My poor brother, still dressed as a pierrot, was absolutely heartbroken at the tragic end to his efforts to amuse his shipmates. Mother and I, very unhappy, drove to Dovercourt to stay the night with relatives of the Gamages.

Watch Your Step was our next production at the Empire, and surely one of the most successful of its revues. There was a superlative cast, and the music was Irving Berlin's—except for my scene. It was set in an opera house; and I was supposed to be Taglioni dancing in *La Sylphide* with a supporting *corps de ballet*. My costume was copied from the famous A. E. Chalon portrait of that greatest of all dancers.

I am thankful to say that, quiet as the scene was, it was an enormous success. It came as a contrast to the noisy ragtime number preceding it, which was sung by Ethel Levey and the chorus. I felt blissfully happy. The whole show was a triumph for everyone concerned, and the house was crowded for months.

I was still dancing my Bacchante role in *The Vine*, which was put on earlier in the programme.

On the first night (4 May 1915) I received a beautiful print of Taglioni from Harry Ainley; that gift started a collection which is now the envy of my friends. Mollie Moss added to it a second print of Taglioni on my birthday that year.

Harry often used to send me comic notes by his dresser, Bob Russell, and he frequently called for me after the performance as he had a regular taxi.

I had begun seriously studying acting with Ben Webster. He gave me private tuition twice or three times a week. Among the plays we worked at were *Trelawny of the Wells* and *His House in Order*, in both of which I took Irene Vanbrugh's parts. It was excellent experience, and made me understand that there was more to good acting than having the desire to act and the ability to memorize the lines.

In May I was asked to appear at the St James's (in aid of The Theatrical Ladies' Guild) in a new one-act play, *The Azure Lily*, written by the Hon. Eleanor Norton, with whom I had become friendly at week-end parties at Dorothy Allhusen's home. There were only two parts in it, the King, played by Ben Webster, and the Spirit, which I played. In the nature of a fantasy, it opened with a solo dance to music by Reginald Clarke. Then followed a

PROGRAMME

Week commencing Monday Evening, SEPTEMBER 13th, 1915

1 OVERTURE ... " Krasnoe-Selo " (March Militaire) ... .. *G. St. Servan*

2 **Pearl Grey**

3 **The Sunshine Girls**

Mr. C. Wilhelm presents

4 **"PASTORALE"**

A "WATTEAU" DANCE-IDYLL IN ONE TABLEAU

Written, Designed, and Produced by
C. WILHELM

Music specially composed by HARVEY PINCHES
Dances arranged by A. H. MAJILTON

CHARACTERS

Girofléc (*a Country Girl*)	PHYLLIS BEDELLS	
	(*Première Danseuse*)	
Narcisse (*a Rustic Swain*)	CARLOTTA MOSSETTI	
Philidor (*a Gallant*)	FLO MARTELL	
Desirée (*a Coquette*)	CONNIE WALTER	
Celadon (*a Page*)	J. HART	

Watteau Dancers by Misses B. Hill, A. Farrant, M Moss, T Cunningham,
L. Osmond, F. Shortis, B. Banks, and W Taylor

The Scene painted by R. C. McCLEERY
The Costumes executed by Miss HASTINGS
Machinist W Sheldon   Electrician C. Winter
Properties P. Corveyson   Wigs by W Clarkson

5 SELECTION . , "Watch your Step" ... ... *Irving Berlin*

By courtesy of the Mander & Mitchenson collection

long speech, which was none too easy as, after dancing, naturally I was rather breathless.

Our effort seemed to be successful, however, as Ben and I were asked to repeat the play at another all-star matinée at the Haymarket at which Queen Alexandra, the Princess Royal, Princess Victoria, and Princess Maud were present. That was a very hot day, I remember; perspiration was trickling down my face. As I was speaking my lines, Ellaline Terriss and Ivy St Helier were standing in the wings, and I had to try hard not to giggle when I saw Ivy looking at me because, in the play, I was supposed to be a very cold, immortal spirit!

In the summer of 1915 Dion Boucicault and his wife, Irene Vanbrugh, invited me to spend a week-end at their cottage. I discovered that 'Dot' wanted to find out if I would like to play Peter Pan that Christmas. He told me he had recommended J. M. Barrie to come and see me dancing. But afterwards I heard that Barrie had decided I was too tall for the part—he had seen me dancing on points, which does make one look taller. The golden opportunity went instead to Unity More. That did not affect our fondness for one another; although I must confess to feeling envious of her, particularly after I had been studying acting so hard and felt I could have done well. However, it was not to be. Unity was a delightful Peter Pan and played it during the Christmas season for two years running. I felt very glad she had such success.

In September a charming little ballet called *Pastorale* had been produced specially for me by the Empire management. It was described as a 'Watteau' dance idyll in one scene, and it ran until my contract ended.

18

ONE DAY I ran into Nelson Keys at the Carlton where I was selling flags for one of those innumerable flag day appeals. He asked me if I remembered meeting a young officer at Mabel Russell's party in January.

'Of course,' I said. 'I remember him. He was on crutches and had a lovely sad face.'

Bunch Keys told me that Ian Macbean had been longing to meet me again but had not liked to write until he knew whether I would be willing to meet him. He was determined not to be considered a 'stage-door Johnny'.

I said that I would be delighted to meet him; and that very evening I was sent some red roses and a charming little note asking me to tea on the following day at Rumpelmayers. Ian waited at the stage-door for an answer. I sent dear Mrs Smith upstairs to tell him we could meet at four-thirty. She returned, full of enthusiasm. 'He's got the loveliest eyes I've ever seen', she declared. 'No wonder you want to go out with him.'

Next day brought our fateful meeting. We were both utterly tongue-tied. I do not think I had ever before been so nervous about meeting anyone. I fell completely in love with him.

Every week-end after that, when he was in London, he sent me roses and spent as much time as he could at Golders Green. He had been back to France since our last meeting and had been wounded again—in the foot. He was on light duty on Salisbury Plain, consequently week-end leave was more easily obtained than it might have been.

Ian had been with the first batch of British soldiers to go to France in 1914 and his regiment, the 2nd Battalion Sherwood Foresters, had fought a rearguard action throughout the retreat from Mons. I discovered that he had lost both his parents before we met, and the loneliness of his life wrung my heart. I longed to be able to look after him. For many weeks, however, there was a barrier between us that I did not understand. He went on sending me red roses and writing the most beautiful letters.

I knew from Bunch Keys that he was in love with me. He would never say so.

He had a little Newton-Bennet two-seater car. On Advent Sunday 1915, he drove me out to Windsor for evensong at St George's Chapel and we heard Mendelssohn's *The Sorrows of Death*, which was always sung by the choir there on that Sunday. From the age of seven, I found, Ian and his elder brother, Ronald, had been King's scholars at St George's and soloists in the choir. Ian told me that when he was fourteen his voice had broken on a top note just as he was singing the line, 'The night is departing . . .'

On this, my first visit, we sat in the stalls of the Knights of the Garter—a privilege enjoyed by the old boys of St George's—and after the service, which was conducted by Canon Dalton, Ian took me to the organ loft to meet Sir Walter Parratt, who had been organist and choirmaster in Ian's schooldays and was still. We visited several of the masters who still lived at Windsor Castle and later went to see Ian's young sister, Muriel (Moulie) who was a boarder at St Stephen's Convent at Clewer, near Windsor. She was then aged about twelve, and was very thrilled to meet a real, live ballet dancer. Afterwards we drove back to London through one of the worst fogs I can remember and were rather late reaching Golders Green.

When Leslie Gamage came on leave I lunched with him at the Carlton Grill. I told him that when I read his letters I had wondered if he had been hoping I would marry him eventually. He had, himself, never broached the subject of marriage; and it was an embarrassing question for me to be asking him. If he were not serious I was risking a rebuff. But out of honesty I felt he ought to know that I could not marry him.

He was terribly hurt, and he left me without a word. I did not see him again; but, when he had gone back to France, I talked to his mother. She appreciated my point of view but said that Leslie felt I had not played fair. When, however, I explained that he had never given me the chance to refuse him, she realized that I could not have done other than I did. I had felt, too, that it was fairer to settle it with him while he was on leave rather than write to him.

The next time I was out with Ian, he asked, 'Where is the military badge you usually wear? Aren't you engaged to someone?'

'No,' I told him. 'It's the badge that belongs to an old friend I am very fond of; but I am not in love with him.'

I realized then that it was Leslie's badge that had been the barrier between us.

On 18 December 1915 we became engaged to be married.

As soon as the news of it leaked out there was far too much publicity. Reporters made nuisances of themselves, arriving on our doorstep at Golders Green in the early morning and refusing to leave without an interview. No doubt they meant well. But it upset me to think that my private affairs must become public property; and I vowed that when I got married it would be kept a secret.

A tremendous number of letters and telegrams of congratulation came from friends and admirers; but one which pleased me most was from Dennis Neilson-Terry in France. At first I had a difficult time with my mother as she had always hoped I would marry Leslie Gamage, and she knew nothing at all about Ian. Eventually, however, when she saw how much I cared for him, she accepted the situation.

Perhaps I did not know much about Ian myself at first. But gradually I began to find out things about his earlier years. When he left St George's he went to Repton, where he excelled in gymnastics. He became captain of the gymnasium eight and later, at Sandhurst, took the advanced army gymnastic course. He had also boxed and fenced for the army before the war.

In our years together Ian often kept me amused with anecdotes of his schooldays and of the time when he was training at Sandhurst; but I think his childhood at St George's must have been the happiest period of his life. There he often appeared before Queen Victoria and sang duets with Madame Kirkby Lunn. He told me that he sang outside Her Majesty's bedroom when she lay dying. I still possess the minute pair of black woollen gloves he wore at her funeral in 1901.

He told me of his excitement during the coronation of King Edward VII when he earned his first decoration. Later he won many more. With other boys of St George's choir he often played cricket and other games with the young princes, the Prince Albert (afterwards King George VI), and his brother Edward. As a boy, therefore, he had been familiar with the pomp and circumstance which surround our Royal Family, but had also come into contact with them in the simple and human pleasures of every day.

19

◆◆

MY CONTRACT with the Empire ended on New Year's Eve, 1915. The management wanted me to stay on until the end of the run of *Watch Your Step*; but I decided it would be better to make a clean break as, after so many years, I felt in need of a change. Also I had been growing discontented. Full-length ballet had been superseded by revue, and only short ballets had been produced for me. This was inevitable, perhaps, as the management was compelled to follow the public taste of the times.

Nevertheless, my last night at the Empire was one of the most thrilling of all. When the curtain fell on *Pastorale* I thought there would never be an end to the bouquets which were handed up and piled high on the stage beside me, and I completely lost count of the number of curtain calls I took. Adeline Genée, sitting in the front row of the stalls, threw at my feet an exquisite Victorian bouquet tied with ribbons that matched my costume— a gesture that meant much to me, as I knew her reluctance to draw attention to herself in public.

The ovation I received from the audience, the orchestra, and the company was something I shall remember always. It would be, I felt, an anticlimax to appear later in *Watch Your Step* the same evening. But even then, when I had finished my Taglioni scene, there was a still greater ovation for me, which was followed by a presentation of a beautiful emerald and diamond ring, a gift from C. B. Cochran and the company. Joseph Coyne made the presentation speech. I had masses of other lovely presents from the *corps de ballet* and from all my friends. I honestly felt that I would willingly die after such a wonderful evening, and that never again could I know such joy and such gratitude for the warmth and love which surrounded me. I had three taxis to carry all my flowers and presents back to Golders Green. The only disappointment—and that a keen one—was that my fiancé was on duty in Newcastle-on-Tyne, having just been posted as Commandant of the Physical Training and Bayonet Training School, Northern Command. He was not there to share my triumph.

Before I left the Empire I had signed an exciting new contract to appear at the Coliseum in a play by Malcolm Watson which had a dancing part in it. I was to receive one hundred pounds a week, which was a big advance on the thirty pounds I had been earning. My doctor suggested that before the show opened I ought to have my tonsils removed, as I had been having sore throats for some time. We thought it would put me out of action for a week or two; but unfortunately it was far worse than that: it took me six months to recover from the operation, and I was compelled to withdraw from the Coliseum engagement.

The Zeppelin raids were on; and, as our lease on the Golders Green house had almost expired, we sub-let it to the photographer, Elwin Neame and his wife, Ivy Close. We took a house at Alexandra Road, Clifton, Bristol, and once again my dear father had a home after so many years of living in boarding-houses and only seeing us in London at week-ends.

Quite rightly, now that I was engaged to be married, Mother

felt it was time she rejoined my father. I lived with them until I regained my strength. Every day I wrote long letters to Ian, who was still in Newcastle-on-Tyne. Then I accepted an offer to appear at Drury Lane in Albert de Courville's mammoth production, *Razzle Dazzle*, in which I was to be given no less than five numbers.

My first appearance was as an Ice Cream Girl, dressed in pink and white tulle and sitting in a huge, silver ice-cream cup which was carried onto the stage by two tall footmen. There was a miniature ballet, which I was allowed to write and arrange myself, which I called 'One Summer's Day'. The first half of the revue ended with a spectacular scene of a Highland Gathering of the Clans, in which a chorus of two hundred and fifty appeared in full dress kit. I wore the Macbean tartan and danced the Highland Fling.

In the second half of the show I was the Maid of the Mist in a magnificent Niagara Falls scene, and after that changed quickly into a Red Indian warrior's costume in which I danced a very 'wild man's' solo as the Spirit of Niagara. Altogether I found the work pretty exhausting, as there were matinées every day, and at each of the twelve performances every week I had to repeat my Highland Fling.

I had been coached in this for two hours a day during the six weeks of rehearsals by a tough Pipe Sergeant-Major of the Scots Guards, who refused to pass even the slightest fault. He piped on and on, and insisted upon my working until I was nearly dropping through exhaustion. I felt that both he and I earned the success the dance had with the public.

It was unfortunate for Albert de Courville that our chief comedian, George Formby, was taken ill. The father of the present comedian, he was then at the height of his popularity. He was unable to appear when the show opened on 19 June 1916, and at short notice his place was taken by Shaun Glenville. Most of the sketches were unsuited to this player's quite different style of humour: in consequence the comedy side of the show was not very successful. Most of the press notices complained of a lack of wit and humour. Its main success lay in the lavish spectacle it presented. But the revue was too long. The curtain fell well after midnight.

Towards the end of July George Formby did take up his part, and a shorter, reconstructed version of *Razzle Dazzle* was given.

87

However, after only a very few weeks at Drury Lane, the revue moved to the Empire and Harry Tate came into the cast. George Formby was still with it, but not for long, as his health again broke down.

I found myself re-installed in my old dressing-room, No. 1, the room which had so recently been the scene of my farewells. George Formby dressed next door in No. 2 and Harry Tate was in No. 3. The Green Room had been converted for Shirley Kellogg into a very charming dressing-room which was actually on the stage, on the prompt side.

For these Empire performances my Summer's Day ballet was cut, much to my regret; but, instead, another dance was added to a new Ladder of Roses scene.

Razzle Dazzle settled down to a long and most successful run. Harry Tate with his inimitably funny sketches was a great asset to it. He was one of the most lovable men it has ever been my good fortune to meet, and he had a heart of pure gold.

That Christmas Eve, I remember, I found the staircases and passages leading to our dressing-rooms completely filled with turkeys and geese which Harry had bought to give away to the stage staff. There must have been thirty or forty birds lying there. As well as for his glorious sense of the ridiculous, which made him one of the greatest comedians, he will be remembered by all who knew him for his kindness and generosity. He died in 1940 and left just over a thousand pounds although, in his lifetime, he had earned enormous salaries. He must have given most of his money away.

I had taken a furnished service flat in Albemarle Street which I shared with Ivy St Helier until her own flat became vacant, and then I went to live with her for a while at 12 Windsor Mansions, which was next door to the Three Arts Club. Mabel (Bobbie) Seymour Hicks joined us there for a while and we spent some very amusing times together. Then we heard that an unfurnished flat was available in the same building and I took it for myself. I enjoyed arranging the furnishings. The flat was on the first floor and had a balcony and French windows to the drawing-room, dining-room, and one of the bedrooms. There were two other bedrooms and a large kitchen and bathroom—all for £120 a year!

My sitting-room, furnished by Burnets, was a joy, with its black, fitted Wilton carpet and hand-blocked printed linen curtains and loose covers. There was ample room for my

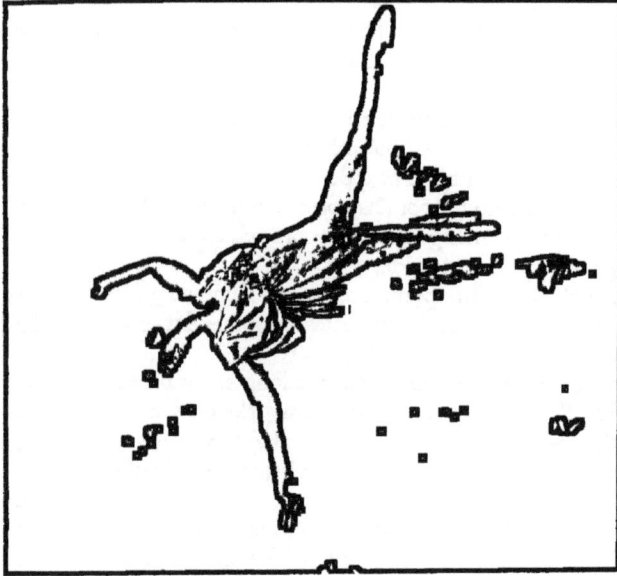

Illus & Walery

Phyllis Bedells and E. Kurylo in *Sylvia* at the Empire Theatre, 1911.

Augus

Karsavina in *Le Spectre de la Rose* at Covent Garden, 1911.

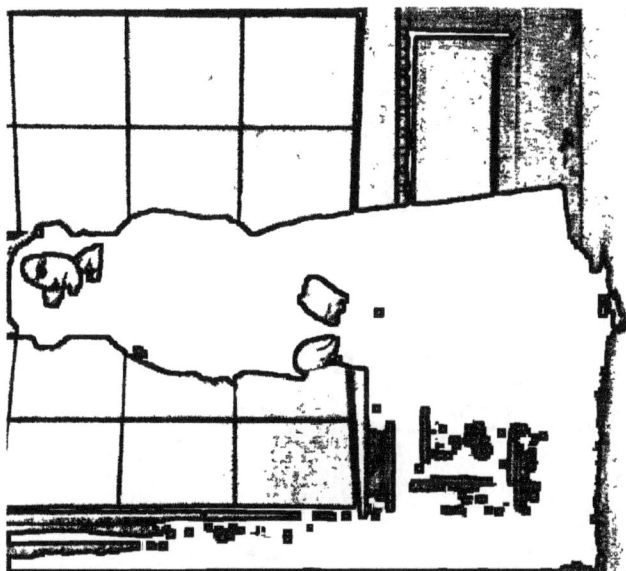

The Squaw in the ballet *New York*, the Empire Theatre, 1911

Ellis & Walery

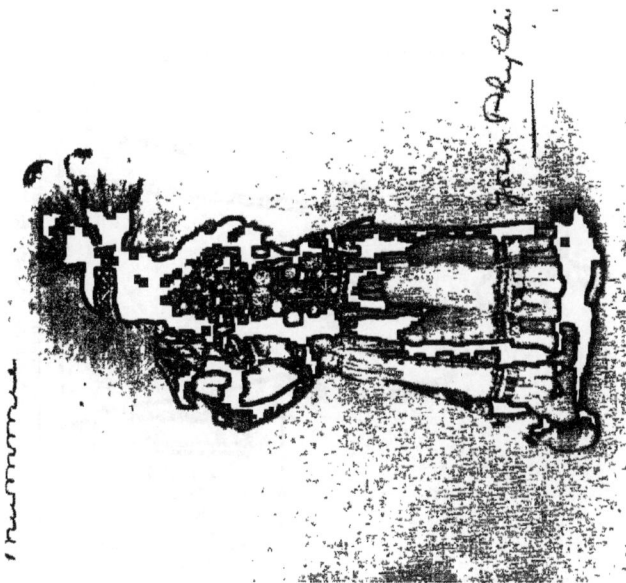

Phyllis Bedells in private life at the age of 18

Bassano

Cecchetti, 1914.

C. Wilhelm, who wrote most of the Empire ballets and designed
the costumes and décors.

Lllis & Walery

Dennis Neilson-Terry, 1912.

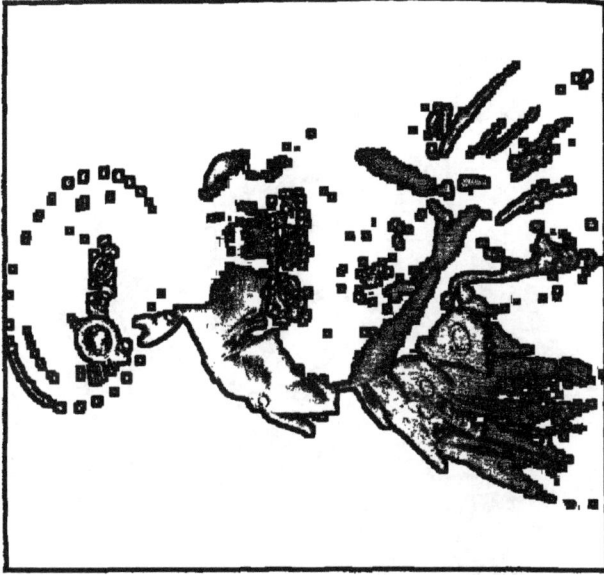

Harris

Phyllis Bedells as the Slave of the Ring in *Aladdin* at the Empire Theatre, 1912.

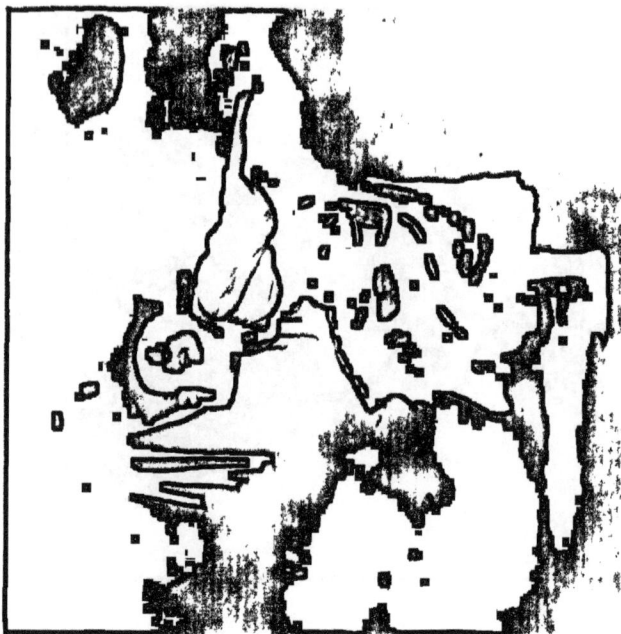

Nightbirds, the Lyric Theatre 1911–12

Harris

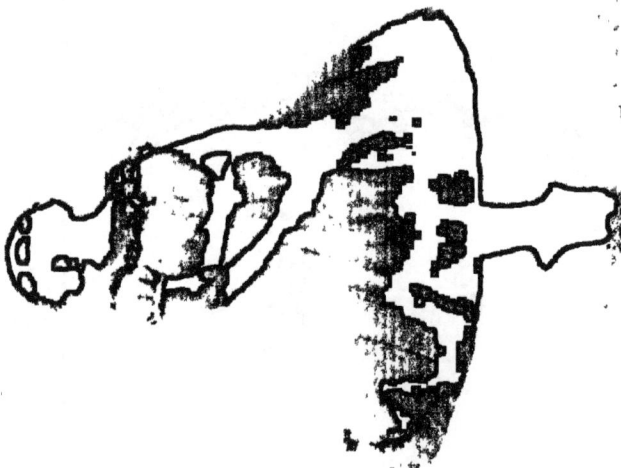

Gypsy Dance, the Empire Theatre, 1913

Barrane

Above Phyllis Bedells with E Espinosa and Miss Sheppard, in the revival of *The Dancing Master*, at the Empire Theatre, 1914. *Below* No 1 dressing-room at the Empire (1914–15)

The Vine, at the Empire Theatre, 1915
Above Carlotti Mossetti, Little June, and Connie Walter *Below*. Phyllis Bedells, Carlotti Mossetti, and four coryphées, including Marjorie Moss (*right*)

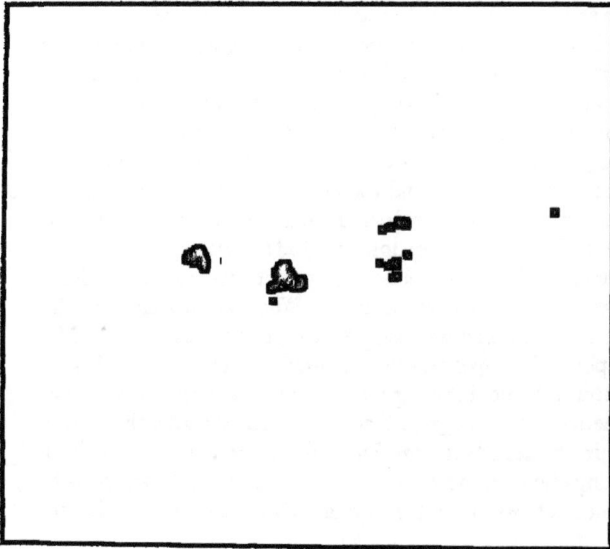

Florence Van Damm

The author in private life, 1915.

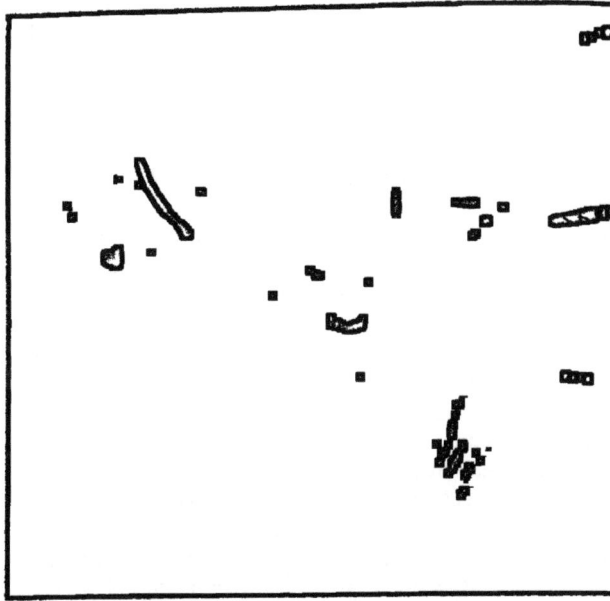

Henry Ainley as Joe Quinney in *Quinneys*, at the Theatre Royal,
Haymarket, 1915.

Blüthner piano. Maples did the bedrooms in pink and white and the dining-room was in old oak. Although at the time it seemed excessively extravagant, after thirty-five years the furniture and carpets are still in use.

Ivy and I had a splendid arrangement: on alternate nights we had supper in each others' flats, so that our maids could get to bed early on their free nights. We would sit and discuss our ambitions or play my gramophone. I had some fine recordings made by the London String Quartet, who were friends of mine. I had met them at Dawsie's musical parties. Albert Sammons, Warwick Evans, Waldo Warner, William Murdoch, and W. H. Squire were some of the other famous musical people I met there and Dame Madge Kendal, Violet Loraine, Marie Löhr, Léon Quartermaine, and Fay Compton would often come in. Later on, thanks to Dawsie, Malcolm Sargent and Prince George Chavchavadze became our close friends.

During the time I lived in Windsor Mansions I saw more and more of Dawsie. Although she was about thirty-five years older we became devoted to each other. While the air raids were on I found the easiest way to get home from the Empire was to walk, and 11a Portland Place was a good 'half-way house'. I would call on Dawsie, have a soft drink and a slice of her home-made cake and, after a short rest and a chat, resume my walk home. If by some chance I had not seen her for a few days, she would walk round to my flat quite late at night and give our code ring on the front door bell to avoid causing me any alarm. If I was in bed, which was often the case, she would sit talking and smoking for an hour or so and tell me stories of her life. She was a widow, but I gathered that her ten years of married life had been perfect. Without ever being morbid I knew she yearned to join her husband, although to her countless friends she was the merriest and kindest of women. Deep down she had a great loneliness.

Number 7 Windsor Mansions, opposite my own front door, was occupied by Max Pemberton. When we had air raids the occupants of the flats were supposed to go to the basement. The head porter, Mr Piper, was most insistent that the rule was obeyed. But how I resented leaving the cosiness of my flat. Often Max Pemberton would suggest that I dance for the assembly down there in the cold basement, but I always refused. Apart from anything else I was never suitably clad. Later on I had to insist that the main passage in my own flat where there was no glass to splinter was a far safer place. There I stubbornly remained for all the later air raids.

In September 1916, Henry Ainley joined the army, too, and afterwards I saw very little of him. He was given a commission in the R.G.A. and served not only in England but in France and Italy until his demobilization in February 1919.

In 1916 I was asked to dance in a film which Lucoque was making called *A Baby Boy's Dream of Fairyland*. Later that somewhat cumbersome title was changed to *Fairyland*. In the film I was Queen of the Dance. I had to dance on my points in a natural woodland setting, which I found far from easy, as there had been a lot of rain and my shoes were soon sodden. I earned very little money from that film and discovered later that I was being featured in it all over the country during the Christmas holidays. This experience finally compelled me to realize that one must always employ an agent to draw up such contracts.

Every week-end I went down to see my mother and father, travelling to Bristol on Sunday morning and returning on Monday in time for the matinée. With twelve shows a week I lived a full life. It was impossible for me to go to classes then. None of the great teachers, owing to war conditions, was in London, so I had to do what I could myself. It was a strict rule with me never to appear without having done some practice beforehand, as I knew that unless I practised conscientiously my technique would quickly deteriorate.

20

✦✦✦✦✦✦✦✦✦✦✦✦✦✦✦✦✦✦✦✦✦✦✦✦✦✦✦✦✦✦✦✦✦✦✦✦✦✦

BEFORE Christmas 1916, Ian was ordered to sail for an unknown destination. I had a terrible time on the day he left. He had been for nearly a year in Newcastle-on-Tyne and, during the twelve months we had been engaged, I had only seen him two or three times when he came for a short week-end and stayed at the Carlton Hotel. Now he was off to the war again. I managed to see his train leave from Waterloo between performances; but, oh, the tears I shed that night, even as I was dancing!

Eventually Ian arrived in Salonika and was soon in the fighting line. He gained the Military Cross, the *Croix de Guerre* with

Palms, and the Order of the White Eagle of Serbia, and was twice mentioned in dispatches. While in Greece he contracted dysentery and malaria, and when he left hospital he was given command of an entrenching battalion at Stavros. General Sir George Milne came to inspect the battalion there and appointed Ian to his own staff, where he was first made G.S.O. 3 and later promoted to G.S.O. 2 and given the rank of Brevet Major. I think the only person I was ever really jealous of was 'Uncle George' (who later became Field Marshal Lord Milne). Ian simply adored him and I knew he would willingly have given his life for him.

One of Ian's best friends of those days, Major the Hon. Dudley Carleton (later Lord Dorchester) came on leave and invited me to lunch at the Berkeley Restaurant. It was from him that I heard of Ian's bravery in the fighting line. Ian himself would never talk about this and deprecated any suggestion that he had done anything out of the ordinary.

The original contract for *Razzle Dazzle* had been for thirty pounds a week for the run of the show; but, even before we opened at Drury Lane, de Courville got Leon Pollock to approach me and together with my agent, Mr Braff, a new contract was drawn up for three years, rising by ten pounds a week each year to fifty pounds in the third year. With these twelve shows weekly to get through I did three years' hard labour, but felt secure financially and was able to live in comfort and to make an allowance to my grandmother who, by paying for my early training, had made my career possible.

I secured the services of a wonderful cook, named Sarah, who made my home a favourite meeting place for my many friends. She was no longer young, but absolutely refused to take any time off. She prepared most delicious meals and kept my flat spick and span, so that I was able to entertain anybody without the slightest anxiety. Of course most of my entertaining was done after the evening performances or at early luncheons. I was at the theatre from 1.30 to 6 p.m. and from 7.15 until 8.45 p.m. I used to stay in my dressing-room for tea between performances and seldom got any fresh air; but this, I thought, did me no harm. Despite the anxiety of having my fiancé at the front and my only brother in submarines, I never ailed.

It was galling to me to find that I could never go to other theatres, particularly as I missed seeing the season at the Coliseum in which Adeline Genée revived *Camargo* and *La Danse* in the spring of 1917.

Early in May *Razzle Dazzle* came off; and during rehearsals for the next de Courville production, he insisted I dance in *Zig-Zag* which was then running at the Hippodrome. This went on until the production of *Smile*, which opened at the Garrick in June.

Those last four weeks of rehearsal were hectic. De Courville got his money's worth. In the final week, from ten to eleven in the morning, I rehearsed the numbers I had arranged for myself. From eleven to half past one there were full-dress rehearsals with the company. Then the rest were allowed a break for lunch, but I had to rush across to the Hippodrome to appear at the matinée there, in the opening scene and in the finale. As soon as the matinée was over back I had to go to the Garrick in a taxi and in full make-up to continue rehearsing until half past seven, when I was again due at the Hippodrome for the evening show. Immediately after the fall of the curtain there I went back to the Garrick to work until four, five and—on the night before we opened—until six in the morning!

Edgar Wallace saved my life. I had no time at all for meals. While the company had theirs, as I have said, I was at the Hippodrome; so dear Edgar Wallace, who had written some of the scenes for both *Zig-Zag* and *Smile*, sat in the stalls while rehearsals were on and fed me between numbers with teaspoonfuls of Brand's Essence. It was rather like a hen-bird feeding her chick. I seemed to be far too tired and too worked up to eat sandwiches. That was the only food I had for days on end, although I drank dozens of cups of tea in my dressing-room.

My contract with de Courville stated clearly that I was to fill the role of principal dancer; but I had signed the usual form of agreement 'to act, sing, dance or perform to the best of her ability'. When rehearsals for *Smile* were in progress de Courville asked me to sing a song.

'It's impossible,' I said. 'I can't sing. I'm a dancer.'

But he said, 'You will be breaking your contract if you refuse.'

He had passed me a song called *Cheero*. I took it and my troubles to Edgar Wallace. I was sure, I told him, everybody would say, 'Why doesn't she stick to dancing—to what she can really do.' Edgar Wallace, however, advised me to learn the

92

song, which I did; but, right up to the last three days of rehearsals, I refused to sing it.

I was talking to Edgar Wallace again and we were discussing Unity More who had previously been under contract to de Courville at the Hippodrome. Everyone in the company knew her, including Julian Jones, the Musical Director; but, because of our long friendship I suppose I knew her funny little mannerisms better than anybody. I was saying to Edgar Wallace that if Unity had been given this song to sing she would have done it like this ... and I gave him an impromptu imitation of Unity singing it. He was immensely amused and said, 'My dear, you've hit on an idea there. If de Courville asks you to sing it to-night, do it like that and see how it goes.'

Sure enough at the rehearsal de Courville said, 'Phyllis, you have got to sing that song. We'll have no more nonsense about it.'

Julian Jones was told to start my music. Without a word to anyone I started to sing and dance. Before I was half way through the whole company and those in front connected with the production, including de Courville himself, and the orchestra, were helpless with laughter.

De Courville clapped his hands and shouted across the footlights, 'That's fine! We'll keep that.'

So the item came to be included in the programme as 'Unity More—or less'. I said nothing to Unity about it and was terrified on the night she came to see the show that our friendship would be jeopardized. While I was singing I mustered enough courage to glance up towards the box where she was sitting and was relieved to see that she was laughing with the rest.

In addition to this imitation of Unity and a lovely butterfly ballet in pure classical style I had an amusing number during what was supposed to be a charity concert. I did a burlesque of a retired Russian ballerina. Wearing a grey wig, and spectacles, I walked on, leaning heavily on a stick, to the music of Tchaikovsky's *1812 Overture*. I grew increasingly excited until finally I threw away my stick, picked up my skirts, and danced as wildly as of yore! The joke came off well, and became one of the hits of the revue. I had to be careful to keep it subtle and not sacrifice the ex-ballerina's dignity.

De Courville's ruthless determination to have his own way was legendary. At the final dress rehearsal of *Smile*, Minerva Coverdale, a pretty American soubrette, sang a song about legs, and was supported by the chorus lying on their backs with their heads towards the audience and 'dancing' with their feet held high in the air. The black tights they wore were of spun silk and apparently of too thick a texture to please de Courville, who sent for the representative of the firm which had provided them and said, 'I want forty-eight pairs of fine, pure silk black tights to fit these girls, in time for the opening tomorrow night.'

It was then three-thirty in the morning. Naturally the man replied, 'That's impossible.'

'Those are my orders,' de Courville told him, 'and they must be obeyed.'

The tights arrived in time. How the manufacturers managed it, with a war on, I cannot imagine. Albert de Courville always had his way!

I was sharing a dressing-room with Madie Hope, whom I had known in the old Empire days. Poor Madie was terribly jumpy about the air raids, and I often had difficulty in calming her and preventing her from communicating her fear to the rest of the company. We had one particularly trying week. One afternoon, while a raid was in progress, I was singing my 'Unity More' song and had just sung the line, 'I've a slight idea I've met my fate', when there was a terrifying explosion which simply rocked the theatre. Even the orchestra burst out laughing at the aptness of the words. We learned afterwards that a mobile A.A. gun, immediately outside the Garrick, had let fly at the enemy overhead.

The strain of twelve shows a week, constant air raids, loss of sleep, together with overwork during the rehearsals eventually caused my health to break down. In July I was ordered immediate and complete rest by my doctor, who found I had a dilated heart. I was hurried off to Newquay, where Mother joined me, and for two weeks was not even allowed to go upstairs. But by keeping strictly to the doctor's instructions I soon recovered, and after three weeks was back in harness.

The press and public alike had hailed *Smile* as a great success, but frequent air raids had a disastrous effect upon the box office. The show was withdrawn after only a four months' run. Once again I returned to the Hippodrome to dance in *Zig-Zag*, which had gone into a third edition. I danced in the Autumn scene and in a Stone Age scene, with funny little Daphne Pollard and George Robey which I found amusing enough; but I told myself

94

that I was only marking time until de Courville could give me something that was a little more interesting.

In one respect it was fortunate I had only two dances at each performance because my stock of Nicolini ballet shoes had almost run out and it was exceptionally difficult to obtain any from Milan. At one time I was reduced to one pair, which had to last for no less than thirty-eight performances. I darned and cleaned them again and again; and just when they were beyond further repair, much to my relief, a new consignment arrived. Had it not done I might have been unable to do any more classical dancing, and become a modern revue dancer instead and, so to speak, hauled down the flag.

When I did not go to my parents at week-ends I often went to Sunday evening parties at Lydia Kyasht's house in Knightsbridge. Always among her guests there were Russian noblemen who had escaped from the revolutionaries. I remember one evening I was playing a quiet game of auction bridge with three other friends and there was another group playing poker when Lydia asked me to change over with a lady who wished to play bridge. I told Lydia I was not much good at poker but would do what I could. Within half an hour I had lost over £50—more than my week's salary. Even although I later managed to win back £30 of it I felt pretty miserable and as soon as I could politely leave I did. After that experience I made it a rule never to play for money—except for very low stakes.

21

AT THE BEGINNING of 1918 I received the wonderful news that Ian was coming home on leave from Salonika. He wrote that he would have nearly three weeks, and wanted me to marry him at once instead of waiting until the war ended, which was what we had previously decided. The newspapers had pages and pages of casualty lists every day. It seemed that the end of the war must be far off. Ian and I had been engaged for well over two years. I naturally felt very anxious, and sometimes wondered if we really knew one another well enough. I felt shy at the thought of marriage within four days of his return to England.

But before he arrived I made all the preliminary arrangements, obtained a special licence, and booked hotel accommodation. I also invited a maiden aunt of his, Miss Ethel Fisher, nicknamed 'Hesh', of whom I was very fond, to stay with me at my flat for the three weeks before the wedding. It was not certain when exactly Ian's ship would dock. I told de Courville I would need three weeks off and begged him to keep my secret, as we wanted a very quiet wedding without any of the usual theatrical publicity. For once I had my way. Only our nearest relations and closest friends knew of our plans.

While Hesh was staying with me I had my first experience of how it felt to have drunk too much. Lydia Kyasht, who was dancing at the Coliseum, invited me to a farewell party given by twelve Russian officers who were leaving to join our forces in Mesopotamia. The only other guests were Lord Lonsdale and Hilda Bewicke. They called for me at the Hippodrome after my show, and we drove to a flat which was used as a club by the Russian officers. We were given an excellent supper, with which I drank white wine. Presently all the officers left the room; but they soon returned in procession, singing lustily and carrying between them a huge bowl of steaming punch. What was said to be a traditional ceremony followed, during which they poured out a small glass of hot punch for me and gathered round, chanting in Russian. At first I refused to drink it, but Lydia said, 'Phyllis, you *must* drink and then turn your glass upside down. They will go on singing until you do. If you refuse you will offend them very much. It is one of our great traditions.' So, of course, I drank it. The same thing happened in turn to Hilda, Lydia, and Lord Lonsdale. I noticed that even Lord Lonsdale, who must have been more accustomed to drink than I, coughed and spluttered a little. It was not until afterwards that I discovered what the brew contained: red wine, vodka, rum—plentifully spiced.

I found the room was spinning round and had great difficulty in walking straight, although my mind seemed quite clear. I was determined not to disgrace myself, and grasped the handrail tightly as I went downstairs to the car. I told Lydia that I wanted to go back home as I felt unwell. She drove me there. Hesh was waiting, and I confessed to her what had happened, and she helped me into bed. She laughed, and did not seem at all shocked. My bed seemed to be floating about the room as I lay on it. It was a most horrible sensation.

Since my engagement I had been busy making my trousseau. Now I had to rush around the shops buying the other things I needed—a new fur coat and some hats. My wedding dress had been hurriedly designed and made for me by Charles Wilson, the firm which belonged to the father of one of my pre-war pupils, Marian Wilson. It was a lovely shade of blue charmeuse with hand-tucked panels of chiffon of the same colour; and, with it, I wore a grey corded silk hat, rather Napoleonic in shape, which was then the height of fashion. How awful it would look to-day!

Ian arrived on 1 February. He stayed at the Carlton Hotel until our wedding, which took place at St Marylebone Parish Church on 5 February 1918, at eleven in the morning. My father and mother came up from Clifton for the night and stayed with me at the flat. Betty Spottiswoode and Ian's younger sister, Moulie, were bridesmaids. The best man was Kenneth Gooch, a friend of Ian's family. Altogether we had only twenty guests, including Lady Crutchley, Ian MacDonald, and Guy Dury (both in the Grenadier Guards), my agent, Mr Braff, and my dresser.

Ian gave me a diamond and enamel wrist-watch. My present to him was a crocodile leather dressing-case. There was a large amount of silver and china, which had been kept by his aunt Jean (Mrs Eden) for Ian after his parents died. For many years, when Ian's father and mother were living in Singapore, all the Macbean children had lived with her at Ower in Hampshire.

I was about to enter the car on my way to the church with my father when another drove up and the chauffeur handed me a small packet containing a lovely sapphire and diamond eternity ring and a message, 'With my love and best wishes for every happiness—Mary Curzon.'

We had a very jolly little wedding party in my flat, and then Ian and I went to Branksome Towers Hotel at Bournemouth for the first part of our honeymoon. During the three days we were there it rained nearly all the time. At the week-end we went to stay with Ian's grandmother, Mrs Fisher, who was well over eighty, at the Dower House, West Lavington, in Wiltshire. I remember her telling me that she had seen the great Taglioni dance.

We went to Clifton for a night to see my father and mother, and so back to London where, in less than a fortnight, we saw a dozen plays. Ian had been starved of good entertainment for so long and I was so much in love with him that I willingly agreed to have this busman's holiday. We spent a small fortune, eating in the best restaurants and buying stalls in theatres. It was an odd sort of honeymoon, perhaps; but so long as Ian was happy I felt that was all I cared. For all the time the spectre of the war hung over us and the day when he must return to duty seemed to come so terribly soon.

I remember vividly the last night together. We sat in the front row of the stalls at the Savoy to see the new success *Nothing but the Truth* in which A. E. Matthews played so excellently. Even although our hearts were so heavy with the thought of parting we laughed uproariously. The play must have been very good.

Ian left early next morning, and I went back to the Hippodrome and was soon rehearsing for a new production, *Hotch Potch*, which de Courville was presenting at the Duke of York's. Fred Kitchen was our chief comedian. One of my numbers was a Spinning Top dance, rather like that in *Jeux d'Enfants*. Everybody seemed to like it. On the whole, however, the show did not go well and was withdrawn at the end of June. De Courville was planning to take *Zig-Zag* to the Folies-Bergère in Paris and asked if I would go with it. I agreed. Our plans were well advanced when 'Big Bertha' began to shell Paris. De Courville said he could not risk taking us there at that time, and I was given my first long holiday.

I joined Mrs MacDonald, Mrs Hugh Spottiswoode, and Betty at Branksome Towers. Quite near there was a convalescent home at which Ian MacDonald, whom I used to call John, to avoid confusion with my Ian, was recovering from the effects of poison gas. He was allowed to leave and join us at the hotel, where we all thoroughly enjoyed ourselves together, bathing and playing a lot of tennis in glorious summer weather, and dancing every night after dinner.

My birthday, 9 August, was spent at the hotel. It was a splendid day. The news had just come through of the Big Push on the Western Front, which eventually proved to be the turning of the tide for us and our allies. We felt very happy.

It was while I was on holiday that I had a nasty accident which kept me in bed for some weeks. The grass on the tennis courts must have been damp. I leapt to return a high ball and somehow slipped, so that I fell on my hip. I had to be carried indoors and in an hour there was a lump the size and colour of a large red cabbage. It was unimaginably painful. The skin was not broken but was stretched like a big purple balloon. For over a week it remained in spite of hot fomentations being applied every hour. However, I was very kindly treated at the hotel and had lots of flowers and an amusing bouquet made of red cabbage tied with ribbon from the MacDonalds. As soon as I was able to get up I went to Clifton for the rest of my holiday.

De Courville then decided that he could risk producing *Zig-Zag* in Paris and wanted me to go. This time I refused. Ian had written, saying he did not wish me to go: Dorothy Turner went instead. Dorothy had been a pupil of mine years before and it was an opportunity for her to make a success.

I agreed to appear in the second edition of *Box of Tricks*, then running at the Hippodrome, and had a wonderful welcome on returning from my long holiday. The press notices were all excellent. I appeared in two scenes: one as Pierrette, with Alec Frazer as Pierrot serenading me, then accompanying me on the oboe as I danced. The setting for this was moonlit and romantic and I had the whole stage to dance on. And I was in an Early Victorian 'boy-and-girl' number with Dorothy Jay.

Dear Harry Tate was also in the cast, and that fine comedian and dancer, George Clarke. Cicily Debenham had a good song to sing called 'When London's Lit Up'. The words of it reflected the optimistic view everybody was taking of the news just then. There was an exciting new exhilaration abroad which, thank heaven, was justified. We heard that Bulgaria had asked for an armistice. It was the first sign that the war was coming to an end, and that it should come from the theatre of war in which my husband was serving gave me a great feeling of thankfulness.

Ian, I heard later, was on duty at G.H.Q. Salonika when a plane brought a personal message from the King of Roumania and Queen Marie to our own king, George V. It was he who ciphered the message and sent it to London. I still have the original manuscript.

When Sir George Milne and his G.H.Q. Staff moved to Constantinople Ian of course went, too, and apparently had a most interesting time. He went with 'Uncle George' on a trip to Baku.

22

EARLY in November my brother Stuart had one of his rare leaves, and on Sunday—it was 10 November—I went down to Bristol to my parents at Clifton with whom he was staying. It was known that an armistice was likely to be signed, and excitement everywhere was intense. As I had to be back in time for my matinée on Monday, Stuart, who wanted to see London again, travelled up with me. As we passed through Reading we saw flags being hoisted and heard the church bells ringing. Everyone on the train began congratulating everyone else. I just wept with joy and relief. It was eleven in the morning.

When we arrived at Paddington we dumped the luggage at my flat and tried to get to the Hippodrome by taxi, but the crowds had gathered all round the theatre, and Piccadilly Circus, Trafalgar Square, Whitehall, were a seething mass of cheering humanity. We had to push a way through.

Both performances that day were quite crazy. Some people from the audience tried to get on the stage, and it was all the management and staff could do to maintain even a semblance of order. We had a battle of flowers from the stage to the stalls. When I was in my dressing-room I could still hear the roar of the crowd outside. When the matinée was over Stuart and I managed to struggle through the mob to my flat. I had invited Admiral Mark Kerr, whom I had known since childhood, and Ian MacDonald for an early dinner at six-fifteen, as it was Stuart's last evening. We spent a delightful time listening to 'Uncle Mark' telling of his experiences. He had been a personal friend of many great figures, including the Kaiser and the Greek Royal Family, and, that evening, he was obviously in a reminiscent mood.

At half past seven we began to make our way to the theatre. We went in Ian (John) MacDonald's car while Uncle Mark departed to attend some function or other. Our drive to the theatre was one I shall never forget. John was in white tie and tails and wearing a silk hat. We had to have the top of the little car down to make room for Stuart's luggage. He was in Naval Officer's uniform and sat beside John; and I sat on his knees. I suppose we were inviting the badinage which we certainly received.

Eventually we reached the theatre with people clinging to the back and sides of the car and sitting on the bonnet—all of them cheering lustily. John's silk hat had been bashed in like a concertina.

While I was hurriedly dressing for the show, Stuart and John went out among the milling mob in the streets and returned in the interval with a special edition of the evening newspaper giving the armistice terms, which they read out to me.

When the show finished we had to take Stuart to Euston, where he was to catch the midnight train to Scotland to rejoin his ship. We got as far as the junction of Euston Road and Tottenham Court Road and found hundreds of people playing ring o' roses round a lamp standard there which had had the blue paint removed from its lights. London was already beginning to be 'lit up'. Stuart barely managed to get his train. When it had pulled out, John came back with me to Windsor Mansions and we sat there, quietly smoking and drinking.

John told me that his mother had expressed her feelings of thankfulness by beating the set of drums which he played when they had dances at their house. She had broken the parchment of one of the drums. As she had three sons in the forces and they were all alive her behaviour could be understood; but for a woman of such great dignity and charm—well, it must have been a strange and amusing thing to see her sitting all alone and beating away at those drums.

About this time the Diaghilev Ballet were in London again with Lydia Lopokova and Massine as principals, but owing to having two shows a day I was unfortunately unable to see anything of them.

I had begun to visit old Madame Guy d'Hardelot at her house in St John's Wood. Ivy St Helier, who had studied singing with her, first introduced me. She gathered her many musical and theatrical friends together on Sunday afternoons, and among her guests I met the most illustrious musicians and singers of the day. Many of them willingly played or sang for us. I first heard Stabili sing there, and also Silveri. Carmen Hill, one of England's finest ballad singers, was another of Madame's pupils, with whom I became friendly through having met at these parties. I met Clara Evelyn, too, who shortly afterwards teamed up with Ivy St Helier in an excellent two-piano act with which they had much success in the larger variety theatres in London and the provinces. They started by playing with great brilliance a shortened version of the Grieg Piano Concerto, and then they sang both serious and light comedy songs, some of their own composition. Clara was tall, fair, and very handsome, while Ivy was *petite* and quaint with large brown eyes. Their being such excellent foils for each other was an additional reason why their performances, so full of wit and charm, were as successful as they were.

Unity More became engaged to Captain Nigel Haig, M.C., during the summer, and before the end of the year they had married and Unity retired from the stage. There must have been many broken-hearted admirers when she made her decision, for she was then at the height of her popularity. Our affection for one another, needless to say, remained as strong as always. Nigel had been in love with her since the old Empire days when she and I dressed together in No. 6, and in the end his quiet, faithful devotion was rewarded.

Rehearsals began in January 1919 for de Courville's next show at the Hippodrome, *Joybells*, in which I was the only member of the *Box of Tricks* company to appear. The book for it was by Albert de Courville himself and Wal Pink, with music by Fred Chapelle, who had also written the music for *Smile*. George Robey was the star comedian and received the enormous salary of £600 a week. Shirley Kellogg sang in all the big production numbers. Leon Errol, a newcomer from the United States and later a well-known comic film star, was very good in several of the sketches. And there was again quaint little Daphne Pollard who had been with me in *Zig-Zag*.

The production cost £35,000 and on the first night ran for nearly four hours—until past midnight.

I was in the Winter to Spring transformation scene, and danced an oriental number in the Hindustan scene; but I was most excited about my part as the Queen Bird in the Bird Cage, which was a really magnificent piece of production. After the dress rehearsal next morning we had a call for cuts, as de Courville had realized that the show was going to be too long. We were told 'The Bird Cage is out'.

It was a nasty blow as, hoping this would be my biggest success, I had put my best work into it. George Robey announced across the footlights to de Courville, 'If the Bird Cage scene is cut, I don't play to-night.' For over an hour he argued, and eventually won my case for me. The scene was left in and, as I had hoped, created quite a sensation.

I felt extremely grateful to George Robey because it seemed to me that he and I had never before 'hit it off' very well.

In one of Shirley Kellogg's songs, 'Good-bye, Khaki', she was supported by a male chorus dressed in mud-stained khaki uniform in which they marched up a gang plank from the stage, through the centre of the stalls, and out of sight, to reappear in the full-dress uniform of the Brigade of Guards, scarlet jackets and bear-skins, as though for Trooping the Colour. It was a rousing number; but John MacDonald and Guy Dury fumed with anger when they saw it. They hated to see chorus men wear the proud uniform of their own regiment.

Joybells was an immense success. When my three years' contract with de Courville ended in June he tried to persuade me to stay on in the show until the end of the run; but I felt I had done my three years' hard labour and firmly refused to prolong the engagement. I had another very good reason for doing this: I was expecting Ian home quite soon from Constantinople.

On my last night at the Hippodrome I was standing on George Robey's right as we were taking a call, and he pressed into my hand a diamond and sapphire pendant on a platinum chain. In his gruff and husky voice he said, 'I hear you are leaving us to-night. That's for you, for luck.' Amid the cheers and applause I wept tears of gratitude.

The first part of my holiday I spent with Mrs MacDonald and her family at their lovely country house, 'High Rough', between Hindhead and Haslemere, where I had often stayed for short week-ends. By now I had become one of the family.

From there I went with Mother to Newquay for a fortnight, played some golf, bathed, and enjoyed feeling that at last I could do as I liked and need not keep up my daily practice. I imagined that I had left the stage for always. We went back to Clifton to await Ian's return.

In August he arrived, burned nearly black with the Middle East sun and looking extraordinarily fit. I again felt shy with him at first. All the time we had been engaged we had had only two week-ends together during 1916, when he had been stationed at Newcastle, and a little over two weeks together as husband and wife in 1918. In nearly four years, except for our letters, we had not had much opportunity to get to know one another.

After we had stayed in Clifton for a while with my parents we visited Aunt Jean Eden, who now had a large house at Lyndhurst. I bought a little car, a Humber two-seater, and Ian and I drove to 'High Rough', where we were given a warm welcome.

When Ian's leave finished he was sent to Catterick as Brigade Major. We drove up together, and booked a room for the night at the King's Head Hotel in Richmond. As soon as we had unpacked Ian reported for duty, only to discover that there was no brigade! It had been disbanded the previous week.

We stayed in Richmond for several weeks, awaiting further orders, and Ian tried without much success to teach me to drive the car. My trouble was that in an emergency I merely stopped the engine. The narrow, hilly roads were difficult for me to manage. Ian, on the other hand, was a first-rate driver. It was soon obvious to me that I had better let him drive or we might easily have got on each other's nerves. He did manage to teach me to play piquet, and we played every evening. There were no theatres or cinemas in Richmond, and, of course, no radio, then. It was a quiet life, but pleasantly peaceful. I remember glorious autumn tints and the beautiful scenery, and walking with my husband beside turbulent rivers and brooks: in retrospect I have come to regard those weeks as our real honeymoon.

Because I believed that Ian would be stationed in Yorkshire for some time I had let my flat furnished. On our return to London, therefore, we had to stay at a small hotel in South Kensington while we waited for news from the War Office.

I decided I would learn to ride, something I had always wanted to do, and just what a serious ballet dancer should never do. My first ride I had in Battersea Park; and after the third lesson—I had paid for a course of twelve—I was riding in the Row with Ian. My riding master said that it was as though I had been doing it all my life. I suppose a feeling for rhythm helped me.

I had only completed nine of the dozen lessons when an offer came from Sir Thomas Beecham for me to dance in Granville Bantock's *Pierrot of the Minute* at the Royal Opera House, Covent Garden, and also in the opera *Naïl* by Isidore de Lara, in which there was a ballet. I felt that it was an opportunity I could not refuse and hurriedly began to practise again. That, of course, put an end to my riding.

23

I BEGAN rehearsals. Alexandre Gavrilow was choreographer, and he also filled the role of Pierrot in the Bantock ballet. He and I were asked to give *Le Spectre de la Rose* as a special attraction at a fancy dress ball, with a full orchestra which Sir Thomas Beecham would conduct. The ball was in aid of an endowment fund for British composers which Lady Cunard had organized. The royal box had been reserved for Their Royal Highnesses the Prince of Wales and Prince Albert.

Preparations for this event meant working tremendously hard; and, owing to the ball continuing well into the early morning, the final dress and orchestral rehearsal for *Pierrot of the Minute* could not be held until four o'clock on the afternoon of the opening performance. The ballroom floor had to be dismantled and the seats replaced in the auditorium.

I was simply appalled at the awful dress I was given to wear as the Moon Maiden. It was more like a young girl's party frock. Made of heavy pale blue and white *crêpe de Chine*, it had sleeves nearly to the elbow. It was well and stoutly made, too, with hems and gauging and a petersham waist-belt! Anything less like the clothing of an ethereal Moon Maiden would be impossible to imagine.

By half past five the rehearsal was over, and I scrambled into my street clothes to rush off to Stagg & Mantle's in Leicester Square, and was lucky to arrive before they closed at six o'clock. I bought some moonlight blue chiffon and some shot blue-and-silver tissue, ate a quick, light meal and returned to Covent Garden.

I cut the offending dress to pieces, and I locked my dressing-room door while I hurriedly fashioned my own idea of a Moon Maiden's costume. As there was no time to make it properly I sewed myself into it. First there was a tight leotard of the silver tissue, then a light covering of the blue chiffon worn crosswise over the shoulder in Grecian style and kept in place with a girdle of silver ribbon, and on my head a crescent moon torn from the original head-dress. Just as I had finished the call boy knocked on the door.

'Please, Miss Bedells,' he said, 'Sir Thomas would like to speak to you on the stage.'

I was worried. Everyone knew what a martinet he could be at times. He had made no comment on that awful dress at rehearsal and, known for his strong likes and dislikes as he was, I was wondering what he would think of my daring to destroy the costume his management had provided. I was quite prepared for a row, and even for the cancellation of my contract.

When I got on to the stage, however, Sir Thomas took one look at me, and then said, 'My dear . . . that's *much* better. I sent for you to say you couldn't possibly wear that horrible dress you had on at rehearsal.'

That was only fifteen minutes before the curtain rose on the first night of the ballet!

I am afraid that it was not what I would call a success. Gavrilow's choreography was too full of 'lifts'. I spent most of my time being carried about, either by him or by the attendant Moon Maidens, which gave me little opportunity to dance. Perhaps if he had not been playing a part himself he would have noticed this and rectified the fault. But while he was so busily engaged he could not possibly get a correct picture of the whole.

The opera *Naïl* was also a disillusioning experience. In my mind I had always idealized Covent Garden, but I discovered that the productions at that time were 'thrown on'. There was the most extraordinary mixture of styles in the costumes. None were properly designed, as they would be nowadays—anything the wardrobe could rake up for the occasion was used. I thought regretfully of the Empire's thoroughness and attention to detail.

In *Naïl* the leading parts were sung by Rosina Buckman, Frank Mullings, Percy Heming, and Walter Hyde who had been in *The Vicar of Wakefield* all those years ago in 1906, when I was making my first appearance in *Alice in Wonderland* at the Prince of Wales. Percy Heming, incidentally, began his career with my father in the Bristol Amateur Operatic Society.

When the opera season at Covent Garden ended, I had a most exciting letter from Laurent Novikoff, inviting me to dance with him in a series of miniature productions to be given by a newly formed Russian society, called Lahda, under the direction of Theodor Comisarjevsky. Comisarjevsky, who later spelt his name with a 'K', had produced *Prince Igor* at Covent Garden in

October 1919. Prior to that he had directed State theatres in Moscow. Naturally, I was delighted to accept the invitation.

We started working together at once. Soon after Comisarjevsky himself began his rehearsals with us.

That Lahda Society, I gathered, was financed by another Russian, Boris Said. The Wigmore Hall was taken for their first programme, and an apron front built out on to the small platform. Comisarjevsky thrived on difficulties, accepted their challenge, and brought to problems a brilliance of mind which made artistic success assured. But the seating capacity of the hall was, of course, small.

I found the work new and refreshing after so long a time in revue. A one-act play, *A Merry Death*, which had been translated from the Russian, was the main item. As well as dancing in the part of Columbine I had some lines to speak. Harlequin was Ivan Samson, now well known on the radio, Pierrot Robert Farquharson, and Death, the only non-speaking part, was danced by Novikoff. There were songs from Vladimir Rosing, and I danced with Novikoff in the Gopak from *Sorochintsy Fair* by Mussorgsky.

After that J. B. Fagan lent Lahda the Royal Court Theatre in Sloane Square, and we extended our programme to suit a full-sized stage. We appeared there in February 1920, in a new ballet written and directed by Comisarjevsky with Novikoff's choreography and music by Grieg. It was called *A Fisherman's Love* and gave me opportunities to act as well as to dance. Pupils from the Astafieva and the Mayfair School (Miss Fairbairn) formed the *corps de ballet*.

Although classical ballet was not much in public favour, Novikoff and I opened the programme with an arrangement of the *adagio* from *Le Lac des Cygnes*, Act II. Novikoff and I both felt that English audiences ought to be given a taste of the serious, traditional ballet which we ourselves enjoyed so much. We closed the programme with a *pas de deux* set to Kreisler's *Liebesfreud* and arranged as a caprice, rather on the lines of Pavlova's *Valse Caprice*. This was a tremendous success with the audience and we had to repeat it. It was good to hear their cheers at the end.

Following that special matinée, Novikoff and I were booked to appear for a week at the Palace in Manchester. We played twice nightly and at matinées on Monday and Saturday. This was my first appearance outside London except for two flying visits to Bristol for matinées ten years before.

When my agent told me he had made this booking I told him that I would not go unless he could secure a really good conductor for us. Our music needed a first-class man. He said he knew the very man, and introduced me to someone who was then unknown in London, although he had previously toured with musical shows. This was Jack Hylton, now the famous theatrical impresario. Jack was invaluable. He orchestrated our music to suit the variety theatre orchestras, acted as Stage Manager, and even attended to our baggage and the tipping of stage staffs.

Our contract for the turn, which lasted twenty minutes, was for £100 a week, out of which we had to provide our own costumes and travelling expenses. We paid Jack Hylton £10 a week for his services and for that he not only helped us as I have said, but at the first performance he sang our music as he conducted, to help out when the orchestra found it too difficult to follow.

I was utterly exhausted after that first night in Manchester. We had had a most tiring rehearsal all morning and three performances afterwards. We danced the *Lac des Cygnes pas de deux*, the Kreisler Caprice, and the Gopak by Mussorgsky. There were two musical interludes while we hurried to change our costumes.

At the top of the bill was Ethel Levey and at the bottom, Lupino Lane, while we were given middle billing and had had no preliminary publicity. In spite of this we were a big success.

Jack Hylton and Novikoff found lodgings together, Ethel Levey and I stayed at the Midland Hotel. She took me back with her after the show and gave me champagne and oysters, as I was too tired to eat a proper supper. Then I just fell into bed. However, I recovered enough to join a party given the following night to celebrate Peggy O'Neil's success in *Paddy the Next Best Thing*, which was on its way to London.

Novikoff and I had our first and only disagreement during our next engagement at the Royal Hippodrome in Liverpool. When we arrived from Manchester we found my name in huge letters across the front of the building and, in small type, 'Supported by Laurent Novikoff'. Naturally enough he was very upset by this. He declared he would not appear, and was preparing to return to London on the next train. However, Jack Hylton helped me calm him and, in the end, all was well. The following week we were back in London and doing a week of matinées under Comisarjevsky's and Rosing's direction at the Duke of York's.

The theatre was being used in the evenings for J. B. Fagan's production of *The Merchant of Venice*, with Maurice Moscovitch as Shylock and Mary Grey as Portia, which was nearing its two hundredth performance.

We were at Brighton Hippodrome for a week of twice-nightly performances and then, the following week, at the Alhambra, Glasgow. We toured the same programme we had given in Manchester and Liverpool. Nelson Keys was on the bill with us in Glasgow, assisted by June who had become a beautiful young musical comedy actress. Five years previously in *The Vine* at the Empire, she had been known as 'Little June'.

We returned to London and gave another series of matinées at the Duke of York's. We added a new ballet to our repertoire, *The Prince and the Groom* by Comisarjevsky to music by Liadov which was based on a Russian folk song, and we introduced two new *pas de deux*: Schubert's *Serenade* and Wieniawski's *Krakoviak* —a gloriously spirited Polish peasant dance which I loved doing. And we still danced *A Fisherman's Love* and revived *A Merry Death* with the original cast, except for Pierrot which was played by Keith Moss.

Our press notices had been consistently good. I was extremely grateful to Novikoff and to my Russian friends, Comisarjevsky and Rosing and Boris Said, for giving me the opportunity to appear in their productions and regain my status in the ballet world. Unfortunately, however, there was not sufficient financial backing to enable them to go on—even though none of us was drawing a large salary.

I had an offer from Sir Oswald Stoll to star in *Johnny Jones*, the new production he was putting on at the Alhambra. As it seemed a pity to break up my happy partnership with Novikoff I asked my agent to inquire whether Novikoff could also be engaged. He managed to persuade Stoll to offer Novikoff £20 a week to appear in one scene with me; but as I was to have £50 a week and to be given more prominence in the billing, Novikoff refused.

We danced one more week, twice nightly, at Portsmouth, and that was the end of our partnership. Novikoff taught for a while at the Mayfair School, but soon gave this up to rejoin Pavlova.

Mark Hambourg arranged an all-star matinée at the Coliseum in aid of the London Fever Hospital. Mary Anderson appeared in a scene from *The Winter's Tale*, Ben Davies sang, George Robey, Felix Salmond, Melsa, Novikoff, Irene Vanbrugh, and Dion Boucicault gave their services; and a 'surprise item' was a Chopin waltz, which I danced to Mark Hambourg's accompaniment. At the end the applause was very enthusiastic; and, while we were acknowledging it together, I was horrified to see him returning to the piano and to hear him saying, 'We'll do it again.' He had not realized that I was already breathless. There was nothing for it but to dance again. It almost killed me!

24

I HAD REGAINED possession of my flat. Ian had been sent to Flensburg for the plebiscite which resulted in part of Schleswig-Holstein being returned to Denmark and he had been away throughout the time I was working with Novikoff. No sooner had he returned from Flensburg, however, than he was off again: this time to act as Brigade Major in Londonderry during the 'troubles'. While there he received a number of threatening letters, and I was terrified for fear that something might happen to him. It was a great relief to see him when he returned to England in 1921, when he was sent to Blackdown Camp to rejoin his old regiment, the Sherwood Foresters.

We had sold my little Humber when Ian first went to Flensburg, so we bought another car in order that he could get into London more easily. It was a second-hand Hupmobile with an English coupé body. I imagined that we might enjoy going for drives in it together; but that was not to be. Soon after I opened in *Johnny Jones* Ian was sent to Alexandria to join the second battalion of his regiment which was already there. As I could not drive, the car—which had cost us £850—was garaged for some months; then I sold it for £400.

The first night of *Johnny Jones*, on 1 June 1920, was something of an occasion for me: I made my first speech in public. At the end of the show we took so many calls that I lost count, but still the cheers went on. I thought I must be dreaming when I heard,

'Bedells, speech . . .' shouted again and again. George Robey pushed me forward, and said, 'You *must* say a few words of thanks.' Absolutely dithering with nerves I managed to mutter a few words of thanks. The following day the press was kinder than ever to me.

I had only two big scenes: one was Versailles and the other A Persian Harem, in which I danced a wild, oriental fire dance. Thick glass panels were lit from beneath the stage with vivid red lights, while in the glow of it I fluttered the flame-coloured scarves I wore more and more excitedly as the dance grew wilder, until, with whirling pirouettes, at last I fell among the 'flames'. This made a complete and effective contrast to the delicate grace of the Versailles scene.

Ivy St Helier was in the cast, too, and Clara Evelyn, Netta Westcott, Eric Blore, Pip Powell, and Arthur Finn. The critics were still complaining of a lack of humour, but in spite of this we settled down to a long run. It takes time for a comedian to develop his part, and there are always weak spots to be cut in every new production. Changes in our cast were made from time to time. Lupino Lane joined us in July, and scored a hit with his acrobatic dance. Later in the year Eric Blore left and Jack Morrison replaced him. Kathleen Destournel came in place of Clara Evelyn, and that brilliant juggler, Rebla, was introduced into the Café scene.

I heard during the run that my brother Stuart was to be married on the morning of 4 August and asked Sir Oswald Stoll if I could be excused from the matinée on that day. He refused. He said the public came first and that I was billed to appear. He was well within his rights, of course, but I could not bear to think of not being present at my brother's wedding. The service was to be at 11.30 at Southsea. As there was a train back from Portsmouth due at Waterloo at 2 o'clock in the afternoon I decided to take the risk and go. My first scene in *Johnny Jones* was not until nearly 3 o'clock. I warned the Stage Manager and told my dresser that I might be late and to have everything laid out ready for me. I reckoned that I could easily be in the theatre by 2.30 when the curtain rose.

At first all went well. I went to the wedding service and stayed for the first few minutes of the reception, long enough to drink the health of the happy pair. A friend drove me to the station, and I caught the train with only seconds to spare. I settled down in the corner of a compartment to read. Then the train stopped, for no particular reason that I could see, between stations.

We were held up for what seemed to be hours. We arrived at Waterloo twenty minutes late. I hailed a taxi.

'As fast as you can to the Alhambra', I said.

'The road's up', the driver replied. 'If you're in a hurry you'd better go by Underground to Trafalgar Square.'

I took his advice. Never have I known a tube train to move so slowly. We stopped twice in the tunnels and reached Trafalgar Square only five minutes before I was normally due on the stage. Though it was a blazing hot day I ran for dear life, bumping into people and nearly knocking them over in my haste. People must have thought I had gone mad.

The Stage Manager was anxiously waiting at the stage door. He said, 'I think you can just make it.' My dresser had everything ready and I got on to the stage just as I heard my music beginning. When the scene ended I almost fainted.

I discovered later that the kind Stage Manager had delayed the rise of the curtain and held up scene changes to help me when he found I was going to be late. He realized I was risking the cancellation of my contract if I had not appeared when I had been refused permission to be absent.

It was in July 1920 that the *Dancing Times* organized the first Dancers' Circle Dinner, which was followed by another similar function in October at which those present discussed the need for an association of experts to guide teachers and young dancers in the correct technique of the ballet and to preserve the great tradition of our art.

There was no State school in England nor any authoritative body such as existed in Russia, France, Italy, and Denmark. These very important meetings resulted in the foundation of the Association of Operatic Dancing. The original committee was elected by those present at the October dinner. Madame Adeline Genée became president and Tamara Karsavina, Lucia Cormani, Eduard Espinosa, and I were elected. We were asked to decide upon the methods by which the aims of the association might be achieved. P. J. S. Richardson, the editor of the *Dancing Times*, was unanimously elected its first Honorary Treasurer and Secretary. It was entirely due to his foresight and perseverance that such an important step forward had been made possible. For years it had been one of his dreams. Many committee meetings followed. They were generally held at 5 Hanover Terrace, Regents Park, the lovely home of our president and her husband, Frank Isitt.

Espinosa brought us a rough draft of a suggested Elementary Syllabus to work upon. We took it to pieces, and thrashed out the pros and cons of the systems we had each thought most suitable for elementary work. This first meeting was very representative of the various schools and methods of teaching. While we were agreed that originally the technique of the ballet came from France, it had through the centuries developed considerably in different directions in other countries; our task was to find agreement amongst ourselves. Genée represented the Danish (Bournonville-Johannsen) school, Karsavina, the Russian school, Cormani, the Italian, Espinosa, the French, while I, having trained in all four methods, was able to appreciate all the various points of view. After a good deal of 'give and take', the first Elementary Syllabus was produced, to be presented at a crowded meeting held in the Grafton Galleries on 31 December 1920, when the Association of Operatic Dancing of Great Britain would come into being as an official body.

The year had been a very full one for English ballet lovers. Pavlova had had another eight weeks' season at Drury Lane. Diaghilev had been to Covent Garden again. Karsavina had scored a big success at the Coliseum in J. M. Barrie's play, *The Truth about the Russian Dancers*, and the Swedish Ballet had appeared at the Palace. And now Great Britain had founded the association which was to develop into the Royal Academy of Dancing with the far-reaching results we see to-day.

During the autumn of 1920 Lasky Famous Players asked me to dance in the film of *The Mystery Road* by E. Phillips Oppenheim. When their representative called to discuss my contract he explained that I would need about four or five days' rehearsal, but that the actual shooting of the ballet sequence would be completed in a day and I could still appear in the evenings at the theatre. He asked what my fee would be. I gulped as I said, 'One hundred pounds', but he immediately produced a contract for me to sign. He had, in fact, been given instructions—I learned later—to agree to any sum up to £500. Once again I had made a foolish bargain. I must say, however, that I felt I did not deserve more than I had asked; and even what I was paid I considered almost excessive.

I appeared as Eve in a cabaret scene. The part of the Serpent was played by Espinosa, who arranged the ballet, and Adam—in a modern dinner jacket!—was played by Jack Morrison. We had the Palace girls as our *corps de ballet*.

Then came an evening in February when I was dancing in the Versailles scene of *Johnny Jones* and found I was unable to get to my feet again after a final curtsy. Something had happened to my left knee.

I had special massage and daily treatments. My doctor said I must not do any dancing that involved making a deep curtsy, but I was allowed to continue in the Persian scene. However, it was eventually considered advisable for me to leave the cast temporarily.

My knee seemed to have improved sufficiently in time for me to be able to dance at the Hippodrome on Warriors' Day, 21 March. There was a record audience and His Royal Highness the Prince of Wales was in the royal box. On the stage Bransby Williams acted as *compère* and each time he appeared was dressed as a famous personality, Lord Beatty, George Graves, Charlie Chaplin, Uncle Sam, Harry Tate, and finally as Lloyd George. They were exceedingly clever impersonations.

Sir Harry Lauder was in the show with Billy Merson, Nellie Wallace, Clarice Mayne and 'That' (i.e. her husband, J. W. Tate), and my favourite clowns, Cornalla and Eddie, who had often appeared on the Empire stage in my earliest days.

I danced the Fairy Ring to music specially written by Ivy St Helier who accompanied me. I think it was one of the most attractive of all my dances. Ivy's music perfectly fitted the subject.

R. H. Gillespie, who had been in the royal box during my performance, told me afterwards that His Royal Highness praised my work and added, 'Her brother served with me in the *Hindustan*.' He did not tell Mr Gillespie that my brother was only a humble E.R.A. who had not, at that time, gained his promotion to commissioned rank. That seemed to me an excellent example of the royal memory and kindness.

That same night I judged the fancy dresses at a big charity ball at Covent Garden, which continued until early morning. And a few hours afterwards I was playing in an important golf tournament for the Ladies' Stage Golf Society!

My mother's wish had always been for a tiny house with a big

114

garden. I now had one built for her—or rather I bought one in process of being built, and had it altered in accordance with her wishes. We called it 'The Dormy House'. It was at Filton, near Bristol, then just open country although accessible for my father from his work. I also bought over an acre of land, which we gradually made into an attractive garden with a full-sized tennis court, a low-walled rock garden, which my mother built herself, a forty-five-foot pergola my father and I made from rustic poles on my week-end visits, and a big kitchen garden. We had young fruit trees and later on we kept chickens.

The first examinations were held by the new Association of Operatic Dancing in May 1921. Over a hundred candidates presented themselves, most of them already well-known teachers and dancers. The examiners were Genée, Cormani, Karsavina, myself, and Espinosa. We had no premises. It was necessary to hire a studio and take about forty candidates at a time. The examination lasted all day, from 10 o'clock in the morning until 5 o'clock. Although a number of the candidates were nearly fifty years of age, even they appeared willing to undergo the ordeal and to appear before us dressed in the regulation white ballet skirts, boned bodices, pink tights, and shoes.

My knee trouble all this time had been growing more acute. I consulted a specialist, who told me it was more serious than I had realized. He sent me to have my teeth X-rayed; and it was found that my crowned tooth—broken when I was knocked down as a little girl at the convent—and two other molars at the back which I had also had crowned had caused the trouble which had developed into arthritis. The offending teeth were extracted and cultures taken for a vaccine. I had injections every five days and visited Harley Street daily for treatment.

Dancing was quite out of the question. I had to withdraw altogether from the cast of *Johnny Jones*. It cannot be imagined how heart-broken I felt when the specialist told me, 'You are fighting a losing battle. You will never be able to dance again. Our one hope is to arrest the trouble so that you do not get any worse.'

By now I could no longer bend my left knee at all, nor could I raise my left arm, as the arthritis had also attacked the shoulder. A few weeks before this I had played a match for the Ladies' Stage Golf Society against the Guards Club, and felt myself a heroine to have beaten my opponent eight and six and won for our team. On the day the specialist's verdict had been given we were to play a return match at Sunningdale; but I was so depressed that I was beaten, ten and eight, in spite of trying hard not to let my troubles affect my play. It was the last time I played golf for my club.

Going by bus for treatment one day I discovered I was sitting next to Vera Gelardi, who had been a student at Gilmer's with me. She had taken me under her wing when I was eleven and she was probably seventeen or eighteen. I had not seen her since; but she told me she was married to a doctor and invited me to dine with them that evening.

I had no idea what her husband—Dr J. D. Benjafield—specialized in, but during dinner I told them about my illness. Dudley Benjafield said he believed it could be cured. When I next visited my regular specialist for treatment I told him what had been said and asked if he would discuss my case with Dr Benjafield, which he at once agreed to do. He warned me, however, not to allow my hopes to rise too high. A meeting was arranged between the two doctors.

They shook hands very warmly and the specialist handed over my case to Dudley in the friendliest spirit. I felt I had to do whatever I could. Dudley's faith had encouraged me to hope that, in time, all would be well again. I cannot say how grateful I was and still am for the interest he took. That I was for several years able to dance again I owe entirely to him. I had been so terribly depressed; but I used to visit Vera and Dudley almost every day and they often drove me to Folkestone at week-ends to stay at the Grand Hotel, where Vera's father was resident manager.

I spent many week-ends with my parents, too, at the Dormy House; but I had to be in London during the week for my treatment. Mrs MacDonald and her family were wonderfully kind to me during those long months of inactivity.

Ever since my Ian had gone to Egypt I had been hoping to get the War Office to give me a passage in a troopship to join him. At the end of September came news that I was to sail on 4 October in the S.S. *Derbyshire* from Southampton.

116

25

I WAS DETERMINED to make a real success of my marriage which so far had had such a chequered career. I wanted children of my own, and I was quite prepared to give up the stage. I had told Ian this many times. He had always insisted that he liked me to carry on with my dancing and that, in any case, it would be foolishness to give up while he and I could not be together.

It was thrilling to be on board the troopship. I had never been out of England before. In spite of having to share a four-berth cabin with three other officers' wives, I enjoyed the voyage. The ship, a small one, was carrying a thousand troops and one hundred first-class passengers. A boxing ring had been fixed up for the troops. At first I hated to see the men fight, but after a while, when I had grown used to the sight of blood, my interest in the sport grew.

I was asked to do something at the ship's concert, and, as I could not dance, I sang 'Coal Black Mammy'. Ivy St Helier had composed the song for Laddie Cliff and had given me a proof copy before I left. So the men on the troopship heard it before the London audience did. I soon had them joining in the chorus.

We reached Port Said on the morning of 15 October—a day early. I had sent a wireless message to Ian two days before telling him of the earlier arrival and expected he would come on board at 7.30 a.m. with the other husbands who arrived to greet their wives. As the ship left for Bombay at noon everyone went ashore for a few hours and left me feeling very depressed.

At 11 a wire arrived which said, 'Go to Casino Hotel and await me there—Ian.' The officer commanding the troops said it was impossible for me to be left alone in Port Said without anybody to look after me, so I was put in charge of the Embarkation Officer on the Docks. I sat in his office and watched the *Derbyshire* as she sailed away with all the friends I had made on the voyage. I was feeling very forlorn.

The Embarkation Officer took me to the Casino Hotel for a late lunch, and waited with me until the only train arrived from Alexandria at five o'clock. Thank Heaven, Ian was on it; but he was burnt so brown that I did not at once recognize him. He had been travelling for twenty-four hours. His linen suit was crumpled and dirty as he had been unable to get a sleeping-car. He had been on Company Training in the desert and my wire had been delayed, which explained his not being at Port Said to welcome me.

We dined together at the hotel and caught the night train to Alexandria. We had a sleeper; but there was a long wait at a station where we had to change trains at two o'clock in the morning. I was bitten by insects and felt utterly wretched. I would have given anything to have gone back to England.

My recollections of Egypt are of dust and heat—and flies everywhere. Ian had to do two more weeks of Company Training in the desert, but he had arranged for me to stay with friends at a lonely bungalow near Ikingi Mariut, three miles from his camp. He rode over on Minnie, the regimental general utility horse, for an hour almost every day.

The heat was intense and almost unbearable that year. Mosquitoes were terribly troublesome to me. Another thing to which I had to accustom myself was a plague of beetles that swarmed in the desert.

At the end of Ian's training we moved to Alexandria, where life became more enjoyable and we had some company. I joined the Alexandria Sporting Club and played tennis and golf with Ian and his brother officers. I watched Ian play polo sometimes. As he was a poor man with no ponies of his own he used Minnie as a mount. Even if by no stretch of the imagination could she be described as a polo pony, she served.

In the mornings we met everybody at Groppi's for coffee and cakes or iced drinks, and heard the gossip of the town.

Just before Ian's battalion was transferred to Cairo he was taken ill with jaundice. He had a severe attack and his convalescence lasted for many weeks. When, finally, he had to rejoin his battalion we found a large and pleasant flat in Heliopolis, a suburb of Cairo. I visited the Pyramids, dined at Shepheard's, and made new friends.

But life was expensive in Cairo, and although we were often entertained we were naturally expected to return the hospitality and give parties ourselves—which we did for some time. I liked having people in, and enjoyed for the first time the feeling that I had a home of my own. I felt that this was drawing Ian and me closer together as husband and wife.

I had begun to practise again, for the first time for many months. I had kept up my treatment and the injections according

118

to Dr Benjafield's instructions and was glad to find I could use my limbs with something like the old freedom.

One day I found Ian sunk in gloom and wondered at first if it could be because I was dancing again. But that was not the trouble. He told me that we were financially on the rocks and he had just heard that he was £80 overdrawn at the bank. It was obviously impossible for us to live the sort of life expected of us on Ian's army pay. His own private income was pitifully small—only some £30 or £40 a year. And I had been earning nothing.

Expenses had to be cut down in every way if, in future, we were to make ends meet: I realized that. Fortunately £300 remained from the sale of the Hupmobile car and, with that, we were able to solve our immediate problem. But the fact was that the cost of living as we had been doing was far beyond our means, and we could not go on returning the hospitality we had been receiving nor invite any other guests.

Needless to say, as the months passed, this was a source of continual worry to us, and hints from the Colonel's wife that we ought to be doing more than we had been doing did not help. Finally Ian decided he must leave the army. The Sherwood Foresters were soon going to India—for ten years. If he went with them it would mean continuing the same expensive life or our separating so that I could return to the stage in order to help financially. Both of us, as I have said, wanted children, but, in the circumstances, it was difficult to see how we were ever going to be able to afford to bring any up.

Ian and I discussed what would be best for us to do when he left the army. I typed out a plan for a joint dance and physical training school and sent a copy of it to Mother to warn her of the serious step we were contemplating. All this time we were constantly being entertained by our many friends. Life was a continuous round of dinners, dances, and parties with, of course, the daily mid-morning visits to the Cairo Groppi's. In the afternoons I slept with all the shutters closed to keep out the heat. A *siesta* was an absolute necessity. Our days began early. Ian usually had to be on parade at 5 o'clock in the morning. It was a topsy-turvy way of living, I felt, to be burning both ends of the candle like this.

Eventually Ian was granted three months' leave and towards the end of April we left Port Said in a P. & O. liner. Ian had to share a cabin with two other men and I was with three women and a young baby that scarcely stopped crying, night or day, throughout the voyage.

I spent as little time as I could in the cabin.

We arrived at Plymouth on 14 May, in the evening, and took the 9.15 train to Bristol. We reached the Dormy House at 3.30 next morning and sat up talking to my dear father and mother until it was time for breakfast. The next two days we unpacked, worked in the garden, and had visits from our friends. Then we heard that the freehold of a beautifully built and equipped Swedish gymnasium in Landsdowne Road, Clifton, was shortly to be offered for sale. It was very near to Clifton College, and surrounded by various big private schools. At once we realized that it was exactly what we needed for our scheme. We were taken to see it and made an offer of £1,000 which, to our amazement, was accepted.

By an arrangement with the family solicitor and Ian's bank we were able to pay at once. We felt now that Ian had done well to send in his resignation. We were full of excited dreams of a successful future; but we realized that, during the summer holidays, little could be done besides making plans and arranging for publicity. I resumed my daily practice and was allowed to use the Bristol Hippodrome stage, as we could not get possession of the gymnasium until the end of June.

Ian suggested that it would be wiser if he started the school of physical training on his own account and I returned to the stage for a while if I could obtain the right sort of engagement. We should then feel safe financially until he had had time to work up a connection. After thinking it over I agreed, but mainly because I felt he would be happier if he could make a success of his new job by himself. With his knowledge of gymnasium work, boxing, and fencing, he deserved the chance to make good without my help.

I went up to London and stayed with Vera and Dudley Benjafield, saw the MacDonalds and Dawsie, and renewed many old acquaintances. The next week I was examining for the Association of Operatic Dancing on Monday and Tuesday from ten in the morning until a quarter to five in the afternoon, at Miss Smurthwaite's Studio in Great Portland Street. We were holding the first Intermediate Examinations and sixty-two candidates had presented themselves. There were thirty-three passes, among whom were such well-known teachers of to-day as Noreen Bush,

Grace Cone, Theresa Heyman, Lena King, and Miss Smurthwaite herself.

I had dinner with John MacDonald one evening, and we had a box at the Palace for *The Co-optimists* and went on for supper and dancing to Ciro's. John told me that while on a short holiday in the United States he had met a very charming girl and they had fallen in love with one another. I could not have been more pleased. Eventually he did marry Helen Babbot and they lived in England: our friendship was never broken.

26

I WENT to London again a few weeks later with Ian to see our solicitors. I had read that the impresario, Edward Laurillard, was putting on a new musical play, *The Smith Family*, at the Empire. When I went to see him and suggested he might find something for me to do, he seemed delighted. As his preparations were well advanced, however, and he had already engaged an expensive cast, he felt I might be offended at only being offered one dance. Neither could he afford to pay me more than £30 a week—for three minutes' work!

It was just what I wanted. As I had been away from the theatre so long, it was wiser, I felt, to make a modest reappearance. Two days later my contract was signed. Until nearer the production date I returned to Bristol to arrange my dance. I had been permitted to select my own music.

The setting was to be the ballroom of Devonshire House. I conceived the idea of appearing as the Ghost of Devonshire House and found a lovely old French *bourrée* arranged by Alfred Moffatt which Nat D. Ayer, who had written the music for *The Smith Family*, agreed was more suitable than his own music. The entire stage was at my disposal, with just a spinet placed down right, and at back centre hung the Gainsborough portrait of the Duchess of Devonshire. My first appearance was behind gauze curtains and I drifted, ghostlike, on points from side to side, each of the gauze curtains disappearing as the lights gradually rose. At the end I disappeared in the same manner behind the gauze curtains.

The show opened on 6 September after a week's 'try-out' in Liverpool. With me in the cast were Connie Ediss, Ella Retford, Mabel Green, Basil Foster, Cora Goffin, Billy Caryll, Hilda Mundy, Charles Brooks, Robert Nainby, Nora Howard, and dear Harry Tate and his company.

Ian was gazetted out of the army on 12 August 1922. As he had only eleven years' service he was not entitled to a pension, but he received a gratuity of £2,000, which paid for the purchase of the gymnasium and left him a balance to live on.

As my own flat was still unavailable I stayed at a small hotel in South Kensington while the show was rehearsing. On 27 August we travelled up to Liverpool, and had a most amusing journey. I was in the carriage with Harry Tate, Philip Page, and Mabel Green which was labelled 'The Smith Family'. Whenever we stopped and people tried to get in Harry Tate would say, 'I'm sorry. This carriage is reserved for my family.' Altogether there were about seventy of us!

That night we had a dress rehearsal which lasted until after midnight, and we ate a late supper at the Adelphi, where several of us were staying. Ian had turned up unexpectedly—which was a lovely surprise for me. He stayed until Tuesday, and so was able to come to the opening night.

The next week in London we had another two days' rehearsing. Ian paid me another surprise visit, and came to the first night at the Empire. It proved to be a most exciting occasion. I was dreadfully nervous, but I received a tremendous welcome from the packed house that made me gloriously happy. And once again I was at home in No. 1 dressing-room.

For that first week in London my salary was only £16 13s 4d as there had only been five performances and the rule in those days was 'No play, no pay'. I went home to the Dormy House for the week-end, then came back to London for the Monday matinée. We had nine shows a week. With my daily practice, photograph calls, and seeing all my old friends, I had little free time.

Ian drove up in a new Sunbeam two-seater which he had bought with the £750 remaining from his gratuity. No one could have been more excited than he was with his new toy. I could not be angry with him, but it was certainly an extravagance we could ill afford.

At the week-end we drove to High Rough to show the car to the MacDonalds; then Ian went back to Bristol on Monday while

I examined for the A.O.D. until it was time for my matinée. I examined again all next day and, at 6.30, went to a Harley Street specialist who told me I was going to have a baby.

I felt extraordinarily happy, but I did not know what to say to Mr Laurillard. On Thursday evening the specialist came to the theatre and I obtained permission for him to stand in the wings. When I had finished he took my blood pressure and tested my heart; then he said, 'If you were my wife you would not dance again.'

He asked if I really wanted a child.

'More than anything in the world', I told him.

It was the specialist who broke my news to Mr Laurillard who was very distressed to hear that I would have to leave *The Smith Family* so soon after it had opened. 'Phyllis, I think you have stage-managed this very badly', he declared, reproachfully. 'You have been away from the theatre for nearly eighteen months and now when you return and have a big success, you go and have a baby. Why didn't you have one before?'

As I had no understudy I agreed to dance until Saturday night, which gave me two days to find and rehearse someone else whom I promised to teach. On Saturday Ian drove Mother and Father up to London to see my performance. I thought I had danced for the last time.

Everyone was very kind and I left with mingled sadness and happiness to begin a new life. Once again I said farewell to No. 1 dressing-room; and that really was the last time I was to see it.

But I did not go back to Bristol immediately, because I had been asked to help with the production of *The Island King* at the Adelphi at the beginning of October, with W. H. Berry and Peter Gawthorne in the cast. I found it thoroughly enjoyable to work with E. Lyall Swete, the producer. He was a charming man who had a quite old-world courtliness of manner. There were two so-called ballets with which they wanted my help, but I could do very little in the six days at my disposal. However, it was a welcome job of work and I was glad of the £100 which was paid me for my services.

The following months were spent in unwonted quietness at home in Bristol, knitting and sewing things for my baby.

I was delighted to hear that Lena King, Judith Espinosa's pupil, had been engaged to take over my number in *The Smith Family*. I believe she was most successful. I had seen her dance at the Association of Operatic Dancing examinations and had admired her exceptionally strong technique.

Ian had begun to teach at the gymnasium. Building up a clientele was a slow process because his name was not well known. He had managed to get one or two schools for one class a week, and the rest of his time was spent giving private lessons in boxing and fencing. We were lucky to be able to live with my parents. The rent from my London flat helped to cover day-to-day expenses, but there was no money to spare for emergencies.

I had a terrible shock the day I received an enormous demand from the Income Tax authorities. I had been assessed on the three years' earnings prior to my going to Egypt. All the time I had suffered from arthritis and while I had been in Egypt I had earned nothing. I had imagined there would be nothing to pay. Obviously I was mistaken. I went up hurriedly to London to see the Inland Revenue representative, with whom I had a long argument; and in the end I broke down and wept. I told him I could not pay, nor could my husband: I had visions of being in prison when my baby was born. Eventually the man must have realized how serious our position was, and I was re-assessed at a much lower figure and told to pay off fifteen pounds a month until the debt was discharged. It was some relief, but it still meant that we had to pinch and scrape.

I took over the housekeeping and cooking at the Dormy House, while Mother worked in the garden and looked after the chickens. This was a good plan, for we were able to provide ourselves with fresh eggs and home-grown vegetables.

Mother had started to write for the *Dancing Times* a series of articles under the *nom de plume* of 'Button Box' with the idea of giving useful and practical advice to young dancers. These articles continued for many years and, in that time, Mother made many friends among her readers and had letters of appreciation from all parts of the country. She never revealed her identity.

In May 1923, Henry Ainley came to our Prince's Theatre in Bristol in John Drinkwater's play *Oliver Cromwell*, and of course we had to go on Monday night—although my baby was already overdue and I was feeling far from well. Harry spent most of every day that week with us. It was lovely to see him again after so long.

My brother's wife, who was also expecting a baby, was staying with us, and we were keen rivals in producing the first grandchild for my parents. I won. David was born on 24 May—Empire Day—and all the flags were flying as they always do on his birthday and, I hope, always will.

The *Daily Sketch* had a paragraph on Mr Gossip's page, headed 'A Future Nijinsky', announcing that I had given birth to a son. What my husband said about this headline cannot be repeated.

All mothers will know how blissfully happy I was. For over five years I had been praying for children and now my prayers were being answered.

As soon as I had recovered, Ian and I had a heart-to-heart talk about our precarious financial position. He suggested I return to the stage.

'Very well', I told him. 'But if I do I shall take the baby with me to London.'

But he absolutely refused to consider that. In the end we came to the conclusion that I had better begin to teach dancing at the Swedish gymnasium, as there were many hours every day when it was not needed by his own pupils. I drew up a prospectus and sent notices to the local press announcing that I would be giving daily classes from the beginning of September at the West of England School of Dancing and Physical Culture.

Applications from prospective students and pupils simply poured in. That was the real beginning of my teaching career, although I had done this sort of work in the old Empire days. I soon realized that I was taking on a full-time job. We engaged a nurse for David.

The dancing classes were started on 17 September. I used the A.O.D. method in training and preparing them to take those examinations. As Ian and I between us had also to teach at eight big schools I engaged an assistant, Eileen Heaven, who had become an Intermediate member of the A.O.D. in June of that year. She would finish off a class in the gymnasium for me while I rushed off to one or other of the schools; and then she might hurry there to take over from me while I drove back to work at our own premises again. We ran a kind of shuttle service. Much to Ian's delight the little car was very useful. However, we soon found Filton was too far away from the gymnasium and decided to move into a pleasant little house in Clifton, 12 Buckingham Vale, where Ian and I could be alone. I gave up the lease of the London flat and had all my furniture and my piano brought to Bristol.

27

IN THE EARLY AUTUMN of 1923 the Association of Operatic Dancing acquired its own premises at 154 Holland Park Avenue, which had a big studio suitable for examinations and good dressing-room and office accommodation. We were loaned the Gaiety Theatre for a matinée at the beginning of November. The performance was to be given entirely by members of the association. Genée, our president, agreed to dance, and I was asked to appear in a revival of *The Dancing Master* and play my favourite role of the Débutante, with Espinosa as the Dancing Master. There were only three weeks to get into training and rehearse; but the temptation was one I could not resist.

The Association held a further series of examinations, Elementary and Intermediate, at the new premises in London during the last week of September; and, on 1 October, the first Advanced examination for teachers took place. Grace Cone, Mrs Freda Grant, Gladys Groom, Irene Hammond, and Theresa Heyman were successful.

I was privileged to appear as Genée's 'male' partner in the dance Le Célèbre Menuet d'Exaudet, which concluded the suite of eighteenth-century dances in which she appeared at the Gaiety matinée. It made me very proud to be supporting so great a ballerina. Afterwards I appeared in *The Dancing Master*. For this we had had only five rehearsals; and even although the company was composed of many excellent dancers, we had not worked together long enough to give a really finished performance. In my heart of hearts I was far from being satisfied with the result.

On the day after this matinée an Advanced examination for executants was held. Noreen Bush, Lena King, Olive Handley, Dorothy Lawson, and Molly Seton were the only five to pass an exacting test.

Marjorie Moss, my old pupil and ex-Empire understudy, with her partner, Georges Fontana, were at this time immensely successful as exhibition dancers in the Midnight Follies at the Hotel Metropole. They owed a great and international popularity to the delightful way they had adapted the technique of classical ballet to the ballroom. 'Mollie' Moss in her 'lifts' was as light as thistledown and Georges Fontana a perfect partner. I was glad to think that I had had a hand in her training.

Another couple who were making a name for themselves in the same style of work at Ciro's and elsewhere were Robert Sielle and Annette Mills. Annette Mills is the brilliant T.V. artist, beloved for her 'Muffin the Mule' series. Then, too, Jack Hylton and his band had become all the rage.

It was really thrilling, buried in Bristol as I was, to read of their successes and to meet them on my occasional visits to London.

In December the *Dancing Times* published the first Association of Operatic Dancing Syllabus for a new series of non-competitive examinations for amateur children taking weekly lessons, which it was proposed to hold in the spring of 1924. A scheme had been put before those present at a Dancers' Circle dinner held in May 1923. It had previously been thoroughly discussed by a small band of enthusiastic teachers headed by Grace Cone. When the final date for entries arrived there were 523 candidates from London and the provinces. For these children's grades the first examiners were Mrs Freda Grant, Grace Cone, Theresa Heyman, and myself. I remember judging the work of one particularly clever and very tiny girl who quite captivated me by dancing a Sailor's Hornpipe. She was Wendy Toye, then Susie Boyle's pupil and now the well-known producer who was associated with the late Sir Charles B. Cochran in many of his greatest successes.

After that initial session we decided that the members of the committee should judge only the major examinations, and that the children's grade examiners should be appointed from among our advanced members, selected by the committee. This, we felt, would emphasize the difference in status between the professional teacher or student and the amateur once-a-week child.

Mlle Yvonne Daunt, *danseuse étoile* of the Paris Opéra, had joined our committee, but, as she found it impossible to attend our meetings and examinations, she tendered her resignation and her place was filled in May 1924 by D. G. MacLennan, the well-known teacher and expert on British national dances, who for many years had taught Highland Dancing to most of the Scottish nobility. 'Mackie' had a keen sense of humour, a dry wit, and at our various meetings could always be relied upon to keep us amused. He and Espinosa vied with each other in telling Scottish and Jewish stories against themselves. Cormani resigned, as she was leaving England, and, in her place, we elected Felix Demery who had already helped us to judge the candidates in the May examinations.

Karsavina was not often with us, as her husband, H. J. Bruce, was at Sofia, and, when not dancing herself, she spent most of her time with him. She remained on our committee, however, and gave us valuable help whenever she could.

Over the Christmas and New Year period I spent a very unhappy six weeks owing to the serious illness of my baby which involved constantly nursing him. He had developed a large lump on his neck. The only way to comfort him was to hold him in my arms. I used to tie a big shawl round me and carry him, gipsy fashion, to take the weight off my arms. Every hour he had hot fomentations; but still the lump grew. Eventually the specialist decided to operate. I went through acute mental agony that day; but the operation was a success and David quickly recovered.

I did not teach much during those anxious weeks, but as it was the holiday season my pupils missed little. In August my baby Jean was born. Until two days before her birth I was teaching, and I had resumed my work by the time she was three weeks old, having promised to present my pupils at a big charity performance.

So, in fact, Jean was a born dancer.

Filton had changed utterly. The fields surrounding my parents' house had been taken over by the local council for a housing scheme which, from our point of view, completely spoiled the rural character of the neighbourhood. Only a year after we had moved into our new home my mother and father decided they wanted to be near us. I sold the Dormy House and bought for them the lease of a house in Pembroke Road, Clifton. Mother's work in her garden had tried her strength. Nevertheless, we were all sorry to part with that dear little house and its big garden which we had seen grow from a rough field.

Ian's fencing classes were particularly successful. In February 1924, he took a team of his Bristol pupils to London to compete in a ladies' competition for the first time. They were beaten only by a narrow margin; and Eileen Mogg, one of his pupils, won the Ladies Challenge Shield of *L'Union des Sociétés de Gymnastique et d'Escrime de France*. The father of another pupil (Élise Desprez) presented what is known as the Desprez Challenge Cup and still one of the most coveted awards in ladies' fencing.

Unfortunately, apart from the one or two schools where he taught and a few private boxing lessons, the physical culture side of Ian's work did not succeed. On most days my dancing classes took up about eight hours and, while I was so busy, Ian had nothing to do. He took up golf and would often play eighteen holes. Some days he completed two rounds. I could only manage to fit in an occasional game at week-ends.

I personally taught character dancing and ballroom dancing. To keep up to date I took lessons from some of the foremost London teachers and I held a weekly subscription dance at one of the large restaurants in Clifton.

For a big charity ball in the district I arranged an exhibition dance—on the lines of Moss and Fontana's—for two of my students, Stephanie Insall and Claude Badcock. Ian and I danced a suite of old-time dances, including the schottische and the polka, and a mazurka we learned from my mother. We wore the clothes of the eighteen-nineties. Ian, who was clean-shaven, wore a false drooping moustache, and with a black waistcoat, tail coat, and deep, stand-up collar, was really very funny. The item proved highly popular.

When Fokine was producing the dances for *A Midsummer Night's Dream* at Drury Lane in December 1924, I sent up two pupils for an audition and, to my delight, both were engaged. To Kathleen McVitie and Claude Badcock fell the honour of being the first pupils of my Clifton School to appear on the stage. It was most gratifying, and an encouragement to all of us. At the end of the engagement they returned to me for further study.

During the next spring term I accepted an engagement to appear for one week at the Bristol Hippodrome with some of my pupils, for whom I revived my old Empire ballet, *The Vine*. Claude Badcock took the part of the Young Shepherd, Mollie Milton was the Spirit of the Mountain Stream, originally created by June, and I played my old part of the Spirit of the Vine. My more advanced pupils formed the *corps de ballet*. It was useful to be able to give them such experience so early in their training.

Euphan Maclaren was arranging the ballets in a very big production of *Hiawatha*, to be given for two weeks at the Albert Hall in June. It had been produced for the first time the previous year, but this year something on an even more gigantic scale was proposed. Euphan invited me to dance the chief role in two ballets. I said I would; but when it got nearer to the date, both my children went down with whooping cough. As David was two it was not so bad for him, but baby Jean was not able to sit up properly or to stand alone, and was very ill indeed. The poor little girl choked and went blue when the bouts of coughing seized her. Nannie took over the night nursing and I took charge in the day-time. It was quite out of the question for me to go to London.

<h1 style="text-align:center">28</h1>

●-●

IT WAS SOON after my children had recovered that something happened which completely changed the course of my life. I was in the middle of the morning class at the gymnasium when I received a telephone call from Lee Ephraim asking me if I would appear in London in a week's time in a second edition of *By the Way* at the Apollo. It was so much of a surprise that I could say neither yes nor no on the telephone. I told him I would come at once to see him and discuss it. Ian was playing golf, and I was unable to reach him. I left my assistant in charge of the classes, saying I might not be back that day. I rushed round to Mother, who seemed delighted and urged me to 'take a chance'.

So I caught the twelve o'clock train to Paddington, lunching on the way, and was in Lee Ephraim's office soon after half past two. He took me to the Apollo where I met Jack Hulbert who told me Betty Chester was leaving that week and that he wanted me to star equally with him and Cicely Courtneidge if I would be prepared to join them for six weeks. For an hour or so we talked. I suggested reviving *The Vine*. He agreed, provided I would cut it down to twelve instead of the usual thirty-five minutes. I was also to be given an opportunity in another scene which I discussed with Graham John, who was to write the dialogue up to my entrance.

I agreed upon salary and hurried off to catch the 4.15 to Bristol, where I arrived at 6.15. When Ian returned from his golf he found me packing my trunk. I told him what had happened since he had left me in the gymnasium in the morning, and he was dumb-founded; but he agreed that I ought to accept the engagement.

I sent for Eileen Heaven, and she promised to carry on while I was away. As my contract was only for six weeks I expected to be back with my school afterwards.

Then I told Claude Badcock that I was taking him to London to

rehearse with me, as I wanted him to play the Shepherd's part in *The Vine* and to support me in a *pas de deux* I was arranging. It was a fine opportunity for him, and naturally he was delighted.

Off we went to London. For six days we rehearsed continuously. I chose Debussy's *Clair de Lune* for our *pas de deux*, which was a most successful scene. It opened with a party of 'bright young things' arranging to go off to a night club and two more serious-minded of them deciding not to go. The girl, Dorothy Hurst, sat at the grand piano, and her friend, Cicely's brother Charles Courtneidge, sat in the dim light of a standard lamp at the other side of the stage. The girl began to play *Clair de Lune*. As the young man stared ahead his thoughts came to life: the curtains at the back of the stage softly opened, revealing a balcony in moonlight and Pierrot on his knees, holding the hands of Columbine. As the music flowed gently on we drifted into a romantic *pas de deux*, making our way into the room where the young couple were. Then, as the music came to a close, Pierrot and Columbine floated back on to the balcony and the curtains fell.

The six weeks' engagement at the Apollo began on Friday 3 July—I had always considered Friday to be lucky for me, and every contract I ever had was signed on that day. I was very warmly welcomed back to London by the public and by the friends who visited me in my dressing-room after every show. They said, 'Phyllis, this is where you belong. You should never give up dancing.'

It was good to walk up Shaftesbury Avenue and see my name in lights with those of Cicely Courtneidge and Jack Hulbert. Yes, I did feel I had come home. I had not realized how much I had been missing the old life of the theatre. Each Saturday night after the show I went back to Bristol so that I could be with Ian and my babies. During the week-ends Ian and I had serious discussions as to the advisability of our trying to make a success of life in London again. I discovered that he had been secretly eating his heart out because he had had so little to do in Clifton while I had been overworking.

On my return to London I found a Georgian terrace house in St John's Wood which was for sale on a ninety years' lease and a ground rent of only £15 per annum. I had told Ian I would look round for a house. Back in Bristol next Sunday I told Eileen Heaven we had decided to sell the gymnasium and the goodwill of the school and offered her first refusal. She was enthusiastic at the prospect of buying it and, within a week or two, had done so. We sub-let 12 Buckingham Vale, unfurnished, and moved to London.

Thanks to my engagement in *By the Way*, the proceeds from the sale of the gymnasium with the goodwill of the school, and a loan from the bank, we had enough money to live on for a while until we could settle down. I wanted to conserve as much of our money as possible. Grace Cone kindly allowed me to use a studio at her school from 10.30 to noon every day and I began teaching again.

I was later invited to teach at the Etlinger School near Baker Street, which was then under the management of May Whitty, D.B.E., the wife of Ben Webster with whom I had studied acting years before. Working with my pupils I kept myself in training. Claude Badcock came with me to London from Bristol, and others in my classes were Kathleen McVitie, Mollie Milton, Irene Smith, and Molly Radcliffe who had been in the pantomime as principal dancer in Bristol and had studied under me daily during the two Christmas seasons she was there; she had previously been a pupil of Serge Morosoff.

Ian and I decided that it might be a good thing if he started an exclusive gymnasium and health club in the vicinity of the St James's Street clubs. Friends encouraged us in the idea by saying that it would be filling a long-felt want. Ian went to various agents, and it was not long before he found what he considered a suitable place in Albemarle Street. It was a basement under a big motor-car showroom at a rent of £300 a year which, for that district, was extremely reasonable. We took the risk. Ian asked Spencer, Heath & George to equip the room as an up-to-date gymnasium. An electric horse was installed, and a pair of fixed dual racing cycles. We had two hydraulic rowing machines as well as the usual punch-balls, medicine balls, wall-bars, and other apparatus. Two tiny rooms adjoining the large main room were fitted up for sun-ray treatment; and there were two dressing-rooms, which needed a good deal of plumbing as well as decorating. We spent much more on getting the club ready than we had at first intended, but we were full of hope. I thought that Ian would have the chance to succeed with the work he loved. On 29 January his first clients arrived in response to some 250 letters which I had written by hand to friends and acquaintances.

Binnie Hale, Irene Brown, Ernest Thesiger, Jack Raine, Rupert Doone, Ivy St Helier, Vera Pearce, Enid Stamp-Taylor, Carmen

Hill, Cyril Richards, Quentin Todd, Anthony Bushel, and Marie Löhr were among the friends who gave the London Health Club a good start.

Then during January and February of that year my grandmother in Nottingham became seriously ill, and Mother went to look after her, leaving my father alone in Bristol. One night I had a trunk call. It was from our doctor, who told me that my father had had a stroke on his way home from business. Could I come at once? I was out of the house in ten minutes.

When I reached him three hours later he was lying speechless and paralysed, with only his 'office boy', aged about fifty-five and stone deaf, to look after him. I was in a quandary, not knowing whether to tell my mother who was with her own mother, who was dying. I decided I ought to wait a while and carry on nursing Father myself. Thank heaven he was soon partially recovered; and, after a week, the doctor allowed me to take him with me to London, where I could give him every care. On the journey there, of course, I was very anxious. When I had him safely installed in my own home I wrote to Mother to tell her that he had been ill and was now in London with me.

Mother hurried down to London, and, while she was with me, her mother died in Nottingham. It was a very sad time, but I am sure that being with their two grandchildren helped them both. My father slowly regained his strength. However, he resigned from the Bristol Amateur Operatic Society and his club in Bristol, because he was told to take life very quietly. He returned to his job in Bristol.

My appearance at a charity matinée, at which Queen Mary was present, on 17 March 1926, brought unexpected results. I arranged a gavotte to music by Dr Arne and was accompanied by Nellie Chaplin on the harpsichord. The dance became one of my greatest successes, and remained a favourite in my programmes until I retired in 1935. It was quite the easiest dance to arrange I have ever known. Somehow the music told me exactly what to do as soon as I heard it. Within half an hour, at my rehearsal, I had completed it, and I never changed a step afterwards. I made my own costume.

A few days later I was approached by H. Bernhardt and asked to become Anton Dolin's partner for a series of dance recitals beginning with two performances at Brighton on Easter Monday. It seemed exactly the chance I had been waiting for.

29

WE STARTED working up a programme together immediately, rehearsing at Serafine Astafieva's studio in Chelsea where Dolin had studied before he joined Diaghilev. Occasionally we worked with her class to 'warm up' before rehearsal. I so well remember changing my clothes in her bedroom. It was crowded with furniture and always in a muddle. On the huge, curtained four-poster bed there was a great fur rug. The floor, too, was covered with fur rugs; and in one corner there was a basket lined with old blankets in which lay a cat with several kittens. The dressing-table was curtained, and covered with a great variety of cosmetics. There was no space to move, and the atmosphere was heavy with perfume. It was all most exotic, but I longed to throw the window open and breathe fresh air.

I had first met Astafieva when she first began to teach in London. After our meeting I had had one or two lessons with her on the stage of the Empire, but I did not like what she taught me. After Pavlova's and Cecchetti's lessons I felt that her style was so different it might spoil what I had been trying so hard to perfect. Perhaps I was wrong. If I had gone to her classes in those days I, too, might have joined Diaghilev. For it was mainly from among her pupils that the great man chose the English members of his company. But I would never have agreed to change my English name as all the others had been required to do.

But Astafieva was very pleasant to me when I rehearsed at her studio, in spite of my not having studied with her. I taught my *Clair de Lune* to Pat Dolin and we made one or two slight changes in some of the supported pirouettes and lifts to make these more suitable to the shorter *tutu* I intended to wear as Pierrette. I had worn a Sylphide length dress in *By the Way*. Together we arranged another *pas de deux* to Percy Grainger's *Shepherd's Hey* and Pat worked up a Danse Moderne as a contrast to my Dr Arne gavotte. Pat also danced Rimsky-Korsakov's *Hymn to the Sun*, and I did an Elfin Dance which was really my Fairy Ring solo.

Those were happy days I spent working with Dolin. As he had so recently left the Diaghilev Ballet he was terribly keen to make a success of the new partnership. We both found we worked well together.

Throughout our partnership Poppy Vanda was constantly at rehearsals, helping us with advice and criticism. She had been friendly with Pat and his family for years, and was one of the few people who never flattered us Because she was so very outspoken she was the most useful friend to have when we were launching our own programme. I am sure we owed much to the help she gave us.

After Brighton Mr Bernhardt booked us for the Winter Gardens at Bournemouth, where we had the Municipal Orchestra under Sir Dan Godfrey to play for us. That involved having all our music orchestrated.

When we arrived for the one and only rehearsal, Sir Dan Godfrey was most difficult. He found fault with all our band parts and seemed in a wretched temper, refusing to conduct at the *tempi* to which we were accustomed. However, at the performance, he seemed entirely different. His rendering of the music was most inspiring; and, when the show ended, he came round to tell us that we must come again soon. We did—in less than a month, to give two more performances.

Ian considered it was his duty to enrol as a special constable when, in 1926, the General Strike seemed imminent. When the strike actually started, however, he developed a bad attack of influenza and malaria and was unable to report. As he was very worried, and anxious for news, I bought a portable wireless set—the first of its kind I had seen. I put it outside the bedroom and switched on as the Prime Minister was speaking. Ian's expression of surprise and wonder was worth a fortune to me.

While the strike was still on I was travelling on a bus which had two university students as driver and conductor. One old lady asked, 'Do you go down Clarendon Road?'

To which the charming young conductor replied, 'No, Madam; but we will to-day.'

And sure enough we drove to the very house she wanted, which was quite off the usual bus route.

I was also amused when, on the same journey, we stopped outside a baker's shop, where the conductor purchased two large bags of doughnuts for himself and the driver, which they ate during the rest of the trip.

At the end of May, Anton Dolin and I had a week's engagement, playing twice nightly at the Bristol Hippodrome, where we were an enormous success. The following week we were at the

London Coliseum. That appearance began a wonderfully happy series of engagements at that splendid theatre.

We kept the *Clair de Lune* in our programme, and had a new backcloth painted by Vladimir Polunin which showed a night sky with a crescent moon and a cypress in silhouette. We danced two solos, which we called Contrasts; they consisted of my Gavotte and Pat's Danse Moderne, now called Raguette extra sec. For my appearance in this I had a lovely new dress made of silver cloth, with which I wore a white wig in the pompadour style. Our final number was Exercises, for which we engaged three of my pupils—Mollie Milton, Irene Smith, and Kathleen McVitie— as a small *corps de ballet*. Our costumes for this were in light powder-blue silk, with which we wore pale-blue wigs. Pat and I wore long-sleeved, tight-fitting little jackets and short trunks. To my trunks a tiny skirt was added, to give the costume a more feminine appearance. To the music of Grainger's *Molly on the Shore* the three girls did their side and centre practice; then the music changed to his *Shepherd's Hey*, with Pat and I dancing together. It was our most successful number and, throughout our partnership, was kept as the finale to our programmes.

With us on the bill at the Coliseum we had Muriel George and Ernest Butcher singing folk songs, the well-known Scots comedian Will Fyffe, and Gwen Ffrangcon-Davies with John Gielgud playing in the balcony scene from *Romeo and Juliet*.

Our performances became so successful that Sir Oswald Stoll extended the original contract week after week until well into July, during which time we added new numbers to our repertoire.

Pat and I had two large and comfortable dressing-rooms on stage level. As we had a matinée every day, Nannie sometimes brought David and Jean in to tea with me, and Arthur Croxton put them into a box to watch our performance. The first time they came we had just begun *Clair de Lune* and, in a quiet moment as Pat was lifting me, we heard clearly the voice of three-year-old David, crying out excitedly, 'Oh, Nannie, look at Uncle Pat carrying Mummy.' It was so unexpected that we were both convulsed with laughter, and found it difficult to sustain the romantic spirit of the dance, especially when the whole audience was laughing too.

Soon after we had opened at the Coliseum Pat came to nursery tea with us one Sunday. Through watching me practise so much Jean had already begun to show an interest in dancing. Nannie said she was sure she would become a dancer.

Espinosa, Phyllis Bedells, and Jack Morrison in the Adam and Eve scene of the film *The Mystery Road*, 1920.

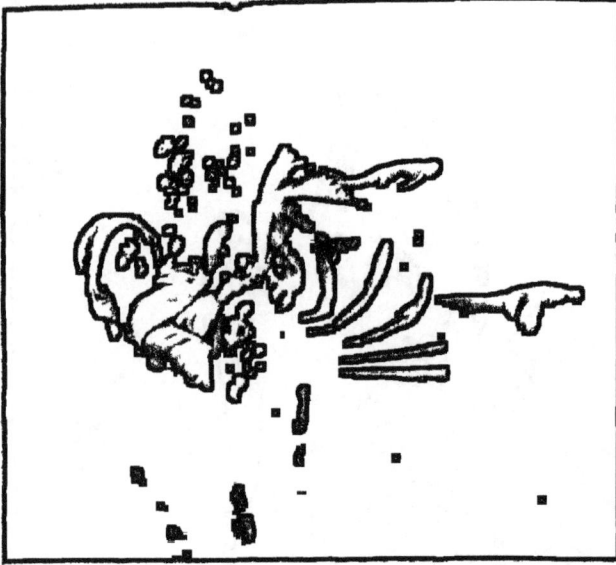

One Summer's Day ballet, *Razzle Dazzle*.

Bassano

Highland Fling from *Razzle Dazzle*, Drury Lane, 1916

Bassano

As the Ice-Cream Girl in *Razzle Dazzle*

Bassano

As the Ghost of Devonshire House, in *His Ninth Parish*, the Empire Theatre 1922

Photo: Studios

Above · The Bird Cage scene from *Joybells*, London Hippodrome, 1919 (Phyllis Bedells in the centre). *Below, left to right* · Clara Evelyn, Phyllis Bedells, and Ivy St Helier in the Versailles scene of *Johnny Jones*, Alhambra Theatre, 1920

Above Phyllis Bedells, her husband Major Macbean, and Hilda Bayley with one of the first car radios, listening-in at Margate to a concert from London in 1923 *Below* The school at Clifton, 1924. Phyllis Bedells with her assistant, Miss Eileen Heaven, and pupils, including Claude Newman.

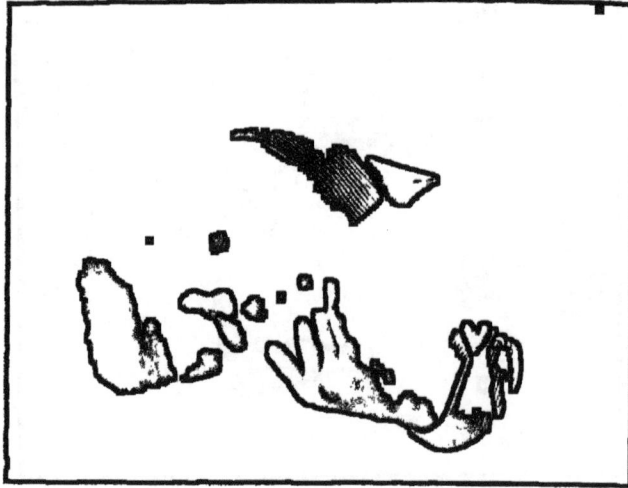

George Robey, 1919.

Stage Photo Co

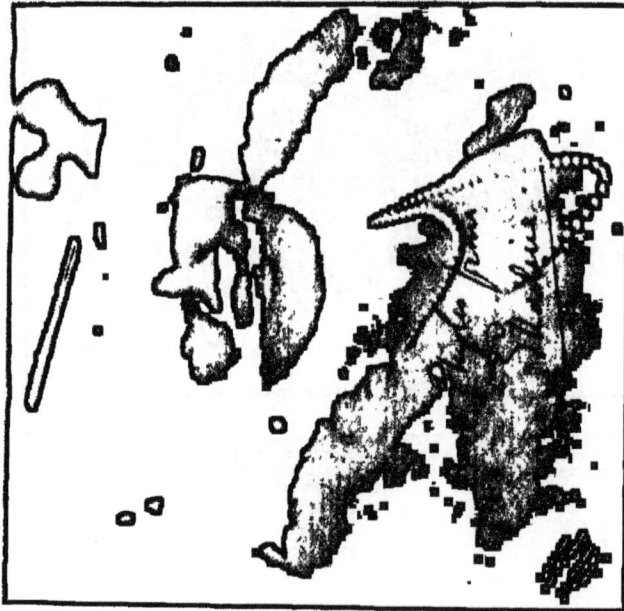

Ellaline Terriss, 1921

Dobson Studios

Phyllis Bedells and Laurent Novikoff in the Gopak by
Mussorgsky, at the Palace Theatre, Manchester, 1920.

Dobson Studios

With Novikoff in the Caprice by Kreisler, at the Duke
of York's Theatre, London, 1920.

Photopress

Photopress

Above Phyllis Bedells going out for the first time with her children, in November 1926, after the accident to her leg. *Below*: Jean and David at their baby dancing class in Miss Cone's studio.

Pat turned to David and said, 'Well, David, are you going to be a dancer, too?'

David solemnly looked him up and down before replying. 'Oh no,' he said. '*Men* don't dance.'

I was fearful lest Pat would be offended; but I am glad to say he only laughed and considered the reply to be most amusing.

As soon as the five weeks' engagement at the Coliseum ended we decided we ought to have two weeks' holiday, as we had important contracts with Sir Oswald Stoll to fulfil at Manchester at the beginning of August before returning to the Coliseum with a new programme. Binnie Hale, who had been making a triumphant appearance in *No, No, Nanette* at the Palace, came with Ian and me to stay at Cannes while Pat and Rex Evans—a friend of his —went to Monte Carlo. On the way we travelled together, but afterwards met only occasionally at parties at Juan les Pins.

At Cannes we saw a good deal of Major Walter Crichton and of Valentine Williams, the well-known author, and his wife. I did my practice every day, clad in a bathing costume, and afterwards ran across the beach for a bathe. It was quite heavenly, but soon over. In no time at all we seemed to be back in London and rehearsing again. The two new numbers we worked out were Boy Blue to music by Sir Edward Elgar, and Lacquer, a Chinese character dance set to music from Ravel's *Mother Goose* suite. We worked at Miss Cone's studio in Stratford Place, which was a modern building with floors of very hard wooden blocks. The intensive work on that hard floor may partly have caused the serious accident I had.

Boy Blue and Lacquer were got ready for the Coliseum; but on 2 August we opened in Manchester with our old programme. There was an orchestra rehearsal throughout the Monday morning; then there was a matinée, which was to be followed by two performances in the evening. I was dancing in Minstrels during the final evening show when I had violent cramp in my right calf muscle. I had been executing a series of *relevés* on points. Foolishly I forced myself to continue. In excruciating pain I heard the crack as the calf muscle snapped. I was in agony. Somehow I managed to hop into the wings where I fainted. The curtain was rung down. Pat went before the curtain to ask the indulgence of the audience while he changed; then he danced his solo, and that was the end of the show.

The doctor who had been called prescribed lead-and-opium

137

compresses, and said I must return to London next day for treatment.

That night Pat and the Hon. Rowland Leigh, a friend of his who had come up from London to see our performance, were simply wonderful to me. I put on the compresses hour after hour. Of course I had no sleep. Next morning I returned to London with our little *corps de ballet*. Pat continued with his solo performance for the rest of the week.

After the accident he had caught a late train and arrived in London at 6.15, managing to contact Ninette de Valois at breakfast time. He arranged with Sir Oswald Stoll that she should take my place at the Coliseum the following week. Then he rushed back to Manchester to dance there in the evening. It must have been a terrible strain for him.

During their London season I was carried into a box at the Coliseum to watch Ninette and Pat dance the new items which he and I had created together.

Time passed; and I began to hope that my leg was getting strong enough to use again. Maurice Cowan asked if I would produce and dance in a short ballet for his new revue *Life*, which was to open at the London Palladium on 30 August. I undertook to try, if I could be given a good dancer as my understudy. Joyce Berry was engaged, a charming young dancer who had studied under Astafieva in London and Nijinska and Spessivtseva in Paris. I worked out a little ballet, *The Chaperone*, to Weber's *Invitation to the Waltz*. Joyce danced in it at every rehearsal until, at the final dress rehearsal, I said I would dance it myself. I had my masseur standing in the wings in case of accident.

Just as I began to dance the calf muscle gave way again. But this time it was even worse than before. I had to be carried to my room, and then to a car and so home to bed. I was absolutely desolate. I had known I was taking a risk, but even so, the shock of the second accident upset me dreadfully. However, 'It's an ill wind that blows no one any good.' Joyce Berry was a great success.

Maurice Cowan was extremely good to me during the run of *Life*. He insisted upon paying me £20 a week because he felt responsible for having persuaded me to dance before I had completely recovered from my injury. Few men in the theatre would have been so generous, and not allowed anyone to know of it.

138

He asked me to arrange dances for his next production, a touring revue called *Lucky Stars*. By that time I was just able to hobble about. I had something to occupy my mind again.

<h1 style="text-align:center">30</h1>

I FOUND Ian was becoming extremely depressed, and discovered that the London Health Club had lost practically all its clients. The early promise of the venture had come to nothing. We had the heavy rent to meet, his assistant's salary to pay, and all the other overheads. Once again we were on the rocks.

I started to teach dancing at the Albemarle Street address and soon had quite a number of young pupils, among them Mollie Milton, Kathleen McVitie, Nina Cassini, Marian Pollacheck (Marian Pola), Pamela Foster, and her sister Eve; also Sheila McCarthy, Molly Radcliffe, and Mark Hambourg's two children, Daria and Michal Hambourg—the latter has become a very fine pianist.

Claude Badcock worked with me for a while, but presently he took a job in a musical show. It was then I suggested he adopt a stage-name. We had thought of several other names before my mother and I suggested Claude Newman. That is the name he still uses. After working in one or two musical shows he joined Ninette de Valois and her small company, which was to make history. For some years he danced with the Vic-Wells Ballet and has now become an important member of the teaching staff at the Sadler's Wells School and an examiner and committee member of the Royal Academy of Dancing.

At Albemarle Street I held daily classes, but we were still not covering our expenses there. It was evident I should have to dance again as soon as possible. By the end of November I managed to get back into training again and Anton Dolin asked me to appear with him at the Piccadilly Hotel in a special cabaret for which I was to be paid £100 a week.

We opened early in December 1926 with *Rugger*, a ballet in which the girls and Pat were the footballers and I was supposed to be a glamorous stage star who had come to kick off. At the end of the cabaret there was a circus ballet, which had wonderfully effective costumes designed by Anna Zinkeisen. The girls were the clowns and *haute école* ponies, and there was a rollicking galop for Pat and myself. That engagement lasted until 27 January.

It was an odd life. I got into the habit of going to bed at 6 o'clock, at the same time as my babies. At 10, Nannie, who had also been to bed, called me and brought tea, and we went off to the Piccadilly Hotel where she acted as my personal maid. We were back about 2.30 in the morning and went off to bed again until the children awoke and another day began.

In February 1927, Dolin and I returned to the Coliseum. This time we had as our *corps de ballet* Ursula Moreton, Doris Sonne, Frances James, and Elizabeth Vincent. We again opened with *Clair de Lune* and ended with *Exercises*; but we added *Movement*, which had music by Leighton Lucas and choreography by Ninette de Valois. This was a more modern number, which we danced in black-and-white costumes designed by Phyllis Dolton. For some reason it was not as successful as we had hoped, and we dropped it from the repertoire, reviving *Jack and Jill* in its place.

While Pat and I were still at the Coliseum Ian received a letter from the Foreign Office asking him if he would go to Peking as a temporary Cypher Officer. If so he should call at the Foreign Office at 3 o'clock. At first Ian did not think taking a temporary job would be much use, but I persuaded him to get particulars in case the work might suit him. I had been worrying over him, as he was often saying he considered himself a failure. Any congenial work he could obtain, I felt, would help him to regain his self-esteem.

After my class at Albemarle Street we lunched together. It was a rather special lunch, as I wanted Ian to 'feel good'. Afterwards he went off to the Foreign Office, and I to my matinée at the Coliseum. I was almost ready for my entrance when he came into my dressing-room, his eyes shining with excitement.

'Well, darling?' I asked him. 'What's the news?'

'I start work at the Foreign Office to-morrow morning and I'm off to Peking on Wednesday—that's in less than a week's time.'

The temporary post, he gathered, might be for two months or two years. No one could say how long it would last. He was to receive £500 a year. As well as this the job seemed to hold many attractions for him.

My heart felt heavy when I realized it might mean another long separation for us and that I had practically pushed him into the job. But I kept telling myself that it was just the sort of work for him. My first thought was for his happiness. As I have said, I wanted him to be given an opportunity to regain his self-confidence.

For the next few days I saw very little of him. He was busy learning all he could about his new work and I was appearing twice a day at the Coliseum. He left London early in the morning on 23 February, travelling with two other men by way of Berlin, Moscow, and the trans-Siberian Railway. Nannie and I and the children went to see him off at Liverpool Street. I remember how amused little David was at the names 'Omsk' and 'Tomsk', towns through which his father told him he would be passing. On the way home in the taxi, in spite of my own feelings, I could not help smiling at the way David was repeating, 'Omsk, Tomsk . . .'

A week afterwards Pat and I went to Bristol and, after our opening performance, we went to a farewell party given to my father, who had retired from the Bristol Gas Company. I had found a little ground-floor flat in Clifton Court, which was opposite my own house in Northwick Terrace, St John's Wood. Mother and Father came to live there, to be near me and the children. With my father's pension there was enough money for them to live quietly, but Mother decided to earn a little extra by playing small parts in films. For this she received about £2 a day and had to provide her own wardrobe; but I think she enjoyed the work, even if it did mean she had to leave early in the morning and seldom reached home until late.

After Bristol we went to Manchester. We rehearsed on the stage there for our next programme at the Coliseum. One day I remember, we broke off our rehearsals to give an audition to a young boy who, I believe, was a pupil of Alfred Haines: his name was Harold Turner. We were much impressed by the promise he showed and Pat advised him as to what he ought to do. Soon afterwards he went to London and studied under Marie Rambert, and it was not long before he made a name for himself. He became a member of the Vic-Wells Ballet and for many years was one of the best English male dancers. Like Claude Newman he now teaches at the Sadler's Wells School.

When Pat and I reappeared at the Coliseum we danced the Blue Bird *pas de deux* from *The Sleeping Beauty*. I thrilled to the cheers of a packed house at every performance. The Blue Bird

141

has always been considered one of the severest tests for a dancer. I was particularly thankful to be dancing it with Dolin, who is undoubtedly the finest of partners. He is supremely skilful in handling his ballerina and never for a moment loses his noble bearing.

My baby Jean made her first appearance on the stage. The Houston Sisters who were on the bill with us were taking their curtain calls at one performance, and saw Jean and David standing in the wings with Mr Crocker, the Stage Director. Suddenly Renée Houston took Jean's hand and led her in front of the curtain to introduce her to an amused audience as Miss Bedells, junior. Mr Crocker told me he would mark it in the log book as the date of Jean's first public appearance at the age of two.

Happy as we were when actually dancing together I cannot say that Pat and I never quarrelled. Temperamentally we were opposites. Pat's Irish blood was very quickly roused. Sometimes he would work himself up into a violent temper over trifles, and then, a few minutes afterwards, it would all be over and he would be laughing and joking as if nothing had happened. Our last week together was in Leicester; and, between the two performances on Friday night, we had an awful row, in the course of which he said something unpleasant about friends of mine. I do not think I have ever been more miserable. Our partnership's ending made it worse.

Pat had already signed a contract to appear in *Whitebirds* at His Majesty's. Before that show opened, however, he danced in *Le Spectre de la Rose* with Karsavina at the Coliseum. We did dance together after that, in June, at a big charity matinée at the Shaftesbury Theatre, for which we created a new number in which two dancers who had quarrelled were supposed to be rehearsing. While actually doing our steps we were smiling pleasantly enough; but as soon as we had finished each step we would walk apart and appear to be completely indifferent to each other. The audience chuckled and laughed in all the right places. A real-life quarrel had given us material with which to work out a new dance. Our reunion on the stage helped us both to bury the hatchet. Since then we have remained friends.

Ian's frequent letters from Peking told how happy he was in his new work. At last he seemed to have fallen on his feet. With another man, he shared a pleasant house in the British Legation. They had several Chinese servants; and Ian's life seemed an enjoyable one, with amusing parties to go to as well as the more official functions which he had to attend.

Several of the senior officers had their families with them. I thought I might go out there, too, but Ian considered it would be unwise as the children were so young. He explained that it would not be possible for us to live on his £500 a year. So he continued to live a bachelor life. Sometimes I rather envied him.

When Pavlova came to Covent Garden in 1927 I took two of my pupils, Pam and Eve Foster, to see her dance. They had neither of them seen her, and it was the last time that I saw her dancing. I was very shocked to find her sadly deteriorated. Her knees were constantly bent, and she appeared strained and tired with the years of touring all over the world and never allowing herself sufficient rest. It was more than I could bear to watch so great a ballerina going downhill, and I vowed I would not again spoil the treasured memory of her greatness. Of course the spirit of her dancing and something of her artistry remained; but, as I say, it was heartbreaking to have to witness such a falling off in the perfection of her performance as a whole.

When I went to see her in her dressing-room she hugged me tightly in her arms, and I loved her still. But I could not join in the flattery and gush which her many visitors were heaping on her. With tears in my eyes and a very heavy heart I bade her good-bye. I longed to say to her, 'Stop, stop . . .'

In September of that year, as well as my classes at Albemarle Street every morning, I had started rehearsals for my show at the Palladium, which was to open in October and to be followed by a provincial tour. My little company consisted of Rupert Doone, Molly Radcliffe, Pamela Foster, and her sister Eve. Eric Coates was delighted with the ballet we had made to his *Three Bears* music, and I enjoyed dancing in it, too, even though I had to wear a flaxen wig. I made Molly my understudy. Costumes and scenery were designed by Miss Werge Thomas, whose ingenuity overcame many of our difficulties. Three large travelling baskets were made in the shape of divans, which could be used during the show for the three beds and were also containers for costumes and properties. The scenery was made to fold up like screens. However, the initial outlay was heavy, and a set of black velvet curtains had to be provided for the tour.

Cuthbert Clarke, who had been the Empire's Musical Director, conducted for me and orchestrated some of our music.

At the Palladium there were three performances every day for two weeks. Thirty-six shows kept us all hard at work. Molly was most helpful, massaging my legs before and after each performance—it was the only thing that kept me going.

I received a note from Prince George Chavchavadze who asked to come and see me after the show on a matter of business. He brought a letter of introduction from Dawsie. This meeting of ours began a very happy association, and led to my enlarging my circle of good friends. He wanted me to dance at a big charity concert, and suggested he accompany me at the piano in the Chopin nocturne which I was dancing in the show as a *pas de deux* with Rupert Doone. Prince George was a Russian who had escaped from the Revolution with his mother and sister when only twelve years old. For some time he had been studying the piano very seriously with Mabel Lander and was already becoming known as a concert pianist.

My father, who had had another stroke, was taken to hospital. I was greatly distressed, and visited him every morning; but there was nothing I could do for him. It was Mother who persuaded me that, for the sake of my little company, I must fulfil my contracts. I went with my company to Newcastle and the following week to Birmingham; but after that I refused to go on as I found I was spending more than I earned. I received £100 a week, out of which I had to pay my company's salaries, transport expenses, and fares.

Pam Foster's mother had to travel with us to look after Pam who, as she was under fourteen, needed a licence to appear. Every Monday our hearts were in our mouths for fear the local authorities would refuse to grant Pam's licence. She had to do so many hours of general schooling with her mother. In the last resort, the tour did not seem worth all the anxiety and hard work. And I felt constantly depressed at being parted from my babies and not being with my mother during the lonely hours she spent while my father was in hospital.

I was thankful, therefore, to be home again, even though there was no chance of recovering my initial production expenses. I approached several agents with the idea of sub-letting the Albemarle Street gymnasium, as I had at last realized that it was never going to pay. When Ian left for China he had given me power of attorney. It was nearly a year later when I had an offer to take over the lease. As it was not to be used as a gymnasium I had to get rid of all the furnishings and fittings at a considerable loss. All that expensive equipment brought pathetically little money when sold second hand. The new tenants turned the place into a night club.

My father was now completely bedridden, but was obviously much happier when we moved him to his own home again. Mother was a most patient nurse, and it was a consolation to both of them that my children were able to pop across the road to see them several times a day. Daddy was able to speak again; but his poor face was crooked and sometimes he found it hard to use the right words. One evening when my mother asked him what he would like for his supper, he mumbled, 'Wine and water.' We could not understand what he meant until it suddenly dawned upon us. The look of relief in his dear eyes when we said, 'Do you mean bread and milk?' was most pathetic.

Under these very trying circumstances he managed to retain his sense of humour and patience. I bought a wireless set with headphones which he could wear in bed. Throughout that long illness, until he died, we used to hear him trying to sing bass harmonies whenever the National Anthem was broadcast.

Maurice Cowan wanted me to dance in one of the revues he was sending on tour. I told him I was anxious to be given small speaking parts in some of the sketches, and that if he would agree to this I would dance as well. He did agree. I purposely said nothing to anyone about this engagement as it was in the nature of being an experiment and, until I had had some experience, I did not want publicity, in case I was unsuccessful.

We opened at a twice-nightly London theatre after only one rehearsal on the stage. During this rehearsal I had called the Stage Manager's attention to a defect in the stage boards, and he had promised to see that it was repaired. At the actual performance we had a stage cloth down and I could not see if anything had been done. All went well on the first night; but on Tuesday evening, I was doing an *entrechat cinq de volé* in one of my dances and, as I alighted, my foot landed on the defective portion of the stage. My calf muscle was severed and, once again, I was a cripple. This time it was the left leg—not the one which had been previously injured. Maurice Cowan brought me home; and that was the end of another engagement.

I was plunged into despair. Mr Dempster, my masseur, gave me treatment every day. I was not even allowed out of bed at

K   145

first; and it was eleven months before I was able to use the muscle again. During that time a lawsuit was pending. My solicitors insisted that I had a strong case against the theatre. The opinions of three orthopaedic surgeons were obtained. It was unlikely, they said, that I would ever dance again. During the long stretch of inactivity I was put to enormous expense. As soon as I was able to, I began to hobble about on two sticks, but to travel to and from my treatments I had to have a taxi. The mental strain and the worry about the future were inescapable. As yet the lease of the Albemarle Street premises had not been disposed of, and I was still having to pay the rent without being able to earn any money. Heavy doctors' bills kept mounting up.

I spent my time with my poor father and gave Mother a little more chance to get out for a while. About once a week I played bridge with Madame Guy d'Hardelot. Signor Bacci, who taught singing at the Guildhall School, and dear Max Strakosch, who was always so kind and lent a sympathetic ear whenever I wanted to grumble, made up the four. His sister and her husband (Lady Lee and Sir Kenneth) had a lovely flat in Knightsbridge where I often went to parties and met important people in the diplomatic and musical world. I saw a good deal of Dawsie, too, who was then giving lots of luncheon parties and musical evenings at her flat.

31

•••

IN THE SPRING of 1928 I paid my first visit to Paris. I stayed at the Hotel Meurice as the guest of Unity and her guardian. In addition to making the usual excursions and visiting one or two of the theatres, naturally I wanted to go to the Opéra to see the ballet. We saw Les deux Pigeons with Mlle Zambelli and Monsieur Aveline. I was very much more impressed by my surroundings than by the actual performance, which was stereotyped. As I had been used to the magnificent productions of the early Diaghilev days, inevitably perhaps I found the Paris Opéra ballet old-fashioned and sterile, and since I had always longed to visit what I had thought of as the great home of ballet I was acutely disappointed.

While I was away Nannie took the children to Mrs Longstaffe at Aldeburgh; and after that visit they often went there and became good friends with young David Longstaffe whose mother I had known for years as Nina Sevening, the actress.

When they returned to London David and Jean had been invited to join the babies' dancing class at Miss Cone's studio. Jean, who was then three and a half, got as far as appearing in a competition in which she danced as a little laundry maid, but David did not work well—he hated it.

In February 1928 the Association of Operatic Dancing held its Annual General Meeting, and our president announced that the total membership had reached 995, which included 45 in South Africa. In 1927 806 candidates were examined in either the Elementary, Intermediate, or Advanced Syllabus in England. Of these 165 passed the Elementary, 80 the Intermediate, and 9 the Advanced examinations. In South Africa there had been 87 candidates, 45 of whom passed the Elementary, 19 the Intermediate, and 2 the Advanced. Special classes had also been given to a number of selected children who were in future to be known as 'Scholars of the Association'. Classes for them had been held in London, Birmingham, and Nottingham. There had been no fewer than 2,288 candidates for the Children's Grade examinations. Madame Genée also spoke of a new solo examination, which was inaugurated in January 1928, open only to holders of the Advanced Executant's Certificate.

In March 1928 Her Majesty Queen Mary had graciously consented to become Patron of the Association. We began to feel that all our hopes and hard work were receiving their reward, and that the art which we loved so much was at last becoming recognized in this country.

In March Pam Foster won the Junior Cup for the All England Solo Dancing Competition at the Scala Theatre, which Madame Genée judged. Her dance was arranged by Miss Cone. For this competition Pam entered herself, because I told her of my rule never to enter my pupils in any competitions. Except for entrants for the Adeline Genée Gold Medal of the Royal Academy of Dancing, I have maintained the rule.

During my time of inactivity I went to see others dance. Anton Dolin was at the Coliseum with Vera Nemchinova as his partner and they both had great success with *Rhapsody in Blue* and *Revolution*. Diaghilev's company was at His Majesty's where

I saw for the first time Stravinsky's *Apollon Musagète*, with choreography by the young Balanchine, which was rather too modern in style for me in those days. But I have no doubt that if I were to see the same ballet again I would appreciate it more.

In the same season I remember seeing *The Gods go a-Begging*, which also had choreography by Balanchine, and was set to Handel's music arranged by Sir Thomas Beecham. I preferred Ninette de Valois's choreography when, later, she produced the work for Sadler's Wells. I felt she captured the spirit of it better. In fact Ninette's production of it is, in many ways, the most satisfying of any ballet I have seen.

In June that year Ninette de Valois passed the Advanced Executant's Examination of the Association of Operatic Dancing at the same time as Molly Radcliffe. The committee had offered Ninette full membership without taking the examinations, which the rules allowed us to do in certain circumstances. She refused the offer, however, saying she would prefer to work her way through all the major examinations as all the other members had done. That I consider to be one of her outstanding characteristics: she must always see everything for herself and find out how it works in the hard way. She will never take a short cut nor allow herself or any of her company to benefit by preferential treatment.

After I had been to Cannes for a holiday with the children, when we stayed five weeks with W. J. Locke and his family, my leg injury was showing signs of recovery. Shortly after my return I tried to practise again. At first it seemed quite hopeless; but little by little, although the muscle was very withered, it grew stronger. The lawsuit which had been hanging over my head all these months was settled out of court. The defendants made me an offer of a thousand pounds which, much to my solicitor's disappointment, I accepted. He assured me I should have been awarded something like five thousand pounds if I had allowed the case to go to court, but I was so afraid that if I lost the case I should be ruined. There were the doctors' bills to pay; I could not sleep at night for worry; and I suppose that when the offer was made I was only too thankful for the chance to pay my debts and have a quiet mind again.

Having got rid of the Albemarle Street premises I started teaching at my house. I moved out of my bedroom, which had three big French windows and a balcony facing south, bought an upright piano on the hire purchase system, and had the necessary barres and mirrors fixed. Soon I found that I was able to make ends meet again. This was at the beginning of October 1928. I was also coaching students at the Bostock and Brown School once a week, as well as giving five classes at the Royal Academy of Dramatic Art. All my former pupils rallied round me; and there were several new ones, including little Jean Coomber, who was later Jack Buchanan's leading lady and adopted the stage name of Jean Gillie. She was a niece of Mabel Green, who had played one of the chief parts in *The Smith Family* with me. Jean was a merry child and I grew to be very fond of her, although she did not work very hard at her dancing and only got as far as becoming an Intermediate member of our Association. However, she was extremely pretty, and her ballet training undoubtedly helped her in her musical comedy career. It was sad to hear of her death a few years ago.

So that I might grow accustomed to using my injured leg again I asked Espinosa to let me work under him for a time. I took only nine short lessons with him. It was all I needed to get back my confidence: after that I practised alone or with my pupils and, by 2 November, I was fit enough to take part in a ballet matinée which Espinosa was organizing at the Winter Garden. He was determined to show the public that such a thing as an all-British ballet was possible, but I am afraid his patriotic fervour rather ran away with him. Though quite a number of dancers with good technique appeared, the lack of a choreographer and of a director with the imagination of a true artist was felt. I am certain that Espinosa's well-intentioned efforts did more harm than good to the interests of a national ballet company at that early stage.

The ballet in which I appeared was called *Pro Patria*. It had Espinosa's choreography, and music composed and arranged by T. E. Atkinson. I was the English Rose to whom homage was paid by soloists representing various Dominions, while a *corps de ballet* representing England, Scotland, Ireland, and Wales gave support. My partner was young E. Kelland Espinosa, who danced extremely well. The press was kind and the matinée audience gave us an enthusiastic reception. Nevertheless I felt unhappy about it. I felt that the experiment had brought us no nearer the desired goal.

If, however, I had felt depressed by this attempt at forming a

149

national ballet, soon afterwards I was full of hope again. At the beginning of December 1928, I went to the Old Vic to see Ninette de Valois's production of *Les Petits Riens* to Mozart's lovely music. It was danced by Ninette de Valois herself, supported by a small company which included Ursula Moreton, Stanley Judson, Frances James, and Hedley Briggs. With this performance at the old Vic I felt my dreams were beginning to be realized. I came away full of excitement, and convinced that no limits could be set to the company's development, if only Ninette were given the encouragement she deserved. We have to thank Lilian Baylis for giving her that encouragement.

For some time we had been reading of a new Central European school of dancing in which, I believe, Mary Wigman and Rudolf Laban were the pioneers. Thanks to the enterprise of P. J. S. Richardson the public saw Mary Wigman at a Sunshine Matinée (one of several series given periodically by dancers in aid of the Sunshine Homes for Blind Babies), which was organized in 1928. There could be no doubt about her sincerity, nor could I help being impressed by her, even though I did not care for such a form of self-expression. To me it has always seemed unhealthily introspective. But the enthusiasm for it swept through Europe and the United States, even if, in England, it was never particularly well received. I think that, except for a few so-called highbrows, we were too level-headed to be impressed.

I was kept very busy with my pupils and examinations throughout the early months of 1929. Betty Ann Davies, now the brilliant stage and screen actress, took four private lessons a week with me. I took over Karsavina's classes for her while she was away. And I gave a week of classes in Liverpool, which was organized by Audrey Butterworth to help the local teachers.

In April I joined Unity and her guardian for another very happy holiday—on Lake Maggiore. We stayed for nearly a week at Stresa, at the Italian end of the lake, and then moved on to Locarno, from whence we were able to make trips in the car. The fruit trees were in bloom. So were the magnolias and camellias. Snow still lay on the mountains and yet we had gloriously warm sunshine and blue, cloudless skies. I was grateful to ' J. T.' for giving me such enjoyment. When I came back I felt fit and well again. The children had been away to Aldeburgh with the Longstaffes.

At the beginning of June I appeared for the first time as

principal dancer in the dramatized version of Coleridge-Taylor's *Hiawatha* at the Royal Albert Hall for a fortnight. I had been asked several times, but something always seemed to prevent my doing it. This time I managed it. There was a wonderful spirit about the whole affair. All the artists gave their services, except for bare expenses, and the Royal Choral Society together with a *corps de ballet* of two hundred and fifty drawn from various schools, brought the number of performers to over a thousand. Dr Malcolm Sargent conducted the London Symphony Orchestra. The principal singers were Horace Stevens, Thorpe Bates, Parry Jones, Walter Glynne, William Boland, Stiles-Allen, Flora Woodman, May Huxley, Elsie Suddaby, Mavis Beckett, and Chief Os-Ke-Non-Ton. Leighton Lucas supported me in my *pas de deux*. Felix Demery was Pau-Puk-Keewis; Myrtle Farquharson was the Great White Chief; Hermione Darnborough was the Herald of Spring; and the two delicious children attending me were Wendy Toye and Elizabeth Miller.

There were two ballets in the show: one was *The Heavenly Ballet* which took place on the stage during the Wedding Feast scene; and the other, *The Spring Ballet*, came between the second and third acts. In the latter I appeared as Flora, my entrance and *pas de deux* set to the well-known *Demande et Réponse* by Coleridge-Taylor and followed by my solo to his *Tarantella Frétillante*, for which I had the huge space of the arena. It was thrilling to have so much room to move in, and I let myself go! At the end of *The Spring Ballet* I made an exciting exit from the stage, down the slope into the arena, then across to the stairs opposite which, keeping time with the music, I took two at a time, and then out through the doors of the main entrance, where two stalwart stewards waited to catch me. By then I had gathered such momentum that I could not have stopped myself. This always won a loud burst of applause, as the entire *corps de ballet* turned towards me with arms raised in farewell. Although that exit always involved my running I had to be careful that I did not lose grace. It was also quite exhausting.

Malcolm Sargent's conducting, I felt, was truly inspired. In my opinion he is by far the best of all conductors for a dancer. He absolutely dances with one.

The members of the Royal Choral Society and the other famous singers taking part were so kind to me that it was like joining a great family party. Nearly every night after the show I went back to Malcolm's house, where he and his wife Eileen had a party for their friends, most of whom had been at the show. I met many interesting people there.

On Saturdays there were matinées, and afterwards the district round the Albert Hall, especially in the park near by, was strangely transformed by the masses of redskins and their squaws who were taking a stroll or eating a picnic tea in the open air.

The dressing-room accommodation at the Albert Hall for such a stupendous show was quite inadequate. There is only one big artists' room next to the stage: that was where all the principal ladies dressed. Stiles-Allen, who played Nokomis, and I, were there for every performance—fourteen shows—but the other ladies interchanged the parts of Minnehaha, Fever, and Spring, while Myrtle Farquharson usually came already dressed, as she only appeared in one ballet. During the interval we had to be dressed so as to allow Dr Sargent to use the room for his short rest.

The male principals dressed behind a curtain in a space opposite the artists' room. The choir and most of the others arrived in their costumes; but the *corps de ballet* used passages and store-rooms and dressed behind screens and curtains. Yet no one objected. I think this was because everyone was appearing for the love of it and not for financial gain. All the profits went to the funds of the Royal Choral Society, and enabled them to sing less popular works during the rest of the season.

I danced in *Hiawatha* regularly every June until 1933.

During that busy fortnight I managed to fit in some private lessons for Ivy St Helier who wanted help with her dancing as Manon la Crevette in the forthcoming production of Noel Coward's *Bitter Sweet*.

I was seeing a good deal of my old friend Sir Herbert Morgan and his daughter Gwyneth, who were living in a delightful house in Park Row, Knightsbridge. At the intimate little luncheon or dinner parties at his house I first met, among others in the literary or theatrical world, A. P. Herbert and James Agate.

James Agate and I had many verbal fights. He made it only too plain that he had no love for the ballet, and angered me one night when he said we dancers ought not to use classical music, but should confine ourselves to dancing to light claptrap music. I did all I could to persuade him to regard ballet as an art; but I do not think I succeeded. Eventually we agreed to differ.

Gwyneth Morgan did not care to go to the big banquets and

other official functions which Sir Herbert was required to attend from time to time. I would often go in her place. I learned to appreciate the art of making after-dinner speeches. At one of Sir Herbert's bigger parties I met Sir Edwin Lutyens, and danced the polka with him. He was so light on his feet and danced with such zest, though he was certainly not a young man then, but nothing would stop him. When the music stopped he called for encore after encore, and after a while everyone else gave up dancing to watch us. Amid much laughter and applause we had eventually to give up. I think I was the more exhausted.

Whenever we met after that, Sir Edwin would say, 'There's my polka partner.'

32

HENRY AINLEY had been away from the stage and seriously ill for three years. During his convalescence, when he was living on the Isle of Wight in a house lent to him by Sir John Martin Harvey, I received letters from him from time to time which told me that he was regaining his strength and hoping soon to return to work. He was glad to have his son, Richard, staying with him. 'Richard is eighteen', he wrote. 'Very spotty and just right; and we are reading Shakespeare together.' I had known Richard since he was five when he used to stay with his grandparents in Regent's Park. The first time we met he sat in a high chair at the tea-table opposite to me and said suddenly, 'Phyllis—what a nice name to say.' I knew then that he had his father's love of the sounds of words.

It was a great night for me when I sat in the stalls at the Theatre Royal, Haymarket, with Harry's sister—whom we called Biddy— for the *première* of *The First Mrs Fraser* on 2 July 1929. No one who was not there that night can imagine the tumultuous welcome Harry received when he first appeared. It was the most heart-warming cheer I have ever heard. Biddy and I sat holding hands and weeping for joy. Marie Tempest played the name part beautifully and all the others were excellent: Robert Andrews, W. Graham Brown, Frank Allenby, Margaretta Scott, and Ursula Jeans. It was a triumphant success and ran for 632 performances.

I also went to the first performance of *Le Bal* at Covent Garden during the Diaghilev season there. Balanchine was responsible for the choreography. The ballet gave Anton Dolin, who had just rejoined the company, a magnificent opportunity. There were character dances for Dubrovska, Woizikovsky, and Balanchine (in a Spanish trio); Lifar and Lipovska danced an Italian *pas de deux* and Danilova had a fine solo, too. But it was really Dolin's night! The audience rose to him.

After the show I went to a party at Dolin's flat in Chelsea, and Diaghilev arrived with Lifar to pay tribute. I remember thinking how very ill Diaghilev looked. He had got up from a sick-bed to come that night. It was the last time I saw him, for he died six weeks later, on 19 August at Venice.

On his death the ballet suffered a cruel blow. But the great work he did will always be remembered with gratitude by all who love the arts—and not only the art of dancing, but music, painting, and literature—for it was he more than any other who fused these together in a perfect whole. His influence is still felt, and will be for many decades. Not all his productions in the nineteen-twenties gave me the joy of those of the earlier days; but he worked always for a living art, and tried to clear a way for others to follow. He encouraged younger artists, and possessed a flair for discovering genius, especially among choreographers. Fokine, Nijinski, Massine, and Balanchine were all young men when he gave them their chance, and gave to us, through them, a legacy of fine ballets which will remain classics in the years to come. Nor must it be forgotten that during the two years that Ninette de Valois was a member of his company she learned from him much that she has developed so successfully as Director of our own Sadler's Wells Ballet.

I began to rehearse hard for a performance of *Coppélia* which the Association of Operatic Dancing was to give at the Gaiety, and in which I was to play Swanilda. It was being produced by Alexander Genée, then aged eighty, with the assistance of his niece. I felt deeply the honour of being coached in the part by those two wonderful people. I thought of the time when first I saw Genée dancing Swanilda and how I had longed to be near enough to her to touch even the hem of her skirts. And now, here she was: teaching me her dances and giving me hints and advice about the mime.

That afternoon there was also Ninette de Valois in her new

GAIETY THEATRE

Sole Proprietors: THE GAIETY THEATRE CO., LTD.
Licensed by the Lord Chamberlain to: WILLIAM C. SALENT.

(By kind permission of LADIES CLUB Esq.)

A Special Matinee

WILL BE GIVEN BY

THE ASSOCIATION OF

OPERATIC DANCING

OF GREAT BRITAIN
Patroness: HER MAJESTY THE QUEEN

President: MADAME ADELINE GENÉE.
Committee: MADAME KARSAVINA, MISS PHYLLIS BEDELLS, MR. D. G. MacLENNAN,
MR. FELIX DEMERY MR. ESPINOSA.
Treasurer-Secretary MR. P. J. S. RICHARDSON.
154, HOLLAND PARK AVENUE, W.11
ON

Thursday, July 4th, 1929
At 2.45 P.M.

The Programme will include

PHYLLIS BEDELLS	ESPINOSA
NINETTE DE VALOIS	THAMAR KARSAVINA
ANTON DOLIN	VERA SAVINA

And other Members of the Association.

ALSO

LUCIENNE LAMBALLE
Etoile de l'Opera de Paris.

There will be presented an excerpt from

"COPPELIA"

Produced by ALEXANDER GENÉE.

"Swanhilda" - - - PHYLLIS BEDELLS
"Franz" - - - FELIX DEMERY
- - And Full CORPS DE BALLET

BOOK YOUR SEATS AT THE GAIETY

PRICES:
Boxes, £5 5s. and £3 3s., Stalls, 24/-, 21/-, 14/6 and 8/6, Dress Circle, 24/-, 10/- and 10/6; Upper
Circle, 8/6 and 5/9. Gallery, not bookable, 3/-. All the above prices include tax.

little ballet, *Hommage aux Belles Viennoises*, Lucienne Lamballe from the Paris Opéra, Vera Savina, Anton Dolin, and Tamara Karsavina. The orchestra was under John Ansell's direction. It was an altogether splendid occasion.

Until the beginning of August, when I took the children to Lyndhurst for a holiday, I went on teaching. I had promised to dance at the Coliseum at the beginning of September with Anton Dolin; but I had to give up the engagement because of an injury to my foot, which although not very serious was bad enough to prevent my working on it. Anna Ludmilla replaced me as Dolin's partner.

My dear father died on 28 September. He had a third stroke about 9 in the morning as my mother was giving him a blanket bath. She telephoned to me and I rushed across the road and found my father obviously dying. I got the doctor to come and, later in the day, a famous surgeon was called in and tried drawing off blood to relieve the pressure; but it was of no avail.

We had a nurse in to help from 6 o'clock onwards. For nine hours I helped to administer oxygen, and held my poor father's head and shoulders up so that he could breathe. It was the worst fifteen hours I had ever spent. Half an hour after midnight our darling was at rest.

Next morning he was moved to a little private chapel, and I took Mother to live with us. She was on the verge of a nervous breakdown herself. As my brother was away at sea I had to make all the funeral arrangements. It was then I discovered what good friends I had. Sir Herbert Morgan put his big car and chauffeur at my disposal, which was a great boon. I sent Nannie and the children to Lyndhurst again until after the funeral.

On my father's death his pension ceased. Mother was left with nothing to live on. For six months she stayed with me, and we let the flat at Clifton Court, furnished, to Henry Ainley. As soon as Mother was well enough she began to play the piano for my classes.

As Father had received his pension for only two years and had subscribed to it for well over thirty years, Sir Herbert Morgan and Henry Ainley wrote to the Bristol Gas Company to see if they could get some money to help Mother. She knew nothing of this; but, as a result of their letter, she received a cheque for £300. Mother used the money to furnish a less expensive flat in Maida Vale and continued to let the Clifton Court flat to Harry.

In the winter of 1929 Jean passed the First Grade in the Children's Examinations of the Association of Operatic Dancing at the age of five. Nannie had made her a white ballet dress specially for the occasion which, I am afraid, was not cut strictly in accordance with the pattern used by professionals. But she looked very sweet wearing it, in spite of her knickers showing below the skirts.

From her earliest days Jean's one idea had been to become a dancer, while David had wanted to be captain of a ship. One morning they came as usual into my bedroom before breakfast and David said, 'Mother, I've changed my mind. I'm not going to be captain of a ship.'

I asked him what he had decided to be instead.

'I'm going to be an Admiral in the King's Navy', he said.

'Good for you', I told him. 'Let's hope it comes true.'

Jean piped up then. 'What can I be?'

'You're going to be a ballet dancer', David said.

'But I want to be something of the King's too', she complained.

David, who was just six, decided it was time to end the argument. 'That's all right,' he said. 'You'll be the King's favourite dancer. Then you'll be the most important lady in the land.'

33

I was among others invited by Mr Richardson to two informal dinners at the Moulin d'Or in November to discuss the formation of a Ballet Society to be run on the lines of the Stage Society. All of us felt there was a great need for something of the kind, to encourage artists, musicians, and choreographers to work together for the production of a really first-class ballet in England. The need was the greater since Diaghilev died and his company had been disbanded. As a result of our discussions the Camargo Society was formed.

Its general committee was composed of Lydia Lopokova, Choreographic Director; Arnold Haskell, Art Director; Edwin Evans, Musical Director; Alfred Tysser, Treasurer; myself, and P. J. S. Richardson. Grace Cone, Ninette de Valois, Tamara

Karsavina, Penelope Spencer, Anton Dolin, and Stephen Thomas formed a very helpful Advisory Committee. M. Montague-Nathan was our Secretary. We were able to count on support in various directions from such friends of the Society as Serafine Astafieva, Margaret Craske, Margaret Emert, Ruth French, Anna Ludmilla, Tilly Losch, Alicia Markova, Marie Rambert, Errol Addison, Frederick Ashton, Grace Lovat-Fraser, Lord Berners, Arthur Bliss, Herbert Howells, Gustav Holst, Constant Lambert, Arnold Bax, Malcolm Sargent, Ralph Vaughan Williams, William Walton, Duncan Grant, Rex Whistler, Augustus John, Paul Nash, George Sheringham, and many others.

With such illustrious people backing us we felt confident that only good could come of our efforts. In the middle of February 1930 an inaugural dinner was held at the Hotel Metropole, and was attended by a hundred and fifty guests, including most of those supporters I have mentioned. Adeline Genée was in the chair. Sir Herbert Morgan, in a witty speech, proposed the toast of the evening, 'The Camargo Society', to which Edwin Evans replied, and gave details of our plan. It was intended to present productions about four times a year on Sunday evenings and Monday afternoons in a West End theatre. All ballet lovers were asked to become members.

It was not long before most of the important supporters of the Diaghilev Ballet had joined. The Society promised to grow into a real movement to establish ballet in England.

In January Jean was very ill with tonsillitis which took a serious turn. My doctor called in Mr Muecke, the famous throat specialist, husband of Madame Ada Crossley, the Australian contralto. After one look at Jean he bundled her up in her cot blankets and rushed her off in his car, then and there, to Hallam House Nursing Home. He insisted that David and Nannie went, too, so that she should not be lonely away from them. He operated the same day, and while he was about it said he would remove David's tonsils and adenoids and the two children could recover together. My doctor told me afterwards that in Jean's case it had been 'touch and go' as she already had septicaemia as well as the acute tonsillitis and he assured me that Mr Muecke had saved her life.

When I discovered how much the operation was to cost I felt desperate.

We were recovering from the shock of Jean's illness and she

was convalescing at home when Lily, my parlourmaid, contracted scarlet fever, and we were all put in quarantine. A few days later Nannie was taken off to hospital as well. So for three weeks Mother and I had to do all their jobs in the house with only Rose, our cook, to help. The children enjoyed having their grandmother and me to look after them, and, of course, I enjoyed being with them all the time and not having to spend my time teaching and sitting on committees.

I had been seeing a good deal of Prince George Chavchavadze and his family, but now we were only able to communicate by telephone. Often he would ring me up and say, 'How do you like this?' and would put his telephone on to the piano and play to me. I was very touched one day when he played a charming little *berceuse* which he had composed specially for 'you and Jean'.

Through being quarantined I was unable to go to the Lyric, Hammersmith, to see the Marie Rambert dancers give an afternoon of ballet on 25 February; but I read and heard of their success and particularly of a new young English choreographer, Frederick Ashton, and a brilliant male dancer, Harold Turner—the same youngster to whom Pat Dolin and I had given an audition in Manchester in 1927.

In those days I had a number of interesting pupils. Many had been studying with me for some time. Among the new ones were Iris Henry; Rosalie Crutchley, the daughter of my old friends Betty and Gerald; Annabel Farjeon, daughter of the well-known critic and playwright Herbert Farjeon, and now an author in her own right; and Felicity Andreae who, as Felicity Gray, has become famous on television both as a dancer and as writer of the script of the *Ballet for Beginners* programmes. Others were Anne Jenkins, whose mother had been in 'Alice' with me in 1906, and Barbara Miles who, after she had studied with me for some years as a resident student, became a well-known member of the René Blum Ballet, under the name of Barbara Barrie.

I was also receiving many requests for lessons from other teachers and dancers, among these Madame Lindowska, Madame Lehmiski of Birmingham, Mrs F. Grant, the Misses T. and D. Carter, Audrey Butterworth of Liverpool, Miss Danetree of Birmingham, Kathleen Newbury (now known as Mrs Constable), Mrs Grandison Clarke, and Vera Savina who had been so successful in the Diaghilev Ballet.

It was the beginning of what is now one of the most important sides of my work. I am proud to be able to help teachers and coach their pupils; but I make a point of seeing that the pupils they bring or send to me for coaching never lose their loyalty to their own teacher. Professional etiquette is as strictly enforced by me as it would be in the medical profession. I have become a sort of consultant in the dancing world.

At a committee meeting of the Association of Operatic Dancing in the spring of 1930 we discussed the need for compiling a selection of suitable music which could be published and used at our major examinations and as a guide to teachers when preparing candidates. The question was who would be the best person to take on this task. Madame Genée asked me if I would find someone.

When I returned home I asked Mother if she would do it for us with my help. I felt it might help her to get over her loneliness and sorrow as a result of my father's death. She undertook to try, and spent every hour she could spare on it for over six months, often working into the early morning. She was still playing for my classes and, of course, that helped her considerably as she was able, so to speak, to 'try it on the dog'. We rejected any music which I thought either too difficult for the average pianist or in other ways unsuitable.

Mother had to pay dozens of visits to Augener's, the music publishers who were to produce the book. There she bought albums of classical and modern music from which to select the sixteen or so bars which might be suitable for our exercises and steps.

Nor did her work end there. In many cases, when copyright was involved, she had to obtain permission to use the music, which meant writing numerous letters. And sometimes permission was refused, and a further search had to be made. After some months there remained a few exercises for which she could find no music. I said, 'Why not write it yourself?' That started something! At the age of sixty she discovered in herself a latent talent. There are several charming pieces of music under the initials C. B. in the Syllabus Albums. Mother also wrote a number of delightful pieces suitable for children's dances which Augener's published. I still come across them when I am judging festival competitions.

The volume was ready for publication in the autumn of 1930 and Mother received a cheque for £20, which was then considered adequate payment for what she had done.

On my return from Locarno where I had been on holiday again with Unity, I went with Adeline Genée and Pouishnoff, the famous pianist, to Clumber as guests of the Duke and Duchess of Newcastle. The Duchess was organizing a charity matinée at the Nottingham Theatre Royal, and we had promised to appear. As well as dancing my solo I took the male dancer's role in a Victorian minuet with Genée. Karsavina, who also appeared, was supported by Keith Lester. Little Wendy Toye danced her hornpipe which I so much admired.

I had a long and interesting talk with the Duke after dinner and found him the kindest and most charming of men. As a child, in the old Empire days, I had often seen him sitting in the front row of the stalls. He was a great admirer of the ballet and particularly of Genée's dancing. He was a very short man and suffered from a crooked spine, but his face always looked sweet and kind. It seemed to me that he must be very sad because he had no children of his own. He asked about David and Jean and told me that the next time he came to London he wanted to meet David and see if he could help with his future. When I told Genée of this she said that I should indeed be lucky if the Duke took an interest in David for his future would be assured. Alas, the meeting never took place, because a few weeks later the Duke of Newcastle died. I was sent a lovely piece of Royal Copenhagen china which had always stood on his desk.

From the earliest days of the Association of Operatic Dancing the work for the candidates had been set by Espinosa, while the judging and marking was done by the rest of the Committee, including the President. One day without any previous warning Madame Genée said, 'Miss Bedells, will you set the work for the candidates, please?' I felt as if I were taking a plunge into the deep end of a swimming bath without being able to swim, but after the first few minutes it was all much easier and more interesting than judging. From that day onwards the examinations have been set by various members of the Committee without anyone knowing in advance who was to do it. In the early days we had about forty-five candidates at a time and each exam. lasted all day.

A few months later Espinosa resigned from our Committee and his place was taken by his sister Judith Espinosa, who remained with us until her death in 1949.

34

In July Prince George Chavchavadze and I gave a joint recital in London, for which the Duchess of Norfolk was kind enough to lend us the big ballroom in Norfolk House. The audience paid a guinea each for their tickets of invitation. The Duchess, her son, the young Duke, and her daughters were all present, and also the Duchess of Portland who was so kind to me when I was a child in Nottingham. One of her sons, Lord Morven Cavendish-Bentinck, was also a pianist and was studying under Irene Scharrer. As he was a great friend of George Chavchavadze I saw a good deal of him at our musical parties.

As the Norfolk House recital was so successful we felt encouraged to embark upon a whole series of concerts together. We did not make much money, but we were happy doing the work we enjoyed. We used to rehearse at my house in Northwick Terrace. My next-door neighbour began to complain to our ground landlords that I was using the house for business purposes, and that the constant playing of the piano was a nuisance. Eventually I had to move.

George and I went to Jersey after our first recital and were very successful there. We stayed for a week. I was at La Pulente Hotel and George staying with his old, English governess, May Southby, who had been with him in Russia before the revolution. She was now retired and living with her sister on Jersey. I used to like listening to George and Miss Southby recalling memories of the old days.

That summer I spent my holiday with Felicity Andreae and her parents on board their Dutch sailing barge *Mareke*, which had been beautifully fitted out in a most up-to-date way. We cruised about from Lymington and the Isle of Wight.

In September George and I resumed our recitals. We made a return visit to Jersey and visited Guernsey also, where we were entertained after our performance at Government House. Lord and Lady Ruthven had been at our evening show with their charming daughters. After supper we sat up until five o'clock in the morning, playing games. There were only a few of us and it was all very jolly; but we had no sleep at all. We had only time to return to our hotels and pack and catch the early morning boat to England, for we had a recital in Bournemouth the same day.

Then on 19 and 20 October 1930, before a most impressive audience, the first performances of the Camargo Society took place at the Cambridge Theatre. I had been very hard at work rehearsing under Alexander Genée and his niece whose part, Princess Elena the Abbess, I was taking in a revival of Meyerbeer's ballet from *Robert the Devil*. The *décor* for this production was designed by George Bissill. I had Constantine Tcherkas supporting me as Robert, Mark Fawdry played Bertram, and the *corps de ballet*, representing the spectres of nuns, was composed of sixteen of the more advanced members of the Association of Operatic Dancing. The ballet was definitely a museum piece and was put on deliberately to show the public one of the older classical ballets. It was, nevertheless, difficult to dance, and I felt proud to have been chosen for the role. But I confess that I would have liked the opportunity to appear in a more modern work.

Robert the Devil resembles the second act of *Giselle*, but lacks the pathos of the latter. The ballerina's role is a little too dependent for its effectiveness upon technical execution. However, it served its purpose, and provided a contrast to the rest of the programme. Ninette de Valois had arranged a *divertissement* to Debussy's *Danse Sacrée et Danse Profane* which was particularly striking as the company wore masks which, like the costumes, were designed by Hedley Briggs. Ursula Moreton led in *Danse Sacrée* and Sheila McCarthy in *Danse Profane*.

The most important item was the first production of *Pomona*, with Constant Lambert's music, choreography by Fredérick Ashton, and *décor* by John Banting. Pomona was danced by Anna Ludmilla and Anton Dolin was Vertumnas. The ballet was the most considerable work Ashton had yet done. This was the first time I had met Frederick Ashton, and it was the beginning of a real friendship.

Another *divertissement* followed, consisting of scenes in a dentist's waiting room. It was called *A Toothsome Morsel*, and had music by Gavin Gordon. Penelope Spencer produced it and danced in it as a Dowager. It was light and witty. Then came a dance suite to music by Christian Darnton, danced by Annie Boalth in the Central European style. The programme ended with a grand finale, *Variations and Coda* to Glinka's music, which

163

was produced by Nicolas Legat. In this Ninette de Valois and Anton Dolin danced a *pas de deux* and all the company appeared in 'snippets' during the coda.

The orchestra was conducted throughout by Constant Lambert.

In October I agreed to join the committee of the new Faculty of Dancing, a branch of the Faculty of Arts, with fine new premises in Prince's Hall, Piccadilly. The other committee members were Margaret Craske, Felix Demery, Anton Dolin, Mrs Freda Grant, and Marie Rambert. Anna Ludmilla, Ninette de Valois, Iris Rowe, Margaret Craske, and Elsa Brunelleschi appeared at our first dance recital in November, with Frederick Ashton, Harold Turner, Anton Dolin, Robert Sielle and Annette Mills, and myself. It gave a successful 'send-off' to a series of similar functions which were all aimed at raising the standard of dancing. Further opportunities were offered to lovers of the ballet to meet and pool their knowledge and talents for the sake of the future of ballet in England.

Marie Rambert and her husband, Ashley Dukes, were in process of forming a Ballet Club at the Mercury Theatre in Notting Hill Gate; and Lilian Baylis asked Ninette de Valois to give regular ballet performances at the newly opened Sadler's Wells Theatre as well as those at the Old Vic.

In November (1930) Dawsie died—and I lost one of my dearest friends. Her courage, good humour, and kindliness, together with her appreciation of the arts, had been a real help to me and an example to all.

At the Dancers' Circle Dinner at Grosvenor House that year P. J. S. Richardson proposed the toast, 'England, the home of ballet!' In his speech he spoke of the remarkable revival of interest in the ballet during the year. Sir Paul Dukes, who was among the other speakers, looked forward to the day when England would take the place of Russia in the world of ballet.

In the December 1930 issue of the *Dancing Times* Arnold Haskell wrote an article with the title, 'The Memorable Year': 'I started the year in a state of extreme depression.' (He was referring to the death of Diaghilev.) 'Now I know that I will see pure dancing again and that the splendid tradition planted here by Adeline Genée will be carefully tended.'

35

IN DECEMBER 1930 I had moved from Northwick Terrace to my new house in Maida Vale which had a large garden and where I had permission to teach so long as I did not advertise outside. I was rehearsing for a series of matinées at the Savoy. *Alice in Wonderland* was being revived as a Christmas show. It was an entirely different version from that in which I had made my *début* in 1906, and had new music by Hugh Marlyn which was very pretty; but I missed the old tunes of Walter Slaughter's to which I had danced all those years before. There were many innovations, including Mickey Mouse and a new ballet called *Penguin Land*. However, I still appeared as the Cornflower.

On New Year's Eve I arranged the suite of dances which my pupils performed at a gala at the Waldorf Hotel. Just before midnight a huge Christmas cake was carried into the centre of the ballroom. At the first stroke of twelve out popped little Jean as 1931. It was most effective. All the lights were extinguished except for a spotlight playing on her as she pointed to the clock. Old Father Time was ragged by the dancers and chased from the room, amid general merriment, and Jean danced a solo. She was welcomed so uproariously, with so much cheering and applause that she was frightened by it all, and I felt thoroughly ashamed of myself for allowing her night's sleep to be interrupted. She soon recovered from her fright, however, and seemed to enjoy herself before Nannie and I bustled her home to bed again.

I resumed my classes in my new home. The studio there was a great improvement on the old one at Northwick Terrace: we had much more space and, in every way, better accommodation. I was also rehearsing nearly every day at Legat's studio in Baron's Court for the new ballet *Straussiana*, which he was preparing for the next Camargo Society performance. Supporting me I had Rupert Doone and a *corps de ballet* of excellent dancers. I was not entirely happy about the production, feeling that Legat was giving very little serious thought to it. For me there was no feeling of inspiration about it. And to crown everything I had to dance in a crinoline which was quite unmanageable in some of the lifts and steps.

The day of our dress rehearsal we were all profoundly shocked to hear the news of Anna Pavlova's death in an hotel at The Hague on 23 January 1931. While travelling there her train had been involved in a collision. She and her company had to wait for some time on the permanent way until help came. She contracted a chill which soon turned to pleurisy; and, within a few days, her condition became critical. I need hardly say what a personal sense of loss I felt. How much I regretted not having been able to meet her when she had been in London only just over a month before!

No other dancer has given so much joy to audiences all over the world. Her name goes down to history as the greatest dancer of all time. She was the inspiration of most present-day dancers. Her spirit lives on. While memory lasts we can still recapture some of the infinite pleasure her dancing gave to us.

At the Sunday evening performance of the Camargo Society, which took place at the Apollo Theatre two nights later, a moving tribute was paid to her memory. The programme was interrupted while the orchestra played *Le Cygne*. The curtain rose slowly on an empty stage, very dimly lit, and the performance she would have given was given in her audience's imagination. We all stood, and I think that many tears were shed.

The programme for the second Camargo production included a new ballet, *Cephalus and Procris*, with Ninette de Valois's choreography to Grétry's music, and costumes by William Chappell. The leading parts were danced by Harold Turner as Cephalus, Alicia Markova as Procris, and Prudence Hyman as Aurora. There were twelve attendants, most of them members of the Vic-Wells Ballet.

Another item was *Capriol Suite*, which Frederick Ashton had arranged to Peter Warlock's music and for which William Chappell had again designed the costumes. It was beautifully danced by the Marie Rambert Dancers—Pearl Argyle, Prudence Hyman, Diana Gould, Andrée Howard, William Chappell, Robert Stuart, Frederick Ashton, and Harold Turner. There were three national dances by Alice Cavoukdjian, followed by another Ninette de Valois ballet, *Rout*, to music by Arthur Bliss. In this Ninette herself danced with Ursula Moreton and a small *corps de ballet*.

The programme ended with our *Straussiana*, with music by the Strauss family and costumes by Vladimir Polunin. The *corps de ballet* which supported Rupert Doone and myself included three

166

of my own pupils, Molly Radcliffe, Pam Foster, and Felicity Andreae.

There were conflicting notices. *The Times* said: 'The importance of what one must call the intellectual element in choreography was made very clear by its absence from the last ballet, *Straussiana*, which remained distressingly vapid in spite of the valse rhythm and the virtuosity of Miss Phyllis Bedells'; while the *Referee* said: 'All the preceding performances were far surpassed by the *Straussiana* ballet, arranged and produced by Nicholas Legat.' The *Sunday Times*, after pulling *Cephalus and Procris* to pieces, said: 'We had no such feeling with the graceful romps of the *Straussiana* devised by Nicholas Legat to some music of the Strauss family. . . . The playing of this by the orchestra had more about it of Clapham Common than the *Prater*; but our imagination could generally supply what was missing in the way of grace and charm. The dancing and miming were less pretentious and the thorough professional skill of Miss Phyllis Bedells vitalized and unified it all.' This critic went on to speak well of *Rout*. The *Musical Standard* criticized our Musical Director: 'Mr Constant Lambert conducted efficiently but wanted a much lighter handling of Strauss. Musically, it was Strauss in clogs; and I wondered why such an essentially good conductor couldn't *feel* it as he went along.'

At our meetings after performances all of us on the committee agreed that we should have to do better in future if the Camargo Society was to thrive; and we were very anxious about the state of our finances which had already been sadly crippled by having to pay out £180 in entertainments tax.

At the end of January Mrs Adrian Crombie was to give a dinner party and dance at her house in London to celebrate the birthday of her husband and Princess Troubetzkoy, which happened to be on the same day. The Princess, whose first husband was killed in the Russian Revolution, was Prince George Chavchavadze's mother. I already knew her well: she was 'Moushka' to me and to all her closest friends and relations. George had introduced me to the Crombies some time before and I was by now very friendly with them all. Several secret meetings were held at my house before the birthday, at which George, his sister, Marina, Lord Morven Cavendish-Bentinck, and I planned a surprise entertainment. It was all beautifully worked out and, on the great night, the whole affair went with a swing.

167

After dinner Major Crombie and Moushka found themselves sitting in state on high thrones to receive their guests. Dozens had arrived after dinner. We gave everybody amusing fictitious names and had them ushered into the throne room in pairs to be announced. Then followed an entertainment. George played while I danced several new numbers and some old favourites. Afterwards we all played charades.

For its third production the Camargo Society had a much better programme. I acted only in an advisory capacity and, of course, regularly attended its committee meetings. I had the pleasure, therefore, of watching its performances.

In *Follow Your Saint* John Dowland's music had been transcribed by Peter Warlock. Frederick Ashton was responsible for the choreography; William Chappell designed the costumes. The part of the Lady was taken by Lydia Lopokova, and her two suitors were William Chappell and Frederick Ashton.

The Marie Rambert Dancers appeared in *Mars and Venus* (Scarlatti), and Frederick Ashton and William Chappell were again choreographer and designer. Pearl Argyle was Venus—and how lovely she was! Prudence Hyman and Andrée Howard were attendant nymphs and William Chappell Mars, the part originally played by Harold Turner when the same ballet was performed in the play, *Jew Süss*.

Tamara Karsavina presented her own *Valse Fantaisie* to Glinka's music and with costumes designed by Grace Lovat-Fraser. Karsavina, dancing in this herself, was supported by Frederick Ashton, Molly Radcliffe, Prudence Hyman, and a small *corps de ballet*.

After that there was a fine new work by Ninette de Valois, *La Création du Monde* to music by Darius Milhaud and costumes and masks by Edward Wolfe. In this ballet the man was played by Leslie French and the woman by Ursula Moreton. There were three heathen gods, Peter Fine, Ivor Beddoes, and Stanley Judson. We were supposed to be watching the Creation as it might have been imagined by a singer of a Negro spiritual. The development from chaos to the gradual growth of trees, plants, and animals, and eventually man, was extremely effectively achieved. The ballet had a queer, uncanny effect; in spite of being most impressive it was certainly not one to make a wide general appeal.

As a complete contrast the programme ended with the first

production of *Façade*. William Walton's witty music, John Armstrong's amusing *décor*, and Frederick Ashton's choreography are familiar to all of us. I treasure the memory of that first performance with Lydia Lopokova as a delicious Milkmaid in the Yodelling Song, and Alicia Markova, triumphantly successful in the gay Polka. She wore on her head a perky little straw boater, and, when she removed her skirt, revealed a naughty pair of knickers. And, of course, there was the Tango Pasodoble with Frederick Ashton and Lydia Lopokova. Her burlesque seemed almost too exaggerated, but Ashton's dancing was most subtly amusing.

In the finale, Tarantella Sevillana, the whole company danced. We came away with the feeling that Frederick Ashton had had a triumphant evening. He had shown us no less than three ballets in the one programme and confirmed us in our belief that here was a choreographer who could hold his own with the best in the world.

I again spent my Easter holiday with Unity, but we did not go abroad. She and Nigel had a house at Selsey which had only recently been built for them. We enjoyed the spring there in a quiet way, with lots of fresh air and early nights. It made a pleasant break from my busy life in London and helped me to gather strength for my future work.

36

I HAD RECEIVED a letter from Ian—the first since the previous October. I began to hope that all would come right between us, and tried to be patient and to forget the sadness he had caused me by his neglecting to write. The children were again at Aldeburgh with the Longstaffes, and in the peace and quiet of Selsey I was able to think things out.

On 5 May 1931 the first full programme of ballet was given at the Old Vic. This was of capital importance to all of us who had been working for the establishment of a national ballet, and a triumph for Ninette de Valois, who was not only responsible for the whole organization under the management of Lilian Baylis but was also responsible for the choreography of the entire programme. There was *Les Petits Riens* (Mozart), *The Faun* (Vaughan

Williams), the ballet from *Faust* (Gounod), *Danse Sacrée et Danse Profane* (Debussy), *Hommage aux Belles Viennoises* (Schubert), a new *Suite of Dances* to music by Bach, with Anton Dolin as guest artist, and a new production, *The Jackdaw and the Pigeons*, with music by Hugh Bradford and *décor* by William Chappell. Ninette danced the role of the Jackdaw which admirably suited her. Dolin also danced one of his own solos.

Although the programme contained no major work it was nevertheless received with great enthusiasm by a packed house. Those of us who were present left the theatre filled with excitement. Anton Dolin helped the new venture considerably by appearing as guest artist for his name was undoubtedly a big draw at the box office.

My school by now had nearly doubled itself and kept me very busy. I was in training, myself, as well, because I had promised to dance again in *Hiawatha* for two weeks in June.

David had started piano lessons under Miss Gibson who was Mabel Lander's assistant and I felt it was time for Jean to begin learning as well. Both the children made progress, and it was not long before I was hearing *The Merry Peasant* and other little pieces. But they were never very good at playing duets because they had such totally different temperaments. Miss Lander used the Letchetizky method and I had a good deal of amusement from watching my children struggling to do their practice with corks held between their fingers. Jean was also keen about her dancing, and had begun to work in my children's classes twice or three times a week. She had passed her second Children's Grade examination of the Association of Operatic Dancing.

The fourth Carnargo Society production took place at the Cambridge on 6 July. Ninette de Valois's *The Jackdaw and the Pigeons* was revived; then came *Job*, with Vaughan Williams's music. The ballet, invented by Geoffrey Keynes, was based on Blake's *Vision of the Book of Job*, from which Gwen Raverat took her inspiration for the *décor*. It was Ninette de Valois's greatest production and, to my mind, it remains her finest work. Dr Vaughan Williams's score is a magnificent one, but is filled with difficulties for the choreographer and the dancers, who have to learn to count their various phrases, which are unusually broken up. The final result, however, is one of the most moving experiences I have known.

There was very little actual dancing, except for Elihu and Satan.

170

In the latter role Dolin reached the heights. He was the very embodiment of evil, terrifying and yet fascinating; and his dancing was brilliant. When, at the end, he was ejected from heaven, his fall down the steps was breathtaking.

That programme ended with a revival of Ashton's *Pomona*, in which Dolin again appeared with Anna Ludmilla. This was delightful enough but inevitably an anticlimax after the sheer magnificence of *Job*. At the Monday matinée, however, the mistake was corrected and *Job* was made the final item of the programme.

Two days after all this excitement I had a communication from the Foreign Office which said they had received the following cable from my husband: 'Please send the following message to my wife: LEAVE FOR ENGLAND IN ABOUT TWO WEEKS. PLEASE TELEGRAPH HONG KONG AND SHANGHAI BANK FORTY POUNDS IF POSSIBLE.'

How excited I was! And that same day I had heard from dear Dawsie's solicitors that the legacy of £500 she had left me had become available. I felt she was still acting as my guardian angel and helping me to straighten out my difficulties. My heart was full of thankfulness as I cabled the reply that £40 was being sent. The next I heard was also from the Foreign Office: a curt note saying that Major Macbean would arrive in London on 30 August in the S.S. *Diomed*.

At the end of that week I travelled to Scotland with George and Marina Chavchavadze to stay for the first time with Major and Mrs Adrian Crombie in their beautiful house, 'Pitmuies', at Guthrie in the County of Angus. I stayed with them for three weeks and was happier than I had been for years.

The Crombie family were the kindest and merriest hosts imaginable. They did everything to make me happy. Driving in their car with them I saw most of the beauty spots of Scotland. Sometimes we went as far as the west coast, where a big party of us would stay the night. I was always included in the invitations they had to tea parties, dinners, and dances at many of the great Scottish houses and castles owned by their friends. I went to Glamis and to Brechin, Kinnaird, and others.

Every Friday there was a dance at 'Pitmuies' to which many people well known in Scottish society came. These were enormous fun, as we danced old Highland Reels and many others such as 'Petronella' and 'The Dashing White Sergeant'. Before the first dance I attended the family taught me all these Highland dances so that I should be able to enjoy them. Learning them was easy owing to my previous knowledge of the Fling and the Sword Dance; but I soon found that most of the steps I could do were those used only by the men. The ladies played a more sedate part, confining themselves to simple *pas de Basque* and similarly easy *terre à terre* steps.

Major Crombie wore the kilt in the day-time as well as in the evening; and at these dances nearly all the men wore their clan tartans. It was all a new experience for me. In addition to Prince George and Princess Marina our house guests were Fanny Baillie, Norman Patullo, Admiral and Mrs Greatorex and their daughter, Clemency, as well as Peggy, Ted, and Adrienne Crombie, the three children of our hosts, and Major Crombie's sister, Kathleen Crombie.

It was a fine eighteenth-century house, approached by a wooded drive and, on the estate, there were many old cottages overgrown with roses. The gardens were the most beautiful I have ever seen. Some parts of them were secluded and seemed remote from the world. There was a fine rose garden, a formal garden; and leading from one to the other, you passed through beautiful wrought-iron gates. Specimen delphiniums grew about nine feet high; 'Hunk', as we called Major Crombie, specialized in growing these flowers and had taken many prizes at the Royal Horticultural Society's shows in London. 'Munk', his wife, was expert at growing roses, which she tended herself with love and care. There were three gardeners, who lived in cottages on the estate, yet work in the garden seemed never-ending.

Frequently we went off mackerel fishing from Montrose. We had plenty of music, too. George would play to us for hours at a time. Every day Hunk, George, and I would pore over an enormous atlas, trying to trace my husband's homeward journey. As he neared England I grew more and more excited.

After those three lovely weeks I again joined Felix (Felicity Andreae) and her parents, for another week on the *Mareke*, sailing in and out of the quiet South Coast ports. We did little except laze in the sunshine.

Ian arrived on 1 September; and I have never seen the children so excited. It was 'Daddy, look at this!' and 'Daddy, look at that!' for days. Jean used the word 'Daddy' about once

172

in every four words. I found it pathetic that she should so love saying it. She had longed to have a father like other little girls.

Ian was delighted with David, who was getting on well at school and seemed more than usually intelligent for his age. He was now eight and Jean just seven years old. I had my classes and the Association of Operatic Dancing work as well as various committees to keep me busy. Ian's job had come to an end and there seemed little prospect of his getting anything else.

37

AFTER ATTENDING a dinner in honour of the twenty-first anniversary of the founding of the *Dancing Times* I went up to Liverpool to dance in two special ballet performances at which Adeline Genée lectured on 'The Evolution of a Dancer'. Karsavina and Ninette de Valois also appeared, and I danced the Blue Bird *pas de deux* with Harold Turner. The following week I presented my own pupils in a Suite of Dances at the Hallowe'en Ball at Covent Garden in aid of the funds of the University College Hospital, and then had a busy time rehearsing for Ninette de Valois's new production, *Fête Polonaise*, at Sadler's Wells. I had been asked by Lilian Baylis to give five performances for her as guest artist both at the Old Vic and Sadler's Wells. I was delighted at the prospect of doing so, especially as I was to appear in a brand new production.

Unfortunately it was not as happy an experience as I could have wished. Ninette came to my studio twice to teach me the solo work. I had one rehearsal at Sadler's Wells to learn the *pas de deux* with Stanley Judson and two other rehearsals with the company, during which everything was pieced together—and that was all! My costume, made in the Wardrobe, which I did not see until the day of the performance, did not fit. The top panniers were made of heavy furnishing brocade of artificial silk, which hung down limply and had to be stuffed with tissue paper to make it stand out. The skirts all came from the waist instead of being set on a basque, and that made them very bulky and cumbersome to dance in. They were also a most unbecoming length, reaching just to the knee. And I was given a white wig to wear, which had an egg-shaped head and made me look hideous. So far as my part was concerned I felt Ninette had not served me well. But the choreography for the *corps de ballet* and *coryphées*, especially the *pas de six*, was delightful.

Then I found that the covering for the stage was a cork carpet which was simply thick with resin.

Altogether, on the first night I was thoroughly miserable—under-rehearsed, looking a fright, feeling uncomfortable. And, when I came to do the pirouettes supported by Stanley Judson, not only did my toes stick to the resin, but his fingers caught in the panniers of my dress. Nothing at all seemed right.

At the end of the performance, among the friends who came to my dressing-room was Philip Richardson, whose only remark was, 'Why on earth did they give you that awful wig to wear?' I knew then that my worst fears had been justified and that, even though Ninette and others said kind things to me, I had not done well. There were good notices in the press, but even they did not cheer me up.

As well as my five performances as guest artist I was hard at work rehearsing my own production for the forthcoming Camargo Society performances at the end of November. We were very fortunate now in having as our honorary treasurer the famous economist Professor J. Maynard Keynes, Lydia Lopokova's husband, who worked miracles in establishing the Society on a sounder financial footing: nevertheless we all realized that we must go very carefully if we were to keep out of debt. I am sure that no one outside the theatre realizes how expensive it is to produce repertory ballet. The cost of a good orchestra and the fact that they have to be paid so highly for adequate rehearsals as well as for actual performances is alone sufficient to cripple the finances of most companies. The costumes worn by the dancers are usually made of flimsy materials which need constant renewing; and the expense of silk tights and ballet shoes is high, as these wear out so quickly. In the ordinary way a play or musical show can be presented on a lavish scale, and there is a chance of its being successful and running for many months with little additional expense. But to build up a good repertoire of ballets, the cost of production and upkeep is never-ending, and continual rehearsal is necessary. These are acknowledged facts and the reason why, even in these days, ballet dancers are paid so little in comparison with dancers in musical comedy and revue. However, money is not everything. The intense satisfaction we feel in our job and the prestige of belonging to a first-class ballet company count for much.

The Camargo Society's programme at the Savoy at the end of November 1931 had the Vic-Wells Ballet in *Fête Polonaise* in which I again danced the leading part; then, *A Woman's Privilege*, a ballet in three scenes to music by Handel selected, arranged, and orchestrated by Sir Thomas Beecham who also conducted. Choreography was by Trudl Dubsky, and the chief parts were danced by Jeanette Rutherstone and Trudl Dubsky supported by Harold Turner, Stanley Judson, and a *corps de ballet*.

Chopin's *Ballade in A Flat* was specially orchestrated by Arnold Bax. I was the choreographer for this and danced in it myself, supported by Harold Turner and eight of my advanced pupils, Felicity Andreae, Barbara Barrie, Ella Bennett, Mollie Bergmayr, Peggy Bullin, Daphne Corbett, Jean Gillie, and Peggy Wickens. Barbara Barrie also designed the costumes.

Finally came the first performance as a ballet of Constant Lambert's *Rio Grande*, which had exotic choreography by Frederick Ashton and *décor* by Edward Burra. Lydia Lopokova was the Queen of the Port, Walter Gore, her Sailor; Alicia Markova was a Creole Girl, William Chappell, a Creole Boy. There was a *corps de ballet* of Women of the Port, Stevedores, Stokers, Loiterers, and Natives; and Sacheverell Sitwell's poem was sung by the New English Singers.

I was asked to dance the *Ballade* again at a special midnight matinée on 15 December 1931 in aid of Queen Charlotte's Maternity Hospital, at the Carlton Theatre in the Haymarket. An hour of ballet was presented by the Camargo Society following the première of a new film. It was a very grand occasion, with Their Royal Highnesses the Prince of Wales and Prince George among the distinguished audience. The Rambert Ballet and the Vic-Wells Ballet also appeared in a new production, *The Lord of Burleigh*, with Frederick Ashton's choreography to Mendelssohn's music orchestrated by Gordon Jacob. After the performances there was dancing on the stage.

The following night I again appeared in *Fête Polonaise* at the Old Vic; and, in the same programme, there was another new work, *The Jew in the Bush*, with Ninette de Valois's choreography and Gordon Jacob's music.

All this time my husband was without work and I was still

heavily in debt to the bank. My work for the Camargo Society was voluntary, as was everyone else's connected with the Society —except the orchestra's! It was necessary for me to keep on teaching, even up to Christmas Eve. I had only two days off at Christmas; but I was glad to have the work to do, and to keep the wolf from the door.

Early in December a new and very good-looking male pupil arrived, aged nineteen, and told me he was a student at the Royal Academy of Dramatic Art and hoped to join my class there in January. He asked me if I would give him three weeks of daily lessons before the term started as he was a complete beginner but 'terribly keen to dance'. I warned him that he was starting much too late if he wished to dance seriously; but, as he was determined to try, I agreed to see what could be done. From his very first lesson I realized I had someone out of the ordinary. He was well built and extremely supple for a man. He was very musical and had a burning enthusiasm for work. His name was Francis Heanley. After only one term he wanted to leave the Royal Academy of Dramatic Art and train as a dancer. There was no denying he had talent. Eventually I agreed to take him, and he persuaded his father and mother to let him come to me entirely after Easter. We both decided that he ought to change his name for stage work; and, when I discovered that his full name was Francis John Byron Heanley I immediately realized that the two middle names would be ideal. So he became John Byron.

Another of my pupils who was beginning to make a name for herself was Pam Foster. She had been principal dancer during the long run of *White Horse Inn* at the Coliseum and had been given the principal dancer's role and been made ballet mistress of the new musical comedy *Paulette*, in which, although the show did not run, she scored a big personal success.

Rita Elsie had become one of Mr Cochran's young ladies at the Trocadero and Iris Henry, who had been at the Cambridge in *This World of Ours*, was now engaged to appear in *The Immortal Hour* at the Queen's. Other pupils of mine were appearing in such West End shows as *Bow Bells*, *The Miracle*, *The Dubarry*, *Casanova*, and *Helen*.

Création du Monde, *Valse Fantaisie*, and *Façade* were all revived for the next Camargo Society performance at the Savoy in February 1932. The new ballet was *The Lord of Burleigh*, which had only previously been seen at the midnight matinée. As I was not dancing I was able to see the performance from the front. Watching it, I felt that here were all the ingredients of a delightful ballet which somehow did not turn out successfully. It consisted of a series of dances suggested by characters in Tennyson's poems and, although there were some lovely moments, the whole seemed long-drawn-out and monotonous.

The number of performances of ballet at the Old Vic and Sadler's Wells was increased in March when the company was joined by Markova and Dolin, and Rupert Doone, who was given the opportunity to do the choreography for a new ballet, *Enchanted Grove*, to music from Ravel's suite, *Le Tombeau de Couperin*. The *décor* for this was by Duncan Grant. Dolin played Eros, Markova, Psyche, and Ninette de Valois made an appearance as a Japanese Courtesan in one of the finest dances in the ballet. I did not greatly care for the ballet: there were some clever things in it, but it was rather a muddle, and difficult to watch. It needed to be considerably pruned and simplified. Had that been done perhaps it would have had a more enduring success.

The Camargo Society loaned *Job* and *Cephalus and Procris* to the Vic-Wells repertoire. The success of the season was assured by Markova's and Dolin's appearances; but Constant Lambert's splendid direction of the orchestra ought not to be forgotten.

An 'old Empire' dinner, held towards the end of April in the club rooms of the Faculty of Dancing, brought back hosts of memories. P. J. S. Richardson presided. Everyone had a most enjoyable time. Adeline Genée was there, Unity More, Madame Zanfretta, Carlotta Mossetti, Beatrice Collier, Will Bishop, Fred Farren. We felt sorry that Ivy St Helier and Lydia Kyasht could not come. Inevitably we spent most of our time recalling incidents from the past and making speeches that were heavy with nostalgia. About seventy-five of us sat around remembering those good old days. In such an atmosphere of sentimental reverie, it was good suddenly to hear Genée saying fine, hopeful things about our modern ballet.

It was decided at the Camargo Society committee meetings to take the Savoy Theatre for a four-week season, which would open on 6 June. Not only were we to have the co-operation of the Vic-Wells ballet, but we were fortunate in engaging Olga Spessiva (sometimes spelt Spessivtseva), the great Russian ballerina. Lydia Lopokova, Alicia Markova, Ruth French, Ninette de Valois, Anton Dolin, Frederick Ashton, Stanley Judson, Walter

Gore, and myself were all taking leading roles. There was a fine orchestra of thirty, drawn from the London Symphony Orchestra with Sir Thomas Beecham and Constant Lambert conducting. There were new works: *The Origin of Design* (Handel) with choreography by Ninette de Valois; *High Yellow*, a Negro ballet by Spike Hughes, with choreography by Buddy Bradley and Frederick Ashton; and a special revival of *Giselle*, which was produced by Nicholas Sergueeff. I was able to dance only towards the end of the season because of my annual engagement in *Hiawatha*, which opened at the Albert Hall on the same day as the Camargo performances. However, I did dance the *Ballade in A Flat* several times, and was able to see Olga Spessiva's exquisite *Giselle*, which was also presented during the latter part of the season, and was an unforgettable experience. She and Dolin dancing together were absolutely superb.

Fête Polonaise had been included in the programme and was put on at the beginning of the month. New *décor* and costumes, designed by Edmund Dulac, had been provided, and Alicia Markova had taken over my part, which she danced beautifully. I must confess to feeling a little envious of her, as Ninette de Valois had rearranged some of the solos and the *pas de deux* and they were, in my opinion, much improved. Alicia Markova also had a delightful costume to wear. In spite of my feelings about it I was glad that Alicia was given a better chance to shine in the ballet than I had had.

By the time the season ended it was estimated that twenty thousand people had seen the ballets. The *Daily Telegraph* declared that we had made artistic history, and went on to say, 'The experiment has been something more than a *succès d'estime*. It has shown that we have plenty of talent among the artists in the many mediums which go to the making of ballet and that there is a public eager to enter into its delights.'

Towards the end of July Ian and I went to 'Pitmuies'. We stayed at Oban for two days and, on the way there, drove past Loch Awe and through the Pass of Brander, where I had not been before. At the Crombies' house we enjoyed ourselves much as I had done on my last visit. We played lots of tennis. George Chavchavadze, Fanny Baillie, and several other friends were of the house party.

Nannie and the children joined forces with Dr Malcolm Sargent's children that summer: they all went to Bexhill, where they shared the same lodgings and used the same beach hut. The children and the two nannies soon became excellent friends. It was a splendid arrangement. My two came home as brown as berries and in high spirits.

In the middle of August I was back in London with Ian, and had resumed my classes in an effort to earn some much-needed money. I was rehearsing every day, and getting into strict training again for a most important occasion. It was one of the most exciting events of my life. I was going to Copenhagen to dance in the Royal Theatre there with an all-English ballet company. As far back as April of that year Madame Genée had arranged for a group of English dancers to gather together to show her native countrymen how we had progressed in recent years in the art to which she had devoted her life.

38

The Danish trip had been arranged by the Association of Operatic Dancing through the initiative of Adeline Genée in the first place. We all left London on the evening of 20 September and arrived in Copenhagen early on the 22nd, after a fearful crossing. We must have looked more like dying ducks than swans or sylphides. Everyone had been sick on the way. The captain told me that only eighteen meals had been served.

We were met at Copenhagen by an army of journalists and press photographers. It was then about eight o'clock in the morning, and we were far from looking our best. Madame Genée had been in Denmark for some time, supervising the arrangements for our performances, which were to coincide with the British Exhibition, for which the Prince of Wales was paying a State visit to the country.

A wonderful breakfast party in the Copenhagen Station Restaurant was our first official engagement immediately on arriving. Genée played hostess while we were interviewed and photographed, and she introduced us to many of the principals of the Royal Theatre ballet. After breakfast we were sorted out and put in charge of the people who would be our hosts during our ten-day visit. I was particularly fortunate in having as my hosts Madame Ulla Poulsen, one of the chief ballerinas at the Royal Theatre, and her husband, Johannes Poulsen, who held the coveted title of King's Actor and was the Henry Ainley of Denmark. It is difficult to speak warmly enough of the kindness of their welcome.

In the afternoon we went to the Royal Theatre and were presented to Andrew Moller, the director, and to the other members of the company whom we had not met at the station. I was glad to find that I was in the same dressing-room as Ruth French, because we had been 'stable companions' all the way from England, sharing the same cabin in the ship and the same compartment on the train. We had got on splendidly together. We decided to unpack our dresses at once. At the Stage Door I found a young man with charming manners who spoke English, and asked him about our luggage. It was only after he had carried all my heavy baggage into the dressing-room for me that I discovered he was the principal male dancer of the Danish ballet, Børge Ralov!

The magnificent theatre with its enormous stage and up-to-date equipment was most impressive. We saw the gloriously large rehearsal rooms and classrooms where Harald Lander, the *maître de ballet*, and Madame Jørgen-Jensen held their classes. On the walls hung fine paintings and photographs of former dancers and ballet masters, and there was a very good bust of Bournonville, the father of the Danish ballet, from whom so much of present-day ballet technique originated.

Among our company, and very much under my wing, were two of my own pupils, Felicity (Felix) Andreae and Francis Heanley—who had not yet changed his name to John Byron. As I discovered that neither he nor Felix had heard an opera I managed to book seats for Wagner's *Siegfried*, which was being performed that evening with Lauritz Melchior singing in the title role.

Our own two conductors, Constant Lambert and Geoffrey Toye, had been in Copenhagen for some days at the preliminary orchestral rehearsals. Stephen Thomas, who is now head of the Drama Section of the British Council, also accompanied us as Stage Director. Formidable tasks faced him, as we were giving four completely different programmes during our short stay, and there would not be much time for rehearsing and setting up scenery on a strange stage. However, Stephen Thomas rose to the occasion and seemed to be in his element with all the

180

modern gadgets and lighting equipment which were put at his disposal.

The high spot of the opening night for Harold Turner and myself was to have been our appearance in the Blue Bird *pas de deux* from *The Sleeping Beauty*; but when we arrived on the stage for our only orchestral rehearsal we were dumbfounded to hear Constant Lambert tapping on the conductor's desk and saying, 'I am sorry, but we shan't be able to play this. There are several important band parts missing.'

It was too late to do anything about it, and I regret to say that both Harold and I were so angry and upset that it completely spoilt our happiness for some days. The cancellation of our chief item was a bitter pill for both of us to have to swallow, and we felt that the loss of prestige involved was very damaging to our reputations in Copenhagen.

Saturday 24 September had coincided with the opening of the British Exhibition, and that evening the Royal Theatre presented a wonderful spectacle. It was a gala performance under the patronage of Their Majesties the King and Queen of Denmark, and of our Prince of Wales. Many members of the Danish Royal house were present. Everyone wore evening dress, or military uniforms, or full diplomatic regalia.

Our first programme was a short one, as the Danish Opera began the evening with a performance of *I Pagliacci* in which Melchior sang the part of Canio. It was about 10.30 before the curtain rose on *Les Sylphides*. I danced the Nocturne with Anton Dolin and Alicia Markova and also the solo Valse, and Ruth French appeared in the Prelude. Markova and Dolin each danced a Mazurka and the lovely *pas de deux*.

This was followed by a *divertissement*, in which Wendy Toye won big applause for her Sailor's Hornpipe. I danced Delibes's *Passepied*, and Ninette de Valois, Pride, while Dolin danced Espagnol—all of this seemed to delight our audience. The programme ended with a performance of *Hommage aux Belles Viennoises*, with Harold Turner, Stanley Judson, Ruth French, and the *corps de ballet*.

Afterwards we were entertained at the Palace Hotel by Mr Hansen, a prominent Danish business man, and his wife. An enormous table was laden with dishes of *smørrebrød*. We were hungry and, for about three-quarters of an hour, ate heartily and drank schnapps and lager beer, believing this to be our supper. We were astonished when suddenly a door was thrown open and it was announced that supper was served. An enormous meal of several courses followed.

Needless to say, we all went late to our beds. We had to be up early next day to rehearse for our evening performance—even if it was Sunday.

We were all invited that same afternoon to the Royal Theatre for a matinée of a play, *Nonnebarnet*, which was followed by the ballet *Tata*, which was danced by the Danish company. We did not understand the play, although we were impressed by the acting and production. But I was excited to see young Børge Ralov in *Tata* dancing a fine Hungarian dance. He had a splendid elevation and a good sense of character. It was interesting, too, to see Harald Lander's expert choreography.

At our second performance, that Sunday evening, the King and Queen of Denmark were again present. We gave an all-British programme, with *The Lord of Burleigh* in which Alicia Markova, Harold Turner, and Anton Dolin danced. Dolin appeared again as Satan in *Job*; and Job's Spiritual Self was none other than P. J. S. Richardson, who had come with us to Denmark and made useful contacts with the Danish press and helped us in a number of ways. It was, I believe, the only appearance he ever made on the stage, but no one could have aspired to a higher role than he filled on that occasion. He looked most impressive, sitting up on his heavenly throne. He confided to me afterwards that one of the angels (Wendy Toye) had to tell him when to stand and when to sit, as the music was far too difficult for him to follow.

Job was followed by a miniature Vic-Wells ballet in humorous vein called *Regatta*, which had Ninette de Valois, Stanley Judson, and Harold Turner in the principal roles. After this there was a short *divertissement*, including *Prince Charlie's Reel* for five of the girls. I danced my *Passepied*; there was also a solo *à la Taglioni* for Ruth French, and a solo for Markova; and then we danced my Chopin *Ballade in A Flat* in which I was again supported by Harold Turner and eight *coryphées*. The evening ended with a Strauss Galop in which all took part, and the soloists were allowed to do more or less as they pleased during their brief appearances. We were, each of us, out to give of our best. Although it might not be an ideal way to make the choreography for a ballet, the effect of this finale was to rouse the audience to a state of extraordinary enthusiasm.

We rehearsed all next morning. In the afternoon we were entertained by the *Berlingske Tidende*—one of Copenhagen's most important newspapers. In the evening another gala performance was given in honour of the King's birthday, which was again attended by the Prince of Wales. We shared the programme with the Danish Ballet, who gave *Gaucho*, in which all their best dancers appeared. Alas, we had to watch this performance from the wings as we were dancing ourselves!

Our *Création du Monde* was not so well liked by the Danish press as the *Italian Suite* with Markova and Dolin. This latter received an ovation in the theatre.

We were invited to yet another gay party after the show, which meant more late hours. We still managed, however, to arrive at the theatre early next morning for our rehearsal. It was then (Tuesday) that Ruth French and I joined the Danish Ballet at their morning class under Harald Lander. We had no perform-ance ourselves that evening, so it did not matter if we were tired. Ruth and I did our utmost to show off our best classroom tech-nique and uphold the honour of England—if we could. I have never felt more nervous than I did on entering that vast classroom and knowing that some fifty critical pairs of eyes were upon us. Harald Lander set us some difficult work and, when we had finished our side practice, Ruth and I were placed in the centre of the front row and so had no one to follow. All went well, however; and, at the end of the class, during a series of *fouettés ronds de jambe*, all the Danish company gradually dropped out, leaving Ruth and me to finish, which we did to a wild burst of generous applause—a gesture which warmed our hearts!

We were the guests at a delightful tea dance on board H.M.S. *Dorsetshire*, one of the warships which was paying a visit to Copenhagen during the Exhibition. Owing to Adeline Genée and Anton Dolin having to rehearse for their appearance together at our final performance they were unable to be present. This made me the senior guest, hence I was mainly in the company of the Commanding Officer and his senior officers, all of whom I found very charming. Five different officers approached me, and enquired whether I was the sister of Commander Stuart Bedells. When I admitted it, I heard that they had all served with him at one time or another. I felt grand and important to be Stuart's sister. It was almost as if I belonged to the Senior Service myself.

Inevitably there was a cocktail party afterwards. By 7.30 in the evening, however, I decided it was time we took our leave. I went in search of the two or three younger members of the company for whom I had made myself responsible. I found them having a whale of a time with several of the junior officers; and when I insisted upon taking them away with me I was not at all popular! I was very firm, I escorted them to their 'homes' and left them with the motherly advice to 'go to bed early'. This was our one free night, and I knew we had a heavy day to follow. I went back with Ulla and Johannes Poulsen in time for dinner. I washed my hair and was in bed myself by 11.30 and very glad of a quiet evening.

It was only after we returned to England that I discovered that those young monkeys whom I had taken back home had gone out again to a party with a bunch of naval officers, and did not go to bed until 5 o'clock in the morning. They were extremely tickled at giving me the slip. When I scolded them for breaking their promise to go to bed early, they only replied, 'Well, 5 o'clock in the morning *is* early!' Among the delinquents was Doris May, now known as Pamela May.

We gave our fourth and final performance on 27 September with the royal box again occupied. The programme opened with *Fête Polonaise*, in which I again danced the leading role with Stanley Judson—but this time I wore the Edmund Dulac costume. Unfortunately, however, for technical reasons, the Dulac scenery could not be used. *The Lord of Burleigh* and *Job* followed, and after that the *divertissement*, in which we each once again danced our favourite solos.

Adeline Genée then triumphantly reappeared, dancing with Anton Dolin in *The Love Song*, an eighteenth-century suite of dances to music selected and composed by Dora Bright. These dances brought tumultuous applause from every part of the house, and curtain after curtain was taken until the stage resembled a bower of flowers, which were looped up and tied around with silken ribbons in the English and Danish colours. The great *danseuse* curtsied again and again in acknowledgment of the warmth of affection which her own countrymen were showing her. It was a great occasion for us all: that she should have emerged from her retirement to grace our official performances in Copenhagen.

When it all ended we were given a magnificent party by the *chef du théâtre*, Mr Moller. The following day, too, we were

184

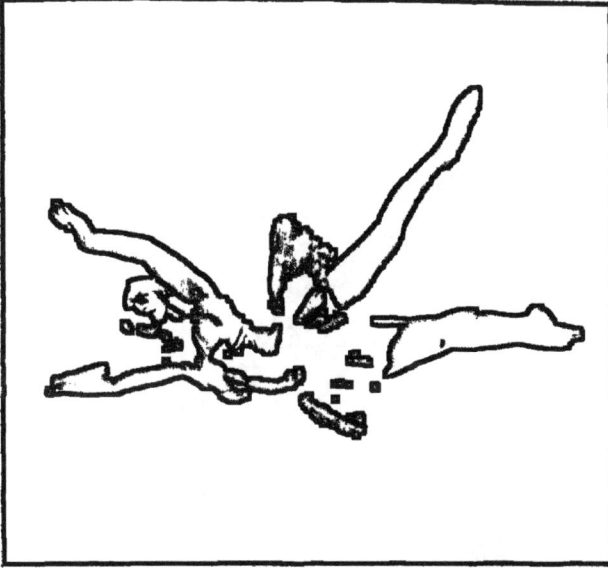

Phyllis Bedells in the Blue Bird *pas de deux* at the Coliseum 1927.

Illed Newspapers

Phyllis Bedells and Anton Dolin rehearsing at Manchester for the
Blue Bird *pas de deux*.

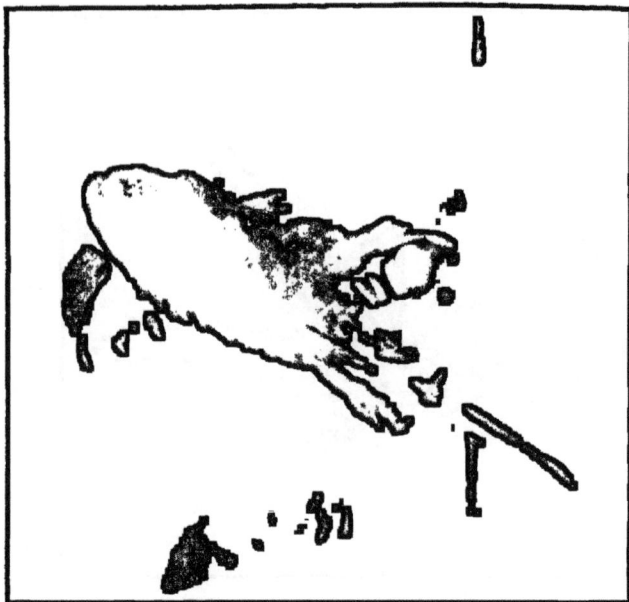

Anna Pavlova, a photograph taken in 1926 during her world tour.

Prince George Chavchavadze.

Gavotte as danced by Phyllis Bedells at her farewell performance at the London Hippodrome, November 1934

Nerina

With John Byron in Clair de Lune at the Royal Charity performance, London Hippodrome, 1934

Debenham

Phyllis Bedells (*centre*) in *Hiawatha* at the Royal Albert Hall, 1950, the Spring Ballet

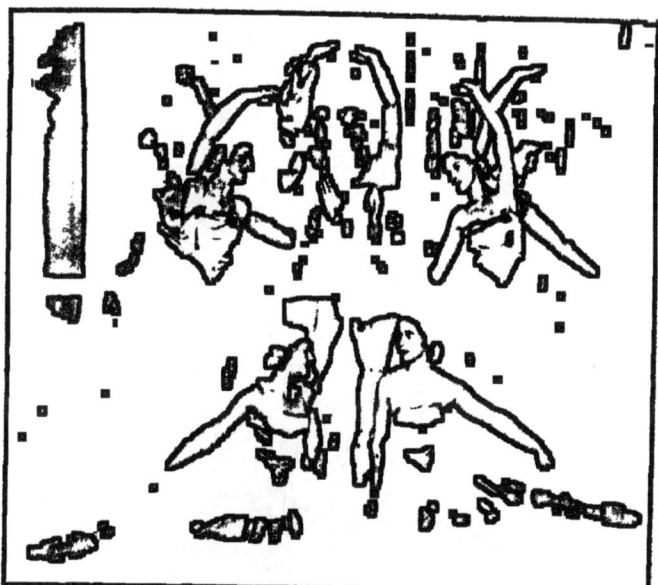

Central Press Photos

London Press Photos

Above · Rehearsal for *Chopin Ballade in A Flat*, produced by Phyllis Bedells for the Camargo Society at the Savoy Theatre, 1931 L to r back row. Peggy Wickens, Daphne Corbett, Harold Turner, Phyllis Bedells, Barbara Barrie, Felicity Andreae, in front, Peggy Bullin and Ella Bennett. *Below* The new studio at Quex Road, 1935 L to r Peggy Masters, Dorothy Dickinson, Laurel Martyn, Joan Turbett, Joan Turner Philippa Godwin, Betty Simpson

Lenare

Action photograph of Phyllis Bedells in *The Débutante* at the Coliseum, 1933.

The author's hus-
band, Major Ian
Macbean, just before
he left England in
1927

Sasha

Phyllis Bedells in
Chopin's *Nocturne*
at her farewell per-
formance at the Lon-
don Hippodrome,
1935.

Gordon Anthony

Picture Post

Above The author with pupils in the new studio, 1935   L to r . Betty Wych, Jean Bedells,
Betty Simpson, and Betty Thompson   *Below* 1951   In the garden at Quex Road with
daughter Jean and grandson Jeremy Newton.

entertained—on no less than eight occasions. We were driven through delightful country in a fleet of private motor-cars to visit such places of interest as Elsinore, the scene of Shakespeare's *Hamlet*. Near here a wonderful lunch was provided by Madame Lausgaard; and later on we were entertained by Madame Hasselbalch, formerly a dancer at the Royal Theatre, Copenhagen, and the heads of the famous Tuborg brewery. In the afternoon the British Minister invited us to his house, and Lady Hohler made us very welcome. Then we attended the Danish Ballet performance in the evening and that was followed by a supper party given by Madame Jørgen-Jensen. Even after that some of us were taken on to one of Copenhagen's better-class night clubs. It was a hectic day of parties and then more parties; but, as time was so short, it seemed that we must cram everything into that last day. We had scarcely any sleep because we had to pack and be at the station early next morning for the return journey.

Thirty-six hours later, on the evening of 30 September, we were home. I do not think I felt tired the whole time we were away, in spite of the late nights and having so little sleep. The air of Copenhagen must have been somehow intoxicating and the continual stimulation of new scenes and faces doubtless helped to keep us going. But when I was back in England, I yawned for a week. I wanted to go to bed and sleep all the time.

39

I BEGAN WORK again with my classes and was soon earning enough for our present needs. I had more pupils than before. Gabrielle Rowley and Nancy Evans, both now well-established teachers, were amongst the new ones. They still work with me whenever they can. Gabrielle won the A.O.D. Choreographic Scholarship, and is one of my best friends and regularly visits me. She is an official examiner for the Children's Grades.

Ian always looked forward to attending the annual Salonika Army Dinner, where he met many of his old friends. It was at one of these dinners that Major Wellings, who was running a successful travel agency, suggested that Ian might like to join the firm. Ian liked the idea and started work almost at once. It was obvious to me that he had found something congenial, for he was much happier and more cheerful than he had been for a long time.

The Vic-Wells Ballet opened their season at Sadler's Wells with Markova and Dolin as their principal dancers. In their first night programme there was a new ballet by Ninette de Valois, *Nursery Suite* to Sir Edward Elgar's music. The Bo-Peep dance from it remains fresh in my memory—it was simple but not at all ordinary. I hope it will survive as a classical example of a solo dance for a little girl. (I did see it danced again at a musical festival I judged in 1950.)

A few nights later there was the first production of *Douanes*, which I found very amusing. The Customs House in a French port was invaded by English visitors, all having the name of Smith. Dolin played a Cook's Man. It was curious how very much the ideas in this work resembled those in *A Day in Paris*, which was produced at the Empire in 1908 when I was one of a family of Smiths and Fred Farren the Man from Cook's. Of course the treatment and Ninette de Valois's choreography were quite different.

By another strange coincidence, within a day or two of the production of *Douanes* we saw a ballet called *Foyer de Danse* at the Ballet Club, which was set to music by Lord Berners. The scene for this was laid in the rehearsal room of a big opera house. This contained many of the same ideas as the Empire ballet, *The Débutante*, afterwards called *The Dancing Master*, in which Genée, Lydia Kyasht, and I appeared at various times. There was more humour in Frederick Ashton's *Foyer de Danse* than there had been in *The Débutante*. It is, however, extraordinarily interesting to notice that the basic ideas of both these ballets presented in 1932 were so much akin to those in the good old Empire ballets. Naturally there was a more up-to-date treatment in the later works.

During October Felicity Andreae gave dance recitals with much success; and in December John Byron was engaged to dance at the Comedy in *Ballyhoo*. After that Lilian Baylis put him under contract and he became a member of the Vic-Wells Ballet, where he remained until 1936.

In November Ninette de Valois produced the *Scorpions of Ysit*, with music by Gavin Gordon and Sophie Fedorovitch's décor. Although this had an enthusiastic first-night welcome it did not long remain in favour.

At the beginning of December 1932 the Camargo Society had a new programme at the Adelphi. There was *The Birthday of an Infanta*, to music by Elizabeth Lutyens, with Penelope Spencer's choreography and Rex Whistler's *décor*. Trudl Dubsky and Hedley Briggs were the principals. *Adam and Eve* had Constant Lambert's music, choreography by Anthony Tudor, and *décor* by John Banting. Anton Dolin, Walter Gore, and Prudence Hyman were the dancers in this. *There is a Willow Grows Aslant a Brook*, to music by Frank Bridge, had choreography by Wendy Toye, who also danced the main role. *The Passionate Pavane*, music by John Dowland, choreography by Frederick Ashton, and with William Chappell's *décor*, was danced by Pearl Argyle, William Chappell, and Walter Gore. And the Vic-Wells company danced *Les Sylphides*.

Negotiations for the engagement of members of the Association of Operatic Dancing for a season of ballet at the Coliseum were finally completed by the middle of January 1933. This was due once again to the initiative of our president, Adeline Genée, who asked me to revive *The Débutante* and dance the principal role in it, with Harold Turner as the Dancing Master. We opened on 2 February. That left me just two weeks for rehearsal. It was a formidable task; but we had the ballet ready in time—although without Genée's help, I feel, I could never have done it. She made herself largely responsible for teaching Harold Turner the mime, and to express the character of the role, in which he achieved complete success. She also helped me to remember the original choreography of some of the dances.

A few days before the rehearsals began I was deputed to meet Sandy Macpherson at the Empire, where he was then the cinema organist. I found him most helpful and, together, we ransacked the Empire music library, which contained the full orchestral scores of almost all the old ballets. They had been purchased by Metro-Goldwyn-Mayer when the old theatre was bought by them to be rebuilt as a cinema. I cannot describe the thrill I felt when I discovered those old scores, and how glad I was to find Sandy Macpherson had taken such good care of them. To have found all the music for *The Débutante* intact was an enormous help.

I persuaded Genée to let Cuthbert Clarke, the composer of the music, conduct for us, as he had done in the old days. We were able to use the original C. Wilhelm designs for our costumes, most of which were made for us by B. J. Simmons of Covent Garden.

It was very exciting, even if hard work for me, to be responsible
for this revival. But our young members rose to the occasion.
It is far from easy to produce a ballet quickly with a company of
dancers who are not constantly together as a team. There were
bound to be shortcomings if we were compared with any of the
fully professional ballet companies. No one knew that better
than I did; but, even so, I was very proud and very gratified by
the success we achieved on the opening night, and still more so
when Sir Oswald Stoll extended our engagement for several
weeks.

The opening night was a specially important one because Genée
appeared with Anton Dolin in *The Love Song*, which they had
danced together at Copenhagen. It was heart-warming to hear
the enthusiastic reception she received that night in a theatre
where she had appeared so successfully nearly twenty years before.

In the opening week's programme there was also a Hungarian
ballet called *The Whitsun King*, with choreography by Derra de
Meroda, in which Anton Dolin played the leading part with
Wendy Toye. They wore some of the loveliest Hungarian
costumes I have ever seen. Later in the season, in place of *The
Whitsun King*, Dolin revived *The Nightingale and the Rose* for himself and had Markova as his partner.

All this time I was kept extremely busy. I was up early every
morning to have breakfast with Ian and my children; then I
taught my pupils all the rest of the morning, had a light meal, and
left for the theatre, where I arrived about 2 o'clock and practised
at the back of the stage for an hour. It took me another hour
to make up and dress; and the curtain went up on *The Débutante*
at 4 o'clock. Between the performances I would rush home by
taxi for another light meal and write letters and do the book-
keeping for the school. Then back I went to the Coliseum for
the evening show. That was my daily programme for five weeks;
but I loved every moment of it.

Genée's return to the stage proved to be such an overwhelming
attraction that she was persuaded by Sir Oswald Stoll to appear
at every performance the following week and during the last
fortnight of the run. It made me proud to be associated with her
on so historic an occasion—it was the last time she danced in
public. We had adjoining dressing-rooms with a communicating
door through which we were able to talk over our experiences
and the many intimate little happenings of the day's work.

The last day of the engagement was nerve-racking for everyone but more especially for me. When I got to the matinée Harold came to tell me he was feeling ill. There was no doubt that he had a severe attack of influenza; but, as we had no understudy for him and it was impossible to teach anyone his part in an hour or so, I begged him to make an effort to appear. He did. I could feel how ill he was as we danced together; the *pas de deux* work with its many difficult lifts and supported pirouettes must have been a great strain for him. When the curtain fell at the end of the matinée he collapsed, and I was almost distraught with anxiety. I did all I could to help him. I stayed with him in his room which I darkened; I dosed him with aspirin and hot drinks. But he lay there in an absolute bath of perspiration. The cushions on the sofa were soaked.

When it was time to prepare for our last performance that evening all of us helped to dress Harold, and he made a super-human effort. By some miracle our prayers were answered and he managed to get through the show; but as the curtain came down for the last time he fell on to the stage, a crumpled heap. Harold was certainly the hero of that night. He saved the situation for all of us. It would have been a disaster for the whole company if we had had to cancel the show on the last night.

After this I had less than a fortnight to get ready for a visit to South Africa where I was to hold examinations for the Association of Operatic Dancing and give recitals. I left my school in charge of Felix Andreae and Ian was to do the office work and book-keeping. Harold Turner had been giving weekly *pas de deux* classes for me, and this he continued to do while I was away.

40

WHEN I EMBARKED on the *Edinburgh Castle* I was welcomed at the gangway by the father of one of my pupils, who was the Chief Steward on the ship. His daughter had given him instructions to look after me 'like a queen', and this he certainly did. My slightest wish was granted almost before I had uttered it. Every steward on the ship seemed to be waiting to do my bidding. I ate at the Captain's table and occupied one of the finest cabins on board.

We called only at Madeira, where we spent about twelve hours ashore, sightseeing. There, nearly all the passengers disembarked, leaving only thirteen first-class passengers to continue the voyage to Cape Town. Those of us who remained got along splendidly together. It was more like being on a well-run private yacht than on a liner.

Early every morning I did my practice on the boat deck before breakfast, and then had a bathe in the canvas swimming pool. The rest of my time I spent playing deck games or lazily reading. After tea we would occasionally play in a tournament with the ship's officers, or swim. After a good dinner we danced until bed-time.

We reached Cape Town on the morning of 3 April as daylight was breaking. I hurried up on deck in my dressing-gown and was so enthralled by the view of Table Mountain in the strange morning light, that I felt I had to run along to the others' cabins and beg them to come with me and see it too. I am afraid I was not too popular at breakfast that morning. I was the only one to whom the lovely scene was unfamiliar. The rest of the passengers lacked my enthusiasm, and would have preferred to be allowed to sleep for another hour or so.

Breakfast was served early; and, while I was eating it, I was told that a deputation of Cape Town teachers and representatives of the South African Dancing Teachers' Association were already waiting to welcome me in the ship's lounge. There were the usual interviews and press photographs to be taken before I could go ashore.

After hasty farewells to the various friends I had made on board and promises to meet again, I was ushered into a car and driven to the Marine Hotel, Sea Point, where I was to stay. At 10 in the morning a tea party was given for me, at which I met all the local teachers and the officials connected with my visit. Hospitality certainly began early in South Africa!

Some of the teachers wanted me to give private lessons that very day in order to clear up some of their difficulties. Such a thing was impossible, I told them: it was against the Association's rules to give lessons beforehand; and I had to begin my work early next morning. However, I offered to compromise by answering any questions while everyone was there, so that there should be no ill-feeling or misunderstandings afterwards. Little did I realize what I was letting myself in for. It was a blazing hot day, and I discovered that I was expected to demonstrate every syllabus from Grade I to Advanced.

It meant going through the entire work of eight examinations and there was scarcely time for me to sit down. I was dripping with perspiration. It surprised me that there could be so many teachers of ballet dancing in Cape Town. All sixteen of them certainly had the best out of me that day. It was 5 o'clock before we finished; then I still had to unpack all my stage costumes as well as my own clothes, and the various papers for the examinations which I had brought over in a crate. I was only too glad to get into a bath and relax before dinner.

I dined at the Mount Nelson Hotel with Herman Eckstein and Mrs Lean, whom I had met on board the *Edinburgh Castle*. Next day I rose very early to practise before I began examining. Examinations took four days, from Tuesday to Friday, and there were nearly a hundred candidates to be judged, both in the Children's Grades and Major Students' work.

Once I did manage to finish in time to go to a symphony concert.

When it was all over, on Friday evening, I was dressing to go to dinner at the Mount Nelson when I received an urgent message from the Cape Town Broadcasting Studios, asking me to give a talk on 'Ballet in England' at 9.15 that night. I felt I could not refuse such an opportunity, particularly as the representative of the Association of Operatic Dancing. But there was very little time to prepare a talk. During dinner with my friends I made a few notes of important points to which I needed to refer; and then we all went off to the studio. Mr Eckstein and Mrs Lean were able to sit behind a glass panel in an adjoining room and listen to me. I was just let loose on the air, to say whatever I liked!

I spent all next morning before getting a train for Johannesburg rehearsing with the Cape Town Municipal Orchestra for the recital I was to give on my return in four weeks' time. Mr Eckstein had pulled some strings and I found I had a very comfortable carriage to myself, convertible into a sleeping-car at night. It was rather a lonely journey; but I could sleep whenever I wished. The sunsets over the veldt were awe inspiring. I had never seen such vivid colouring in the sky. Whenever we passed slowly through the wayside stations coal-black piccaninnies, completely naked, would come to the windows of the train, begging for food. I had been presented with several baskets of fruit and a big packing-case containing honey-dew grapes before I left Cape Town. I could not possibly hope to eat it all myself; I gave those hungry babies peaches and pears and grapes and was happy to see their wide, beaming smiles of gratitude.

For many months there had been a serious drought and, in consequence, the most awful dust was everywhere. The train attendants came in to clean my carriage several times a day, but very soon afterwards dust was lying thickly over everything again. Even the food got gritty. I found it difficult to keep clean. And the heat—the heat was intense.

I arrived at Johannesburg on Monday 10 April, and was met by one of my oldest friends, Mrs Cora Lawrence, who had been Edgar Wallace's great friend during my de Courville engagement. For the first week I was hard at work judging the dancing competitions at the Festival from early in the morning until late evening. Even so, I had to rehearse for my recital with my pianist, Mrs Wellbeloved.

I saw some excellent work at these competitions. Two little girls made a particularly good impression on me. They were Fanny Levy, who danced an operatic solo in the 11–13 age group, and Zoe Stapleton, in the Open Class, who was a budding Binnie Hale. I often wonder what became of them.

In the teachers' section of the competition Marjorie Sturman gained 100% marks for her operatic (ballet) solo dance. I had never expected to encounter a candidate with her quality. Technically her performance appeared absolutely faultless. I was obviously not alone in my opinion for, when I announced the result, deafening cheers from the audience showed plainly enough that others shared it.

I gave my first recital in South Africa at His Majesty's Theatre, Johannesburg, a week and a day after I arrived in the country. Because of the difficulty of transporting costumes and heavy orchestral parts I had deliberately confined my programme to five solo dances, and had the help of pupils from local schools, who also danced. There was a full house and I realized that I should be facing a critical audience and was very nervous; but I need not have worried.

Although everyone expected I would be affected by the altitude, except for a slight breathlessness I felt on top of my form. In my wildest dreams I have never expected such a wonderful response. It was almost embarrassing. Afterwards my room was full of flowers and gifts. One woman, not a dancer, insisted upon giving me a beautiful first-water diamond which had been found on her father's country estate. She had it cut and set as a single-stone ring for me before I left, in gratitude, she said, for the pleasure my dancing had given her.

Even over the Easter week-end I was working solidly to get through the examinations in time. I managed to get away for half a day to attend the Horse Show, and had another short break on the day I was taken to see the native mine-workers doing their tribal dances. It was a thrilling experience. The fanatical enthusiasm and the throbbing rhythm of these dances was terrifying sometimes. For days afterwards I could feel the thudding of it in my head. The dancers wore most extraordinary garments; some of them, I noticed, decorated themselves with safety pins which had been stuck through their flesh. They leapt furiously about, working themselves into a frenzy, until finally they dropped to the ground through sheer exhaustion.

One evening, when I had finished work late and was too tired to eat, Cora Lawrence took me to visit Uncle Sam (Alexander), a Johannesburg personality, an elderly, jovial man who seemed to know dozens of my own theatrical friends. He had a collection of wine bottles from every country which I believe must have been unique. There were hundreds of them, many with strange labels I had never seen before.

Durban, which was the next stage of my journey, I found tropically hot; but, although I had far too much work to do—examinations and making the arrangements for my recital—I enjoyed my five days there enormously. I found everybody so kind and hospitable and more pro-British than elsewhere—although wherever I went in South Africa I was well treated. In Durban, however, there was an atmosphere of sheer goodwill.

I was entertained delightfully by Mr and Mrs Seals-Wood and their daughter, and danced at the Marine Hotel in a roofless ball-room open to the night sky. Mr and Mrs Otto Siedle gave a reception in my honour, and I attended a big luncheon arranged by the Goodwill Club. My recital at the Theatre Royal was quite extraordinarily successful.

By Friday the 5th I was back in Cape Town, where I stayed at the Hotel Assembly, which was nearer to my work than the

Marine Hotel had been. In the week which remained to me before I was due to return to England there were another 112 dancers to examine and rehearsals for my farewell recital to be fitted in.

I began the examinations at once, and on Saturday I also rehearsed with the orchestra for three hours, which meant that I did not finish work until 9 in the evening. Each day was as strenuous. I had no time to relax.

However, my recital at the City Hall in Cape Town was the biggest success of the three I gave in South Africa. This was mainly due to the fact that I had a first-class symphony orchestra to play for me. My programme for each of these recitals consisted of *Romance* (Rubinstein), *Gavotte* (Arne), *Humoresque* (Dvořák), *Russian Court Dance* (to a traditional tune), and *Coquette* (Frank E. Tours). The orchestra played several items; Delis Rohr, who had been a pupil of my friend Elsa Brunelleschi in London, danced a Spanish solo; and there were three charming group dances by pupils of local teachers.

I received masses of flowers. The Mayoress, who, with the Governor-General, Lord Clarendon, and the Mayor, had been present, made a gracious speech and presented me with an enormous ostrich feather fan on behalf of the S.A.D.T.A. This, mounted on tortoiseshell, was so large that I could hide behind it when it was opened.

Next day I was in the middle of examinations when a message was brought from Government House inviting me to lunch with Lord and Lady Clarendon. As I had to carry on with my work until a few minutes before lunch time, there was no time for me to change for such an important occasion. When I arrived, however, I was very soon put at my ease: praise was showered upon me by those who had seen me dance on the previous evening.

I returned rather late for the afternoon session of the examinations, but, after I had explained the delay, everyone agreed that it would have been impossible for me to have left the Governor-General's party before it ended. I put in extra time with the candidates that evening and, in consequence, was too late for dinner at the hotel. I had something to drink and half a dozen oysters, and then went for a drive with Mr Eckstein up Table Mountain to see the twinkling lights of Cape Town below.

For my last day in South Africa the time-table was extremely full, because a large number of 'late entries' had been accepted

194

for examination, many of whom were candidates who had passed lower grades earlier in the session and now wished to attempt more advanced work. The Association sent an examiner only every second year, which caused this congestion. To make matters worse I was suddenly extremely ill. I was writhing in agony and fainting all the time. Once before, I had had a similar attack when I had been in a box at the Albert Hall with Mrs Malcolm Sargent for a performance of *The Dream of Gerontius*. I had seen a specialist, who had diagnosed gall-stones, but when I was X-rayed the diagnosis was not confirmed. Now I began to think the specialist had been right after all. I had two hours of this appalling pain before I was able to pull myself together and continue the examinations. There was no time to see all the extra entries; there were, I am afraid, not a few disgruntled candidates whom I had had to disappoint. I tried to be fair and selected those who had travelled great distances, but, even so, there must have been many who did not forgive me!

As I had so much packing to do I scarcely had any sleep that night. I sailed the following morning in the *Arundel Castle*, and arrived home on 31 May.

Felix, to whom I was very grateful, had kept the classes together splendidly in my absence. And she at once became a pupil again and worked amicably with the students whom she had been teaching. It was evident that they had all grown fond of her.

41

My appearance in *Hiawatha* that year (1933) was to be my last. As Malcolm Sargent was seriously ill our performances were conducted by various conductors, Geoffrey Toye, Foster Clarke, and Muir Matheson. We all missed Malcolm so much that it occurred to Myrtle d'Erlanger and me that we should send him some token of everyone's good wishes. There was unanimous agreement upon this. Myrtle and I opened a fund, and had contributions from everyone who appeared in *Hiawatha* that season—members of the Royal Choral Society, the orchestra, the ballet, and from all the principal singers. With the money we bought a beautifully tooled leather-bound book in which we all signed our names. On the Sunday after the show ended Myrtle and I drove to Alton in Hampshire, where Malcolm was in hospital, and presented him with the album and a substantial cheque.

It was touching to see his pleasure at receiving this gift from so many devoted well-wishers.

In the months after my return from South Africa and before my retirement from the stage in 1935, much was happening in London to delight the lovers of the ballet. The programmes of the Vic-Wells Company had all the rich diversity and the unpredictability of adventurous youth. We who had worked and hoped for the founding of a national ballet felt excited by the promise of their work. I can well recall my personal excitement.

The Vic-Wells season opened with *The Wise and Foolish Virgins*, with Ninette de Valois's choreography, which was followed by *Job*, in which Robert Helpmann appeared as Satan. He made a good impression; but as he was more slightly built than Anton Dolin he seemed at first to lack some of the strength and attack to which we had become accustomed in Dolin's interpretation. Markova also danced beautifully in the Blue Bird *pas de deux* with Stanislas Idzikowsky. He, as always, was magnificent. He was guest artist with the company that season, as Dolin was appearing at the Gaiety in a play called *Ballerina* by Eleanor Smith, and, as well as dancing in it, had a long speaking part. Lydia Kyasht played the part of a retiring ballerina, and had to make a charming speech of farewell.

The chief role was taken by Frances Doble. I found it interesting to see how cleverly Pat Dolin supported her and succeeded, so far as the public was concerned, in completely disguising the fact that she was not in fact an accomplished *danseuse*. The dancing scenes were doubled by Wendy Toye, who wore a mask.

Elsewhere interesting things were also happening. At the Savoy the Kurt Jooss Ballet made its first appearance with *The Green Table* and *Les Ballets, 1933* from the *Théâtre des Champs-Elysées*, a company which had Balanchine as choreographer. I found the latter company's work modern and also ugly. In *Mozartiana* Balanchine had arranged some extraordinarily ungraceful movements for Tamara Toumanova, whose *tutu* was far too short. Mozart's delightful music and Toumanova's quality seemed wasted. Tilly Losch danced in *Errante* to Schubert's lovely *Wanderer* music; and here, too, the Central European influence was evident.

196

I took my mother to the Alhambra for the opening night of Colonel de Basil's *Les Ballets Russes de Monte Carlo*. A charming performance of *Les Sylphides* was followed by the first of Massine's symphonic ballets, *Les Présages*, set to the music of Tchaikovsky's fifth symphony. When the curtain fell on this both mother and I were crying for joy; and I heard myself shouting 'Bravo!' at the top of my voice, as any gallery girl might do. This was a company to be seen as often as possible, I decided. Baronova and Riabouchinska were mere children in their early teens and yet they had the 'grand manner' and the technique of true ballerinas.

At a party after their first performance I was amazed at their extreme youth. Upon being introduced to me they made charming little curtsies; and I realized with something of a shock that, had they been English, they would hardly have been out of their nurseries.

Alexandra Danilova, who was also dancing with the company, was then at the height of her powers. Massine himself was dancing; also Eglevsky, Helene Kirsova, Shabelevsky; and Anton Dolin made an occasional appearance with them as guest artist.

A company called Les Ballets Leon Woizikovsky came to the Coliseum. Amongst other items they revived *Petrouchka* and *Carnaval*. Eglevsky and Nina Tarakanova were in the company. Woizikovsky gave a thrilling performance as the Tartar Chief in *Prince Igor*—as impressive a show as Adolf Bolm's in 1911, when I saw him dance it for the first time with the Diaghilev company. My pupil Barbara Barrie had joined this company, and, at the end of the season at the Coliseum, she toured with them in Germany, France, and Spain.

The Camargo Society, after an impressive gala performance at Covent Garden attended by Her Majesty the Queen and Their Royal Highnesses the Duke and Duchess of York, and a second performance at which the Prime Minister, members of the government, and delegates to the World Economic Conference were present, was once again in funds. Its finances had been in a precarious state. The programme on this occasion consisted of two acts of *Coppélia* and the second act of *Le Lac des Cygnes*. Lydia Lopokova played Swanilda and I liked her most when she was impersonating the doll in Act II. I was not so impressed with her performance in Act I; perhaps my memories of Genée in the part made it difficult for me to enjoy Lopokova's interpretation. Markova and Dolin, supported by the Vic-Wells Ballet, danced excellently in *Le Lac des Cygnes*.

In December 1933 Frederick Ashton produced *Les Rendezvous* set to Auber's music—a jolly affair of brilliantly arranged dances. The company had begun to make regular weekly appearances, and was building up its repertoire and becoming more firmly established with its audiences. On New Year's Day *Giselle* was produced, with Markova and Dolin. The choreography of Ivanov was used, with the help of Sergueeff, who had brought the notation from Russia.

The Camargo Society decided to take stock and to consider its position anew in the changing circumstances. We held many meetings before deciding what was the right thing to do. Everyone felt that the regular special Sunday performances, involving as they did heavy expenses, were no longer necessary now that the Vic-Wells Ballet was so well established, and the Ballet Club under Marie Rambert was catering for the 'intimate' ballet audiences. We had served our purpose. Our existing funds amounted to about £200. This sum, together with anything further we could collect, it was decided should be devoted to helping the Vic-Wells Company to extend its repertoire. With the same object we gave the company all the scores, scenery, and costumes we had collected during our few years of existence.

To celebrate the decision Mr Richardson and the *Dancing Times* organized a Dancer's Circle Dinner at the Criterion Restaurant one Sunday in January 1934. The guests of honour were Lilian Baylis, Ninette de Valois, and the principals of the Vic-Wells Ballet. It had been intended that the chairman should be Anton Dolin; but owing to illness he was unable to be present and his place was taken by Philip Richardson, who made an excellent speech and then read what Dolin had intended to say, paying high tribute to both Markova and Ninette de Valois and also acknowledging the splendid support given to English ballet by Lilian Baylis.

Professor Maynard Keynes then spoke, and told those present of the Camargo Society's decision. After Lilian Baylis had returned thanks in an amusing speech, Ninette de Valois spoke of the various difficulties which arose when producing ballets to please everyone. It fell to my lot to propose the toast of the Chairman, who made a characteristically charming reply.

A first production in England of the complete version of Tchaikovsky's *Casse Noisette* followed at the end of January. On this occasion it was again Sergueeff who was responsible for reviving Ivanov's choreography. English ballet owes him much, and without his help might not be in so strong a position to-day, for ballet is to be judged by the standards set in the full-length classical works as well as by its ability to move with the times. Subsequently Sergueeff reproduced Petipa's choreography when *Le Lac des Cygnes* was first produced in its entirety; but, before that, there were two new Ninette de Valois ballets, *The Haunted Ballroom*, which is still a favourite work, and *The Jar*, which had music by Alfredo Casella and was based on a story by Pirandello. This somehow just missed being good.

Rio Grande was given its first performances by the Vic-Wells company; and this was also an eventful evening because a new star appeared, who had been promoted from the *corps de ballet* to dance the Creole Girl. She was Margot Fonteyn.

On the opening night of a two weeks' season at Sadler's Wells given in association with Mrs Laura Henderson of Vivan Van Damm Productions, we saw Ninette's new ballet, *The Rake's Progress*, with Gavin Gordon's music and excellent settings and costumes by Rex Whistler, inspired by Hogarth. It was an immediate success; and I still consider it, together with *Job*, to be Ninette's finest work.

After that fortnight at Sadler's Wells Mrs Henderson took the Shaftesbury Theatre for two weeks in order that the company might be seen in the West End; but it was not the right theatre for them. I think the company felt out of its element.

This was the last time London saw those great dancers, Markova and Dolin, leading the Vic-Wells Company, although they remained with the company during their provincial tour that summer. There was much speculation and discussion among those who had become *habitués* of the Sadler's Wells Theatre about the loss of Markova and Dolin, and the effect this was likely to have upon the prestige of the Vic-Wells Company. Both Lilian Baylis and Ninette de Valois were determined that their efforts should not be harmed by Markova and Dolin forming their new company, to tour under the management of Mrs Laura Henderson and Vivian Van Damm. Time has shown that this apparently stunning blow was a blessing in disguise for the company. There is nothing more beneficial to youth and ambition than to be up against rivals. The way was opened to the younger members to grasp their opportunities and prove their worth in important roles.

This they did. On the opening night of their next autumn season the air seemed electric. Margot Fonteyn had a personal triumph, dancing the part originally created for Markova in *Les Rendezvous*. *The Rake's Progress* had Robert Helpmann, Elizabeth Miller, and Harold Turner. And Fokine's *Carnaval* was revived with Helpmann again dancing as Harlequin, Pearl Argyle as Columbine, Frederick Ashton as Pierrot, and Mary Honer as Papillon.

A fortnight later the company was seen for the first time in *Façade*, which Frederick Ashton had produced with so much success for the Camargo Society in 1931. A new dance was introduced for Pearl Argyle, with Robert Helpmann as a Squire amusingly flirting with a country girl. To everyone's delight Margot Fonteyn danced the Polka. There was no doubt this young dancer was quickly winning all hearts. But the whole company seemed full of enthusiasm and eager to win through. It was, as I have said, exciting and exhilarating to watch it steadily grow in strength and prestige.

42

THE NUMBER of my pupils continued to increase. I had several from the Dominions, among whom were Bettina Byers and Alison Sutcliffe from Canada. Alison was herself a teacher and had previously studied with Fokine. She had joined my school while I was on holiday at 'Pitmuies'; and, in my absence, Mother had commissioned her to teach Jean a Mexican Hat Dance. It was a delightful surprise when Jean danced this for me, dressed in the correct costume, which Mother had made for her. By now Jean was nearly nine. This was the very first character dance she learned.

May Warren and Joyce Catherine were from South Africa. Others who came to me from the Dominions were Signe and Courtney Green, Daphne Lane, Joan Turner, Verity Sweeney, and Laurel Gill. Laurel Gill came from Brisbane. She had arrived with her mother, father, and brother, who were paying a short, holiday visit while they made arrangements to leave Laurel in England. They asked if I would take her into my house as a resident pupil. I was able to do so as Barbara Miles—whom I had renamed Barbara Barrie—had just left to take up an engagement after having lived with us for some years while she trained. I have never known a more enthusiastic or conscientious worker than Laurel, even if she was inclined to be temperamental sometimes when she was dissatisfied with the progress she was making. She studied with me for several years and, within two years, she passed the Elementary, Intermediate, Advanced, and Solo Seal examinations, was awarded the Choreographic Scholarship of the Association of Operatic Dancing, and given a contract by Lilian Baylis for two years with the Vic-Wells Ballet. That, I think, must be a record achievement.

We changed her name to Laurel Martyn, which was a family name. Now she is in Australia, where for several years she has been *prima ballerina* of the Australian Ballet Company, and head of the Ballet Guild of Australia and its chief choreographer.

As my school grew so quickly I soon needed an assistant, and engaged Edna Slocombe, who had been trained at the Studio School at Liverpool. This was a small revolution as far as I was concerned: previously I had given all the lessons myself. She had not only passed some of her A.O.D. examinations but was expert at tap and musical comedy dancing. I knew that some of my young pupils would not 'make the grade' for a first-class ballet company and, for this reason, included all branches of dancing in my full student's training. They could leave me to become proficient 'G.P.' teachers or to go on to the musical stage.

My house was already too small, and I applied for permission to build a large studio in the garden. For many months negotiations continued with the ground landlords, but eventually fell through—much to my disappointment.

I felt the time had come to give a students' recital. We spent a lot of time rehearsing. I thought it would be a good idea if, instead of the usual matinée or evening performance, I made it a more informal affair. I booked the Rudolf Steiner Hall for 26 March 1934, and we had the show from 5.15 until 7 o'clock in the evening.

Tickets were sold unnumbered so that those who came could sit next to any friends they might happen to meet there. When the performance ended I had a light buffet supper on the stage for both audience and dancers.

Among my dancers were Pamela Foster, who had just returned from a Continental tour as *première danseuse* of the Gsovsky Ballet, and Felicity Andreae. Both had already passed the Solo Seal Examination with Honours. One of the most successful items was a dance I arranged to Tchaikovsky's *Humoresque*, which I called *The Proud Mother*. Olive Killingback, a very tall girl, was dressed as Mother Hen who had two little chicks, danced by Jean Axten and my small daughter. All three of them danced *sur les pointes*, the chicks copying whatever Mother Hen did; and the dance ended with the two chicks cuddling under their mother's wings.

Pamela Foster and John Byron danced *Clair de Lune*; and later John performed in *The Blue Danube* with Felicity Andreae. This, I had previously arranged when John danced it with me at a big charity ball in the Albert Hall.

The recital was very successful, but I did not repeat the experiment of the buffet supper in later pupils' shows as I found it took too much organizing and was far too expensive.

Here I must mention a production of the dramatized version of Handel's *Messiah* which I regretted none of my London friends saw. It was given at Sheffield's City Hall, under the musical direction of Eva Rich. In the first of my two appearances in this I danced to the music of the *Pastoral Symphony*. I wore a long, dark blue, clinging georgette dress, off one shoulder, and a very long veil of a lighter blue which completely concealed my hair and gave the impression of a figure in stained glass. The lighting was dimmed; and, seated at one side of the stage, I had the shepherds watching their flocks. The idea of the dance was the approach of a Heavenly Messenger who was to tell in mime and movement of the coming of Christ.

At dress rehearsal many people said they thought it was very beautiful. I told them that if the audience applauded after my exit I would know I had failed. At each performance there was an extraordinary hush and, I am glad to say, no applause. However I did receive a number of letters telling me how much those who saw it had loved my dancing.

My other appearance was in a ballet scene showing King Herod's Court. I played Salomé. Bransby Williams gave a fine performance as Herod. For my dance I used Saint-Saëns's

Bacchanale which, strangely enough, fitted in extremely well and did not upset the music critics unduly. It gave me a good opportunity to work up to a climax as I danced round the head of John the Baptist which had been brought to me by an enormous Negro. Gradually all at Herod's Court shrank away in horror, leaving me gloating; then, as I realized that, except for the single Negro slave, I was alone with the head of my victim, I became terror-stricken and ran.

At every performance I was completely exhausted after that dance; but I knew in my heart that it was one of the best things I had ever done.

In May 1934, John Byron, Barbara Batrie, Ella Bennett, and Felicity Andreae were all engaged for a new ballet company which was to tour the large provincial towns during the summer. Kathleen McVitie appeared at the Windmill in London and Jean Gillie was at the Trocadero. Pam Foster—certainly a versatile pupil—made a big success in cabaret at Grosvenor House, dancing the Can Can!

I had promised to dance in *Hiawatha* as usual, but had to break my word because I had hurt my foot and dared not risk making it worse, and I was also suffering a good deal of pain from time to time with attacks similar to the one I had had in Cape Town.

During the June session of the Association of Operatic Dancing examinations Jean passed the Advanced with Honours, her examiners being Felix Demery and Judith Espinosa, who told me afterwards that owing to Jean's extreme youth they felt she ought not to be given honours if they could catch her out in anything. But her work had been quite faultless that day and there was nothing for it but to give her what she deserved. She was then nine years and ten months old. At the same session Laurel Gill passed the Intermediate examination with Honours; and that year the Adeline Genée Gold Medal competition was won by Felicity Andreae.

Ian and I were again invited to 'Pitmuies' during July and August; but it could not be the same again, for 'Hunk' had died some months before. It seemed to all of us who knew him that a great, shining light had been extinguished. He had been so much the centre around which our happiness had revolved. I could not believe that I should never see him again. The last time we met he had seemed so full of life with that glorious, boy-like sense of fun of his. I remembered that on our walks together he had told me his doctor had said his heart was not strong and that he should run no undue risks. He had begged me not to tell his family as he did not wish them to be anxious.

It seemed that he had gone on a shoot with some friends, and it had rained. He had caught a chill which turned to pneumonia, and, while lying ill, he had had some teeth extracted. His heart failed and he died.

Ian and I travelled up to Scotland by the night train. It was fortunate we had a sleeper for, during the journey, I was seized with a violent attack of pain which lasted longer than any of the previous ones. After we arrived at 'Pitmuies' I had three more attacks, each more agonizing than the last. The Crombies' family doctor was called in. He at once decided I ought to go to hospital—possibly for an operation.

I begged to go back to London and the doctor made all the arrangements by telephone for me to be given a private room in the Woolavington Wing of the Middlesex Hospital. Within thirty-six hours Ian and I were there. We had driven straight from the station to the hospital; and Ian went home to a lonely house as I had given the maids a holiday and the children had gone to stay at Parkstone in Dorset with their old Nannie and her husband. Ian managed to look after himself and spent much of his spare time with my mother in her flat. They were good for each other, as Ian was very calm and unruffled while Mother had always been anxious if I had had any sort of illness.

Four weeks after the operation I returned home and by then the maids were back from their holiday and looked after me until I was able to travel. I returned to 'Pitmuies' alone to convalesce. Dear 'Munk' was very sweet to me and her son, Teddy, and two daughters, Peggy and Adrienne, were there, too, and so was George Chavchavadze. But how we all missed dear 'Hunk'. I spent hours remembering him as I lay in the lovely garden which he had planted and cared for.

Another of Mrs Crombie's great friends, Captain Hugh Binney, R.N., came to stay while I was there and talked to me about David. He was interested to hear of my son's ambition to join the Navy, and I gathered that he had been for some time a member of the Selection Board at the Admiralty for candidates entering Dartmouth. I asked him if, when next in London, he would talk to David and give us his advice. This he promised to do. Shortly afterwards he came to see us at Maida Vale and saw David alone for about three quarters of an hour. He told me he felt sure that David was the type of boy the navy required but advised me to send him to a boarding-school which specialized in preparing boys for Dartmouth, as generally boys who had been to boarding-school were preferred to those who had always lived at home. It was decided to send David to Stubbington House School in Hampshire, to whose headmaster, Mr Foster, I was introduced by Admiral Greatorex, whom I had also met at 'Pitmuies'.

While I had been away in Scotland Edna Slocombe had been taking my classes for me. By the end of September, however, I was fit enough to begin teaching again, though I was still unable to demonstrate the work. It was then that I learned the art of teaching verbally which, now I am too old to dance, I find invaluable. It is a little wearing for the voice, as it involves making a continuous running commentary of corrections.

Among new students who arrived were Christopher Casson, the son of Sir Lewis Casson and Dame Sybil Thorndike, and a bright-eyed girl fresh from school, Iris Truscott, who showed much talent and, twelve years later, became my head assistant. Then she was a beginner; but she was soon making great progress. Christopher worked with me until he took his Elementary examination; but then he decided to give up dancing, which I think was wise as he was starting rather late and had not the same facility as John Byron had had. John Byron had been appearing with success on Television with Doris Sonne.

In the September session of the A.O.D. examinations Elizabeth Kennedy became an advanced member. During the forty-six working weeks she had studied with me she had passed the Elementary, Intermediate, and Advanced examinations—which I found most gratifying.

John Byron then joined the Vic-Wells Ballet. With Claude Newman also in the company I had the pleasure of seeing two young men who had received all their early training with me making a success in their chosen careers.

In November 1934 the Annual Competition held by the Association of Operatic Dancing for the Pavlova Casket was won for my school by Felicity Andreae. This much-coveted trophy had been presented to the association by P. J. S. Richardson, who had bought the casket at a sale of the late Anna Pavlova's treasures. The competition was for the best group number performed, and composed by members of the Association. It was the first time

Felix had attempted choreography, except when arranging her own solo dances, and I was naturally proud of the good work she did. For a whole year we had the casket on show in my studio until the next competition. So far we have not won it again; but we have only made two other attempts: one by Laurel Gill in 1935 and one by my daughter in 1948.

That autumn, 1934, my mother went hunting for more suitable premises for the school. I had been on the books of local house agents for some months, ever since I had been told I could not build a studio in the garden of our present house, but nothing of interest seemed to come on the market. One morning during the lunch break Mother came to me, full of excitement.

'You must come and see what I've found', she said.

I left my classes in Edna Slocombe's charge, and with Mother and a Kilburn house agent went to 28 Quex Road. It was just what I had been seeking for so long—only a short distance from where we lived, but in a district I had not previously visited. We found it conveniently situated, with excellent bus services and not far from the Underground. Opposite to the house was a Catholic church: so we were not overlooked; and next door to the church there was a Unitarian church with a big hall attached to it which could be let to us whenever we needed a second studio.

Another advantage was that Quex Road was a turning off the Kilburn High Road, which had every kind of shop and many inexpensive restaurants, where my students could have lunch and tea without disturbing my kitchen staff.

I could scarcely believe my eyes. There it was: a big, detached house with a ready-made studio with dressing-rooms which occupied the entire ground level of the house and led on to a large garden.

I immediately made an offer to buy the thirty-one-year lease, but was told that only ten minutes before a previous offer had been accepted by the agent and an agreement signed. To cut short a long story: I bought the house from the people who had forestalled me by offering them several hundred pounds more than they had paid for it. It was the only thing to do. I had to have this ideal house for my school. Imagine my chagrin when I heard that for over two years Mr and Mrs Randall (Edith Bishop, who had for many years been a well-known teacher of ballroom dancing and was now retiring), the original owners of the lease, had been trying to sell it and that the purchasers were only buying it as a speculation.

206

There was a great deal of work to be done, inside and outside, before the house looked as I wished, but in those days there were not as many difficulties as there are now. It was an exciting period. Every few days I managed to go along there to see how the work on the house was progressing. I had to visit firms about bathroom fittings and interior decoration. Generally I managed these calls during my lunch hour. We moved in just before Christmas.

As soon as we were settled in I re-opened my school. That was at the beginning of January 1935. In addition to taking at least four classes a day myself I had the help of Edna Slocombe and Stanislas Idzikowsky for character (Polish) dancing, Ann Driver for eurhythmics, and Zelia Raye for tap dancing—the last three were guest teachers. I was thus able to offer my students very good value for their money and, possessing such a lovely big studio, my school could expand in every direction.

We had a jolly house-warming on the Sunday before we opened for classes. All my friends were delighted that I had at last found what I wanted. Some asked me why I preferred living where I worked. I told them it saved me a great deal of time and energy and that it was pleasant to be home and to be able to relax whenever I had a free hour. I remain of that opinion.

43

THE AIMS for which the Association of Operatic Dancing had striven had always been my own. Its work was—and is still—near to my heart. I have watched and helped it grow in strength and authority.

After discussion, a revision of our examination methods was undertaken: instead of taking forty-five candidates at a time with the whole committee judging, which meant that a single examination lasted all day, we decided to take only four candidates at a time, with two examiners, and that each examination should last for an hour. The method is still used. It is far less exhausting for the entrants and also, we feel, better for the examiners.

Among the first of the functions I attended on my return from South Africa was a dinner organized by a small committee, consisting of Tamara Karsavina, myself, Felix Demery, and P. J. S.

Richardson, to pay tribute to Adeline Genée. We had the help of a large honorary committee of very famous people headed by His Excellency the Danish Minister, Count Preben Ahlefeldt-Laurvig, G.C.V.O., and his wife, the Earl and Countess of Albemarle, and many connected with the theatre and the arts. It gave us all an opportunity to show our gratitude for Madame Genée's interest in the welfare of English dancing as well as our love for her as an artist and a friend.

The dinner was an outstanding success. Two hundred and fifty guests were present. Sir William Llewellyn, President of the Royal Academy, took the chair; and, at the beginning of the evening, one of the youngest scholars of the Association, Marjorie Richards, presented a bouquet with the inscription, '*To Adeline Genée with love from the young dancers of England.*'

Speeches followed—by Sir William on behalf of the painters, Sir Landon Ronald for Music, Mr (now Sir) Kenneth Barnes, principal of the Royal Academy of Dramatic Art, for Drama, Madame Karsavina, representing the Diaghilev Ballet, myself as a life-long subject of this Queen of the Dance, and P. J. S. Richardson for the Association. Then the chairman made a presentation on behalf of subscribers, who numbered nearly a thousand. The tribute was a very beautiful, specially made fitted dressing-case, and a cheque, which was given by Madame Genée to the Association of Operatic Dancing Building Fund.

When she rose to reply there were loud and prolonged cheers, which must have proved to her—if proof had been needed—what great affection and gratitude we all felt.

Another happy occasion was the large tea party which the Association gave to honour Colonel de Basil and his wonderful company shortly after their Alhambra season opened. I had Danilova and Baronova at my table. Dear Judith Espinosa was with us, too, and her fluent French helped to keep conversation flowing easily, because at that time Baronova knew very little English.

At the end of April 1934, the Association held a special general meeting in order to make certain alterations to the rules, including the creation of a Grand Council, which was to consist of distinguished persons interested in the objects of the Association, who would act in an advisory capacity. There was also to be an Executive Committee in whose hands the main business—and hard work—was to be left. For the historical record, I give the names of those on the first Grand Council and on the first Executive Committee:

Grand Council

Chairman: The President

The Earl and Countess of Albemarle; Sir Hugh Allen, K.C.V.O., Principal of the Royal College of Music; Kenneth R. Barnes, Principal of the Royal Academy of Dramatic Art; Lady Barrett, C.H.; Lilian Baylis, C.H.; Phyllis Bedells; Mrs Beresford; Comyns Berkeley, M.D.; Ormond Blyth; Dora Bright; Lady Butterfield; The Marchioness of Bute; Sydney W. Carroll; Francis W. Chamberlain; Grace Cone; Lucia Cormani; Sir Frederick Cowen; Lady Crutchley; Kathleen Danetree; Yvonne Daunt-Stein; Basil Dean; Felix Demery; Ninette de Valois; Anton Dolin; The Lord and Lady Ebbisham; R. C. Elmslie, O.B.E.; Judith Espinosa; Professor L. N. G. Filon, Vice-Chancellor of the University of London; Sir Francis and Lady Fladgate; Sir Johnstone Forbes-Robertson; Colonel Sir John and Lady Gore; Lady Cicely Hardy; Edmund Heisch; The Lord Horder, K.C.V.O.; The Rt Hon. Sir Ellis W. Hume-Williams, Bart, K.B.E.; The Hon. Mr Justice Humphreys; Lady Humphreys; Frank S. N. Isitt; Sir Barry Jackson; Colonel Sir Weston Jarvis; Sir Maurice Jenks, Bart; Lady Jenks; Tamara Karsavina; Dame Madge Kendal; Mrs Kinnell; Dr N. F. R. Knuthsen, O.B.E.; Mrs Liddell; Sir Ernest Graham Little, M.C.; Sir William Llewellyn, G.C.V.O., President of the Royal Academy; The Marchioness of Londonderry, D.B.E.; The Earl of Lonsdale, K.G.; Sir John B. McEwen, Principal of the Royal Academy of Music; D. G. MacLennan; Mrs Emile Mond; Lt-Colonel T. C. R. Moore, M.P.; Mrs Moore; Charles Morley; The Lord and Lady Moyne; The Duchess of Newcastle; Lady Muriel Paget, O.B.E.; E. A. Parry; Mrs Parry; Sir Arthur Wing Pinero; The Lord and Lady Plender; Philip J. S. Richardson; The Duke and Duchess of Richmond and Gordon; The Lord and Lady Riddell; Lt-Colonel Frank Romer; Sir Landon Ronald, Principal of the Guildhall School of Music; The Earl of Rosse; The Viscountess Snowden; Sir Arthur Stanley; Mrs Lyne Stivens; Sir Oswald Stoll; The Dowager Lady Swaythling; Geoffrey Toye; Mrs Jepson Turner; Irene Vanbrugh; T. Sidney Vickery; Mrs Vickery; Sir Archibald Weigall; Sir William H. Willcox, K.C.I.E.; Lady Willcox; Ralph Vaughan Williams, Mus. Doc.

The Executive Committee:

Chairman: The President.

Kenneth Barnes, Phyllis Bedells, Ormond Blyth, Francis W. Chamberlain, Grace Cone, Kathleen Danetree, Felix Demery, Anton Dolin, R. C. Elmslie, Judith Espinosa, Edmund Heisch, Frank S. N. Isitt, Tamara Karsavina, D. G. MacLennan, Charles Morley, Philip J. S. Richardson, Mrs Jepson Turner, and Sir William H. Willcox, K.C.I.E., M.D.

It will be noticed that as well as dancers and teachers the Executive Committee was composed of others whose assistance could be of great value to us.

In August 1935, we received the news that 'His Majesty the King has been graciously pleased to command that the Association of Operatic Dancing of Great Britain shall be known as the Royal Academy of Dancing.'

What great joy it gave us! After only fifteen years of existence such an honour was intensely gratifying. The granting of the privilege of the title 'Royal' was an expression of approval of our work; but most of the credit must go to Adeline Genée, who had given so many years of her life to raising the prestige of English dancing.

For some time the special sub-committee, known as the Royal Charter Committee, had been working hard for this honour under the chairmanship of Sir William Willcox. We had numerous meetings at his house, and the help he gave us was of incalculable value. Now our hopes were realized. On 20 December 1935, we were granted the Royal Charter; and on 17 January 1936, one of the last official acts of His Majesty King George V before his death, was to affix his Great Seal to the document.

While all this excitement was afoot the Royal Academy of Dancing—as we must now call it—had been arranging to give me a most impressive Farewell and I had been keeping myself in strict training.

The new Markova-Dolin Ballet Company had been formed, but, as yet, they were only rehearsing. As well as the two stars there was a *corps de ballet*, thirty-nine strong, including such artists as Wendy Toye, Prudence Hyman, Kathleen Crofton, Diana Gould, Molly Lake, Freddie Franklin, Stanley Judson, Algeranoff, Keith Lester, Guy Massey, and Travis Kemp. Busy as they were with their rehearsals, Pat Dolin still found time to rehearse with me every day for my farewell matinée at the London Hippodrome.

LONDON HIPPODROME

Leicester Square, W.C.2.

Proprietors: MOSS EMPIRES LTD
Man. Director: R. H. GILLESPIE.   Director: GEORGE BLACK.
Manager: FRANK BOOR.

FRIDAY, NOVEMBER 8th
at 2-45 p.m.
THE
PHYLLIS BEDELLS
FAREWELL MATINEE

PHYLLIS BEDELLS
NINETTE DE VALOIS
ANTON DOLIN
RUTH FRENCH
ROBERT HELPMANN
ALICIA MARKOVA
ATTILIA RADICE
(*Prima Ballerina—La Scala, Milan*)

The "BALLET CLUB" Company in
'BAR AUX FOLIES-BERGÈRE'
with Pearl Argyle, Maude Lloyd and Frederick Ashton

The "VIC-WELLS BALLET" in
'RENDEZVOUS'
with Harold Turner and Margot Fonteyn

The SADLER'S WELLS ORCHESTRA
(By permission of Miss Lilian Baylis)
Conductors: CONSTANT LAMBERT and JOSEPH SHADWICK

Organised by
The Royal Academy of Dancing
Patroness: HER MAJESTY THE QUEEN.

The great day arrived. Friday 8 November 1935 was the most wonderful day of my life: the tribute paid to me by all the leading dancers and ballet companies in generously giving their services made it, I think, a unique occasion. As well as the English dancers who appeared Signora Attilia Radice, *prima ballerina* of La Scala, Milan, travelled from Italy specially in order to dance.

One small sorrow was that David was not allowed to come from Stubbington House School. The headmaster said that, even on such an occasion, he could not permit the rules to be broken. But while I was making up for my first dance, a telegram arrived. 'Good luck, Mummy darling, for this afternoon', it read. 'Love from David.' I was so touched that my young son should have thought of sending it that I could not help weeping with gratitude. There were over a hundred other telegrams and cables.

During my rehearsals with Pat Dolin he had wagered I would be dancing in public again before two years had passed, but I had assured him that I meant to stop once and for all; I was so certain it was the right thing to do. I dreaded to think of hearing people say, 'Ah! you should have seen her when she was at her best.'

Nevertheless, while the actual performance was on, I could not realize that this really was my final appearance. Just as Pat leapt into the wings, leaving me alone on the great Hippodrome stage at the end of *Exercises*, the curtain fell. Then I did know. And it was awful. I had a huge lump in my throat and tears were streaming down my cheeks.

All who had taken part in the performance came crowding on to the stage. There were masses of flowers for me and other presents. The curtain rose and fell, again and again, to the tumultuous applause and the cheers of audience and artists alike.

Eventually Pat pushed me forward to make a speech. At first I was unable to utter a sound; but then I did manage to say something in an effort to thank everyone for the great honour they had done me. I really cannot remember what I said; but I was told afterwards that it was something about 'how glad I had been to help blaze the trail for all these wonderful dancers who were now appearing in English ballet'.

At the end of the performance my friends used their cars and taxis to help me bring home all my flowers and gifts. There was a basket much taller than myself from the committee and members of the Royal Academy of Dancing and a silver tray with a cocktail shaker and six glasses. Inscribed on the tray was: '*To a great artiste—a tribute of admiration from the Markova-Dolin Ballet, November 8th 1935.*' With this was a small leather-bound book with the signatures of the new ballet company. On the first page Laura Henderson had written, '*We have all loved to show a tiny appreciation of all you have done for English ballet, an inspiration to me to carry on the good work!*'

Mr and Mrs Frank Isitt (Madame Genée and her husband) gave me a very lovely Royal Copenhagen china flower-vase. The Cecchetti Society sent Svetlov's fine book on Tamara Karsavina. There were dozens of other gifts.

A beautiful basket of orchids and violets had a card attached, saying, 'To the *Débutante* of British dancing from a *Dancing Master.*' It came from Espinosa; and, in this charming way, he reminded me of the parts we had played together in the old Empire days, as well as of our roles in life. This gesture of his pleased me greatly, as there had been so much ill-feeling between us since he left our Association and formed his own.

I was also very touched by the message with some lovely flowers from Euphan and Dorrit Maclaren, '*To the Cornflower from her friends, the Lobsters*'—a very happy allusion to the time we were together when I made my first appearance in London in *Alice in Wonderland* in 1906.

There were roses sent from Mrs Smifkins—my childish nickname for Mrs Smith, who had been my loyal and devoted dresser for so many years at the Empire. She was very old now; but she had managed to come to my Farewell.

It would take too long to tell of all the kind thoughts from old and new friends and so many of my past and present pupils. All I can do is repeat that it was the proudest day of my life and that my heart seemed to be bursting with gratitude to everyone for making it so memorable.

Many friends came to join me at an informal party at my home, which went on for several hours. Prince George Chavchavadze sat at the piano and played for us.

The critics next morning were all extremely kind.

The *Manchester Guardian* devoted nearly a full column to the performance. 'One's regret that this was Phyllis Bedells's last appearance on the stage was greater than ever when one saw again how dignified, how faultless a classical dancer she was . . .'

The *Liverpool Post*: 'Nobody quite understands why she is retiring for, although it is many years since she won laurels at the Empire, her technique shows no sign of falling off, and this afternoon she looked positively radiant with youth . . .'

The *Daily Telegraph* had two headlines to a notice written by Arnold L. Haskell. And a few days later, among many other charming letters, I received this one from him.

My dear Phyllis,
                    All my congratulations on the matinée. I did not come round as I had to dash off to the *Telegraph* and, in any case, you must have been surrounded. It was an immense success, impressive, moving and dignified—so few people know how to retire in time and you have done so before your powers have been in any way impaired. I am sure that with a talented daughter's career to foster and follow you will not feel it too badly. Once again, all good luck,
                                        Yours,
                                            Arnold.

There were many other notices which there is no space to quote here; but I cannot end this chapter without recalling what the *Dancing Times* said in its December 1935 issue:

'The Farewell Matinée in honour of Phyllis Bedells, organized by the R.A.D. at the London Hippodrome was an event in every way worthy of the occasion. . . . It was impossible not to be moved by the tremendous ovation which Miss Bedells received after cutting her final *entrechats*—and what clear-cut *entrechats* they were—and making her last bow as a public performer. Might one say that in that applause there was crystallized the thanks and appreciation of the public for the great service she has rendered the Art of Dancing in this country during the past twenty-five years, ever since she became *première danseuse* at the Old Empire and so proved than an English dancer with an English name *could* succeed. The matinée witnessed the close of an era— an era which saw the birth and childhood of an English ballet. That era is past: English ballet has now reached the period of adolescence and a bright future stretches before it. How precarious its very existence was in the early days, and what a wonderful tonic the precept and example of Phyllis Bedells proved, only the more elderly of us can know. How hopeless it seemed at one time for an English dancer even to try to succeed cannot be realized by a younger generation. We who are old enough to remember these things understand how much the present secure position of native ballet in England is due to the inspiring influence of the lady we paid tribute to last month at the Hippodrome.'

That was written by 'The Sitter Out.'

Epilogue

So ENDED my dancing days. There had been ups and downs; but I can say honestly that if I had my life to live over again and could choose afresh I would change nothing.

Since my Farewell much has happened. I end the story of my active dancing life here. Maybe some day I will tell of the years since 1935, during which my daughter made a successful career as dancer and Ballet Mistress in her twelve years with the Sadler's Wells Ballet, and my son became a Lieutenant-Commander in the Royal Navy.

Our own English ballet has won international recognition and its dancers hold their own with the finest in the world.

Adeline Genée and Ninette de Valois have both been honoured by being created D.B.E. Margot Fonteyn and Marie Rambert became C.B.E., and Philip Richardson was awarded the O.B.E.

My school still thrives, I am glad to say, and I have had the honour of teaching most of the best-known English ballerinas, which gives me joy in my loneliness since my dear husband and my mother have died.

Ian had rejoined the Army in June 1939, but was taken seriously ill in 1940 and invalided out. For over four years he suffered terribly; but, in those years, we grew closer together than we had ever been—there was real devotion, companionship, and understanding between us at the last.

Now both my children are married and living elsewhere. I am a proud grandmother—and life still holds much happiness, for which I continue to thank God.

Index

217

227

Lightning Source UK Ltd.
Milton Keynes UK
UKHW020830130123
415295UK00008B/848

9 781376 191899